About the authors

María Soledad Segura is professor at Facultad de Ciencias Sociales and Facultad de Ciencias de la Comunicación of Universidad Nacional de Córdoba and is a researcher at Consejo Nacional de Investigaciones Científicas y Técnicas of Argentina. She edited *Los medios sin fines de lucro entre la Ley Audiovisual y los decretos. Estrategias, desafíos y debates en el escenario 2009–2015* (2016) and *Agitar la palabra. Participación social y democratización de las comunicaciones* (2014).

Silvio Waisbord is professor of media and public affairs at George Washington University. His most recent books are *Reinventing Professionalism: Journalism and News in Global Perspective* (2013), *Media Sociology: A Reappraisal* (editor, 2014), and *Vox populista: Medios, periodismo, democracia* (2013).

MEDIA MOVEMENTS

CIVIL SOCIETY AND MEDIA POLICY REFORM IN LATIN AMERICA

María Soledad Segura and Silvio Waisbord

ZED

Zed Books
London

*Media Movements: Civil Society and Media Policy Reform
in Latin America* was first published in 2016 by Zed Books Ltd,
The Foundry, 17 Oval Way, London SE11 5RR, UK.

www.zedbooks.net

Typeset in Plantin and Kievit by Swales & Willis Ltd, Exeter, Devon
Index by Rohan Bolton
Cover design by roguefour.co.uk

A catalogue record for this book is available from the British Library.

ISBN 978-1-78360-463-0 hb
ISBN 978-1-78360-462-3 pb
ISBN 978-1-78360-464-7 pdf
ISBN 978-1-78360-465-4 epub
ISBN 978-1-78360-466-1 mobi

Printed and bound by CPI Group (UK) Ltd, Croydon, CR0 4YY

CONTENTS

ACKNOWLEDGEMENTS

This book began life during conversations between us at the conference of the Nordic Latin American Research Network in November 2013 in Oslo. We realized our shared interest in citizen participation and media policy reform in Latin America as well as our familiarity with local and national cases. We agreed that the regional trend of citizen-initiated reforms was a watershed moment in the history of media policy in the region, and that it was packed with innovations to further understand the nexus between civic society and media policy change. We believed that a wide-angle interpretation of the phenomenon was necessary, so we decided to take up the challenge and collaborate in a common project.

We are grateful to Kika Sroka-Miller for believing in this project from the beginning and trusting us to carry it out to its conclusion. We would like to thank Eduardo Bertoni and Des Freedman for their careful reading of the text and illuminating comments. Many thanks to friends and colleagues with whom we discussed ideas: Martín Becerra, Gustavo Gómez, Damián Loreti, and Guillermo Mastrini. We are indebted to everyone who agreed to be interviewed for this book, shared valuable insights, and provided us with relevant documents and key data.

INTRODUCTION

If media policy does not result from social participation, then, policies are the product of the intervention of groups, sectors, and agents whose interests are different from the collective interest. (Margarita Graziano, 1986)

What would be the conditions of a communications system in a genuine democracy? First, it is fundamental that no group within the society would have the right to control what can or cannot be said, and that there should be no control by fear, by censorship, or by physical liquidation. (Raymond Williams, 1962)

Media movements and policy reform

Since the mid-1990s, Latin America has been an exceptional laboratory of media policy reforms. Until recently, most media systems in the region have basically functioned according to legislation enacted decades ago, at a time of completely different technological developments and laws passed by authoritarian regimes. Transforming media legislation according to democratic principles and the new realities of technological developments has been long overdue.

A raft of proposals and laws have been intensely debated and passed in the region in the past two decades. These were not just minor pieces of legislation or amendments to existing laws. Rather, they were ambitious attempts to overhaul key aspects of media systems and public communication. Dozens of freedom of information laws were passed at municipal, provincial, and national levels throughout the region. Currently, only four countries, Argentina, Bolivia, Costa Rica, and Venezuela, do not have national laws allowing public access to government information. Contempt (*desacato*) laws that criminalize speech critical of authorities and institutions have been abolished or the associated penalties have been eliminated in most countries. Also, new broadcasting and telecommunications laws have completely transformed the legal framework of media systems in Argentina, Bolivia, Ecuador, Mexico, Uruguay, and Venezuela.

Recent levels of policy activism and legal changes are unprecedented. Considering the traditional reluctance of political elites and media owners to engage in public discussions about media policies, let alone shake up legal frameworks, the current state of policy debate and action is remarkable. Media owners traditionally espoused the notion that the best law is "no law" out of fear that any policy would interfere with their business interests. Political elites were unwilling to sponsor regulations that would negatively affect powerful media companies and, instead, preferred media laws to protect their power and the interests of media allies.

Our interest in this book is to examine the contribution of citizens' movements to a uniquely intense period of policy reforms in public communication in Latin America during the 2000–2015 period. We examine a range of experiences of citizen participation to reshape media systems and change media policy-making processes in the region. The analysis dips in and out of cases of media activism at both national and regional levels. Because we are interested in understanding the overall characteristics of media activism and policy reforms as well as similarities and differences in the region, we cast a wide analytical net by looking at various experiences. We are less interested in producing a granular analysis of particular experiences by country or type of media reform than in finding connecting threads among media movements in terms of goals, strategies, and impact. Whereas our analysis primarily draws from the cases of Argentina, Ecuador, Mexico, and Uruguay, we also make references to experiences in other countries. We chose these countries because, although they present similar levels of citizen activism on various media policies, the outcomes have been notoriously different.

Although focusing on a single country might be appealing to produce nuanced, close understandings of particular experiences, we have chosen a different methodological approach. Given a new era of policy reform in the region, we believe that a regional analysis focused on four countries is better suited to understanding a cross-national phenomenon. A regional approach also allows us to gain insights about the transnational interactions among organizations, networks, and movements. By doing so, we hope to produce generalizable conclusions about contemporary media governance that, hopefully, will inform the analysis of citizen participation and media policy-making in other regions of the world.

The analytical focus is on "media movements" – civic initiatives aimed at transforming media policies to promote pluralism in public communication. We approach "media movements" as social movements – networks of citizens and associations that aim to achieve social transformations through collective actions such as advocacy, education, and protest. Just like other social movements, media movements "are sustained, organized, public efforts making collective claims on target authorities" (Tilly, 2004: 3). Media movements belong to the broad family of media activism aimed at expanding democratic expression and contesting power in contemporary societies. Indeed, media activism is not a unified field around tactics and goals to promote media change and democratic speech. It includes an array of practices – grassroots production, cultural jamming, online organizing, media protest, community dialogue, media watch, critical media literacy. While we recognize the sheer diversity of media activism, we concentrate on civic mobilization focused on spearheading policy changes.

Media movements are forms of collective action concerned with the production, distribution, and consumption of informational, non-material goods that target the state to introduce changes in media systems. Certainly, these efforts are part of broad struggles for the democratization of society, politics, and markets. They not only reflect the expansion of forms of civic engagement through new agencies, repertoires, and targets. They also express forms of civic participation in the information society concerned with improving the distribution of opportunities for civic expression.

The study of "media movements" requires the examination of goals and strategies. Here we analyze experiences with different policy goals, namely, changing legislation about ownership, funding, content production, and access to public information. Organized citizens have aimed to legalize community media, curb media concentration, promote domestic production of audiovisual content, regulate official advertising, ensure public access to government information, increase media accountability and transparency, eliminate contempt laws, and decriminalize libel and slander in cases of public interest. The examination of a broad set of policy objectives and movements gives us an opportunity to draw conclusions grounded in the analysis of similarities and differences across movements and countries.

Also, we discuss various strategies used by media movements, including critique, collaboration, and consensus-building with state and market actors. Although some movements are grounded in the strong tradition of alternative media and the politics of resistance against states and markets in Latin America, they have considered and deployed an array of tactics to achieve wide-ranging goals. This is another reason why the region is an exciting place to study citizens' activism in media policies: movements have resorted to various strategies to advance goals. Revisiting a tradition of resistance and alternative media that had characterized progressive media activism in the past (Krohling Peruzzo, Tufte & Vega Casanova, 2011), today's media movements utilize a range of strategies and actions to effect substantial changes in public communication. Because the state remains a critical site of political power, it is at the center of media policy-making. These experiences suggest, then, an understanding of civil society as a countervailing space to established political and economic powers that eventually finds it strategically beneficial to partner with state and market actors.

Civil society, citizenship and participation

What is the theoretical relevance of the study of media movements in contemporary Latin America? We believe that this is an important subject to gain a better understanding of fundamental issues at the center of recent studies in media policies and democratic theory. Our study aims to provide insights to gain a better understanding about participatory politics, citizens' mobilization, and impact on democratic quality and media governance.

By placing the study of citizens' policy activism within emergent forms of media governance, we hope to make a contribution to understanding whether citizens contribute to new styles of policy-making. As Des Freedman (2008: 4) writes, policy-making is

> a battleground in which contrasting political positions fight for material advantage … Every step of the way is marked by fierce competition for, or development of, resources, influence and power. … The policy process is both structured – circumscribed by institutional, economic, technological and governmental

dynamics – and actor-driven in the pursuit of different norms
and goals.

Following Manuel Puppis (2010: 135), we understand "media governance" as "the entirety of rules that aim to organize media systems." At the core of media governance are principles, institutions, and regulations that shape the fundamental characteristics and dynamics of media systems. It prominently features various forms of citizens' participation in the way policies are brought up, discussed and implemented in both civil society and policy-making (see Donders, Pauwels & Loisen, 2014; Ginosar, 2013).

Also, we aim to contribute to debates about participatory policy-making and democracy, a subject that has attracted considerable attention in recent decades. This is a well-plowed field with a long and distinguished philosophical lineage in political theory and sociology that has underscored the centrality of civil society in democratic theory and practice. No doubt, civil society is a complex concept and a perennial subject of semantic debates and conceptual disputes. Civil society has been used as a normative ideal about "the good society" as well as an analytical approach to assess the state of contemporary politics. It is generally understood as a space outside the state and the market for citizens to engage in debate and action about common concerns (Edwards, 2009).

Contemporary interest in this topic has generated voluminous scholarship interested in assessing civic deliberation and participation opportunities and contributions to democracy. Interest has been driven by both troubling and promising trends in contemporary polities. Pessimism about the contemporary shape of civil society and citizenship is grounded in several findings: low political knowledge, political malaise and apathy, public disenfranchisement, weak political organizations, the disproportionate power of entrenched interests, abysmal social inequalities, and the disconnection between the state and civil society. Critics find a yawning gap between the contemporary state of citizenship and the democratic promise of participatory politics (Dryzek, 2006).

Optimism, instead, has been sparked by waves of protest and other types of collective action, municipal and national experiments in participatory politics, the rise of social accountability movements, and the wedding of digital technologies and insurrectionary politics.

In contrast to gloomy conclusions, this argument finds positive signs of active citizenship in contemporary democracies. It concludes that pessimistic accounts paint an incomplete picture of the state of contemporary citizenship. One doesn't need to embrace absolute optimism to recognize that specific forms of citizens' participation are a counterpoint to democratic politics beset by concentrated political and economic power. Yet neither absolute hopelessness nor excessive enthusiasm is warranted. For every promising case, one also finds counterexamples that render a complex picture of the state of participatory politics.

A starting analytical point is that participatory processes contribute to expanding the range of perspectives and demands that eventually become articulated in specific policies. This is the basic premises of the model of deliberative democracy which assumes that open, unrestricted participation of citizens in public debates is necessary to produce better outcomes (Fishkin, 2009; Parkinson & Mansbridge, 2013). Democracy is premised on the idea that myriad voices need to be expressed and heard (Couldry, 2010; Dahlgren, 2013).

Applied to policy-making, deliberative politics serves to correct a well-known problem of contemporary democracies: policies "captured" by political and economic elites who typically benefit the most from government decisions. The imperfections of contemporary representative democracy make it necessary to institutionalize participatory mechanisms. Imperfections include the disproportionate influence of moneyed interests in politics, the distortion of public and parliamentary agendas by political and economic elites, and politicians' narrow interests. Because policy-making is too important to be left in the hands of politicians, technical experts, and lobbyists for companies with vested interests, it is necessary to institutionalize different forms of civic expression, feedback, consultation, and persuasion. Participatory processes, then, bring in a wider spectrum of voices to express demands as well as to identify problems and solutions that might result in policies with broader benefits and that effectively serve broader constituencies. In principle, then, citizen participation might broaden the debate about issues and perspectives and contribute to passing legislation that favors public interests.

Also, citizens' participation in policy-making might have other positive, spillover consequences for democracy (Altschuler & Corrales, 2013; Baiocchi, Braathen & Teixeira 2013; Coelho, 2014).

Citizens can increase their knowledge about fundamental aspects of democracy (e.g. individual and social rights, the inner workings of institutions, positions held by various parties and organizations). They might also become more confident in democratic institutions. They can also bolster a sense of collective efficacy – that is, the idea that organized people can effectively drive and institutionalize positive changes. They might contribute to bringing civil society and government closer together by building and maintaining bridging mechanisms that increase accountability, transparency, and effectiveness. It is also hoped that public participation helps to cement sentiments of inclusion and cohesion in society which are considered central for a well-functioning democracy. It also promotes citizenship outside electoral periods and other forms of personal and collective engagement. It bolsters the institutional texture of civil society by mobilizing myriad organizations behind specific initiatives – that is, the kind of institutional social capital that is considered the backbone of democratic life. In summary, it is expected that participatory experiences may not only produce socially inclusive policies that address citizens' demands, but that they also have positive ramifications for democratic governance and the quality of citizenship.

Recent studies about participatory politics have probed normative expectations as well as personal convictions to find out if the evidence actually supports theoretical visions and normative hopes about the "good democracy" (Geissel & Newton 2011; Nabatchi, Gastil, Weiksner & Leighninger, 2012; Pateman, 2012). During the past decades, dozens of participatory experiments have been implemented with uneven results across the world. The intersection of several factors helped to drive interest: grassroots demands for more inclusion in policy-making, the interest of selected governments in novel institutional mechanisms, the decentralization and devolution of decision-making to municipalities and provinces, and support for the implementation of democratic innovations among global aid institutions such as the World Bank and United Nations Development Program (which have funded various projects). Consequently, we have an unprecedented number of cases through which to revisit arguments about the dynamics and effects of citizens' participation on policy outcomes and democratic quality.

Studies about citizen participation help us refine our thinking on these matters (Brock & McGee 2012; Gaventa & Barrett, 2012). It is not our interest to summarize this extensive literature here. For the purpose of our study, it is important to highlight the spirit of this line of inquiry – namely, to probe theoretical arguments and empirical realities by asking important questions. Why is participation in policy-making normatively desirable? How do citizens make policy-making better? What difference does it make if citizens take part in public debate, parliamentary discussions and procedures, and policy implementation and monitoring? What are the benefits of public consultations, participatory budgeting, the inclusion of citizens in parliamentary debates, and other forms of participation?

Wrestling with these questions is important to move beyond simple hosannas to civic participation and get closer to understanding the shapes and benefits of citizen participation. Rose-tinted views of civil society do little to promote a better understanding of when and why citizen participation makes a difference to democratic governance. By tackling these questions, studies help to contextualize normative expectations and interrogate the gaps between arguments for citizens' participation and empirical cases in diverse contexts (Cornwall, Robins & Von Lieres, 2011). They yield sober conclusions about the impact of citizen participation.

First, we should not overestimate positive impact but should take a realistic, nuanced approach to assess strengths and limitations (Speer, 2012; Woodford & Preston, 2013). Findings about contemporary participatory experiences cannot be elegantly summarized in terse statements. The fact that participatory processes have been implemented fully or partially across very different political settings, with dissimilar objectives (from environmental to health policies), and resorting to multiple mechanisms (from public consultation to citizens' testimonies in parliamentary hearings) makes it difficult to draw parsimonious conclusions. While theoretical and normative blueprints share important premises about why citizens' participation matters, empirical cases are affected by too many variables for drawing succinct conclusions.

Second, participatory policies have made positive contributions in some cases, such as increasing health and educational budgets (Boulding & Wampler, 2010; Gonçalves, 2014).

Third, we need to be cautious about assessing "citizens' participation" at face value. Not all forms of participation are embedded in civic ideals or pursue citizenship goals. Not all civic organizations have democratic ideals or promote the respect of human rights. Also, various forms of collective action could be participatory but they do not necessarily represent vast sectors of society (Sorj, 2010). Governments have used "citizens' participation" such as public consultation and soliciting input without changing top-down decision patterns, to justify ready-made decisions, coopt civic demands and mobilizations, or leave established procedures (e.g. control of decisions, lack of autonomy of consultative bodies) unchanged (Haughney 2012; Roya, Yetano & Acerete, 2011; Turnhout & Van der Zouwen, 2010). What might seem participatory in terms of formal process or channels for citizens' activism is not necessarily empowering if it means the ability to affect decisions or act autonomously. Because examples of "citizen participation" may serve as window dressing for entrenched interests or are controlled and strengthen existing powers and autocracies, we cannot automatically assume that they effectively channel popular views or redress power relations. Close inspection of actual initiatives is necessary to assess their nature and impact.

This line of inquiry lays out important questions that still await detailed attention and evidence-based, rigorous answers (Michels, 2012). How do explain the different impact of participatory policy-making? How is impact measured? Are all impact indicators similarly important? What factors explain differences across experiences and countries? Are they comparable? What local variables shape outcomes? The institutional texture of civil society as well as local traditions of civic mobilization? The particular configuration of the state? Specific political junctures? Does the impact of citizens' participation vary across the kind of expertise demanded to speak authoritatively about specific policy issues? What about counter-cases – that is, policy-making processes that, despite weak citizen engagement, may produce positive results in terms of democratic and social values?

Citizens' participation in media and information policies

These questions have also attracted attention from media scholars interested in studying the role of civic society in promoting and renewing media pluralism (Flew, 2013; Hintz & Milan, 2012).

Media pluralism refers to a system of public communication that features institutions and platforms that promote a diversity of views, reflect heterogeneous cultures, and provide systematic coverage of a range of public issues and demands (UNESCO, 2008). Interest in this question underlies research focused on the success of civic efforts to broaden news coverage, the proliferation of citizens' media, the legalization of community media, and the rise of media monitoring institutions. These actions are aimed at redressing chronic problems of media systems, specifically the disproportionate influence of markets and political elites, the weakness of civic voices in news coverage, limited content and ownership diversity, and the lack of accountability of media organizations. What underlies disparate experiences of citizens' participation is the notion that civic engagement is necessary to shore up pluralist media systems and strengthen the quality of democratic life.

Obviously, the challenges for media democracy are not identical across political regimes and media systems. Media democracy in the global South is beset by long-standing problems grounded in the quality of governance and the particular structure of media markets. Some problems are firmly grounded in the persistent deficits of governance: official discretionary manipulation of public resources, lack of access to public information (as well as erratic implementation of laws), contempt, libel and slander laws, and weak public media tilt the balance in favor of political elites. Other problems are caused by specific aspects of market structures, namely, ownership concentration and runaway commercialism which reduce opportunities for comprehensive and regular coverage of public issues and channeling citizens' demands and solutions. Also, the collusion between media business and governments undermines opportunities for citizens to express demands that don't fit powerful agenda and to challenge industrial corporations and political wrongdoing. Finally, anti-press violence by state forces (the police and the military) and parastatal and criminal groups (drug traffickers, gangs, vigilantes) amidst situations of statelessness in vast swaths of the global South makes public expression extremely dangerous for citizens and journalists.

The argument

Our argument can be summarized in three propositions.

First, the cases considered here demonstrate that civil society plays a fundamental role in the process of media policy reforms.

Civil society organizations (CSOs) have deployed various strategies to achieve goals and have gained newfound positions as legitimate actors in the policy-making process. The experiences analyzed here amply demonstrate the maturation of media activism.

Second, civil society engagement is not enough to make policy changes happen. Support from powerful elites in strategic positions is necessary, too. CSOs can persuade key allies through forms of collective action from below. Citizens and influential allies have formed coalitions that resulted in progressive media policies. Certainly, they have not always succeeded given changing political opportunities. What is important is that the dynamic interaction between mobilized activists and political elites attests to new forms of collective action.

These coalitions reflect the consolidation of the state as an arena for struggles to redefine and strengthen public communication in new democracies. The state should not be narrowly seen as the enemy of media democracy, whether because it distorts the market, limits media independence, or suppresses the vitality of civil society. Certainly, plenty of historical experiences in Latin America demonstrate that "the state" has not been exactly amicable to civic participation. It has been the censor, persecutor, and executor of policies that benefit authoritarianism and corporate interests. The state, however, can also enable and guarantee media democracy through appropriate policies. The state performs different roles in media systems, and it is subjected to the influence of competing interests. The fact that media movements target governments to promote policy changes suggests that some forms of bottom-up activism do not see an insoluble contradiction between civic goals and state intervention. They equally deviate from free-market orthodoxy that flatly rejects any form of state intervention, and radical views that see the state as nothing but the agent of corporate business and self-interested political elites. They do not hold simplistic views about the state but, instead, assume that mobilized publics may influence state policies to support civic interests under certain circumstances.

Finally, the experiences analyzed here suggest that the state remains a crucial actor for media democracy in a globalized world. No doubt, globalization has made power dynamics more complex, and reinforced the ability of supranational actors to supersede state sovereignty. Also, the ascendancy of transnational bodies and global forms of activism indicate important forms of participation beyond state borders. When it comes to media matters, however, the state is hardly irrelevant. Key decisions affecting press structures and news content are intimately linked to the state, the nature of the political regime, the ideological platforms of governing parties, the relations between governments and the press, and so on. The globalization of media citizenship does not necessarily entail the globalization of decision-making or the evisceration of the power of the state on media issues.

The structure of the book

Chapter 1 provides a summary of the main characteristics of media systems in Latin America in order to comprehend citizens' demands and proposals to address central problems that undercut democratic public communication. Media systems are characterized by limited pluralism given the domination of market interests, the absence or weakness of public broadcasting, discretionary government practices over economic matters affecting public communication and media systems, and the inchoate state of community and alternative media. These characteristics have been the result of a legacy of elite-controlled media policies and the policy-making process that excluded public interests. A long history of the politics of media patrimonialism by which policies favored commercial interests and benefitted government officials explains why media systems exhibit limited conditions for the public expression of multiple publics. This scene-setting chapter gives a historical background to contextualize the analysis of how contemporary media movements tried to affect public policies to redistribute opportunities for public expression.

Chapter 2 surveys the field of media activism – the organizations and the demands of media movements in the region. The focus is on CSOs that have worked on three issues: broadcasting systems, public access to government information, and speech laws. The field comprises a variety of CSOs and networks that are essential to articulate citizens' demands, translate debates into proposals, and turn ideas into public policies. It represents the expansion of institutional opportunities for citizen participation and representation in media policy debates.

The focus of Chapter 3 is on the strategic playbook of media movements. Strategies refer to the tactics used by CSOs and coalitions to achieve specific objectives. Media movements have tried to influence various actors (the state, the media, the general public, potential allies, and opponents) through the utilization of various strategies across several public arenas – public opinion, courts, legislature, the media, and elections. They have been flexible in terms of selecting strategies according to specific conditions and goals. The strategic flexibility of media movements is a remarkable new aspect in the context of a strong tradition of protest and resistance in media activism in Latin America. The broadening of strategic decisions and tactics is indicative of shifts in the way media movements envision how media reforms are possible in specific political contexts.

Chapter 4 discusses the impact of media movements on new legislation. Media movements have had noticeable impact on policy reforms in three areas: broadcasting, public access to government information, and speech laws. The passing and the content of major policy reforms are unimaginable without collective actions. Mobilized citizens played central roles in the processes that culminated in important reforms that changed the legislative landscape in several countries in the region.

Chapter 5 examines political junctures in order to explain the uneven impact of media movements. The successes and failures of media activists need to be understood by addressing specific political junctures shaped by the presence of elite allies and political circumstances. As important as it is to drive reforms forward, collective action is insufficient to crystallize effective policy changes without support from selected government conditions and favorable timing. The significance of these political factors demands understanding how media movements are positioned vis-à-vis state politics. Only then we can explain the divergent policy outcomes of collective action.

Chapter 6 places local media activism in the context of transnational collective action in support of progressive media reforms. Transnational organizations and coalitions contribute to strengthening the organizational infrastructure and to supporting the strategic goals of local activists. They provide opportunities for connecting them with transnational communities of practice, obtaining funding, raising the legitimacy and visibility of local organizations, and mobilizing the power of "moral persuasion" among governments and other actors. Notwithstanding these important contributions, transnational activism doesn't single-handedly drive changes in media legislation. Only when connected to local activists can they effectively contribute to media reforms in supportive roles. The reason is that the prospects for policy reforms are essentially grounded in local movements and political junctures. Globalization has not fundamentally changed the fact that media policy-making politics are local. They continue to be firmly tied to domestic dynamics and calculations. Media movements think "transnationally" but they act locally.

Chapter 7 focuses on the analysis of the participation of civic society in policy implementation – a remarkable new development in the history of media governance in the region. New legislation includes participatory mechanisms whose performance has been uneven. CSOs have participated in the rolling out of new policies in different ways. They made important contributions to the application of public information, freedom of speech, and broadcasting legislation despite numerous problems as well as limitations of several laws. Recent experiences confirm that permanent civic mobilization is necessary to ensure that progressive laws are implemented and to criticize and modify laws that are contrary to media pluralism.

The Conclusion offers an overview of the main findings of the book and the contributions of media movements to deliberative politics and participatory media policy-making. It concludes by raising questions about citizenship, media policy, and collective action that require further attention. We hope that the findings and arguments presented will inform future research and debates about these questions.

1 | LIMITED PLURALISM AND "ELITE-CAPTURED" POLICIES

The analysis of media movements and their impact on policy-making and media structures requires a historical background of key aspects of media systems and policies in Latin America. Only then we can understand the demands, strategies, and impact of contemporary media movements. The analysis presented here has no ambition to provide a comprehensive and detailed survey. Rather, our interest is to provide a snapshot that captures essential characteristics of media systems and policy-making in the region in order to contextualize the analysis of media movements.

The analytical premise of our study is that media systems across the region can be considered part of a common "Latin American" model. In line with a tradition in media studies, we believe that national media systems in the region share distinctive characteristics (Fox & Waisbord, 2002; Lugo-Ocando, 2009; Matos, 2012). This approach goes back to foundational research in communication and media studies in the region that emphasized common attributes of media systems based on similar historical developments as well as the contemporary situation.

Certainly, media systems in the region are not identical. Economically, the size of Brazil's and Mexico's systems, with an estimated $66 billion and $34 billion in revenues respectively, loom large in the region (Lizama, 2014). Also, advertising investments are not equally distributed within the same countries. Large metropolitan areas as well as resource-rich provinces and municipalities typically attract the lion's share of investments. Also, some media systems have historically been more stable largely due the particular evolution of political systems. Not all countries have been equally vulnerable to cycles of democratic and authoritarianism, and political violence that, to say the least, greatly affected the structure and performance of media systems.

In what follows, we analyze core components of Latin American media systems. Media systems were chiefly subject to the logic of the market and politics rather than the demands and expectations of multiple publics. Despite a long history of public media and "third sector" media in the region, neither one became solid alternatives. Both have continuously suffered from several problems that undermined their prospects of becoming consistent alternatives to commercial offerings. Also, poor democratic governance, namely legal frameworks and practices that favored state opacity and discouraged public scrutiny, further deepened problems for democratic communication.

Consequently, media systems in the region are beset by "limited pluralism" – that is, they offer restricted opportunities for diverse perspectives and issues bounded by commercial priorities, industrial interests, and government designs. Adverse conditions for pluralism have been grounded in the structure and the functioning of both markets and states. The domination of the market model has relegated non-commercial, public interest media to a marginal position particular amidst the concentration of ownership and funding. The state has also contributed to undermining media pluralism by failing to guarantee suitable conditions for different forms of public expression. The persistence of laws restricting critical speech coupled with the tenuous respect for basic democratic rights in areas plagued by violence further weakened media pluralism. "Limited pluralism" was the result of a history of elite-captured media policies that primarily benefitted private companies and governments rather than the public good.

The market model

The market model has historically dominated Latin American media systems. Core principles of the market model, namely private ownership, commercialism, and advertising funding, have anchored both print and broadcasting industries throughout their modern history (Fox & Waisbord, 2002).

The policies of privatization, liberalization, and transnationalization of the 1980s and 1990s deepened historical characteristics of media systems across the region. What happened was not a sudden overturn of public regulations or the dismantling of state monopolies, as in European broadcasting during the same period. Instead, market policies refashioned fundamental aspects by furthering ownership concentration. Although this was not an entirely new feature given that media markets already showed important levels of concentration prior to the 1980s (Fox & Waisbord, 2002), neo-conservative policies forged the horizontal expansion of selected companies into other media industries – newspapers, broadcasting, and pay television (both cable and satellite), the vertical concentration of companies within audiovisual industries, process, and also the concentration of companies from leading economic sectors such as agribusiness and banking, and strengthened the position of media giants (Huerta-Wong & García, 2013; Luna Vásquez, 2014; Sunkel & Geoffroy, 2001; Trejo Delarbre, 2010).

The decision by many governments to privatize state-owned broadcasting stations put the finishing touches to systems that were already dominated by private interests. Although broadcasting systems were organized around commercial principles since the beginning, some licenses had been reserved for governments. In some cases, state-owned licenses were the result of the policies of expropriation ordered by governments in the late 1960s and 1970s such as in the cases of Argentina and Peru.

Second, the liberalization of media industries in the past decades lubricated the expansion of media corporations. The removal of limitations on media ownership (including the number of radio and television stations and cross-media properties) contributed to the rise of multimedia corporations and strengthened the grip of market interests in media systems. Consequently, in a few years, companies were able to expand horizontally and vertically by controlling assets across media industries as well as moving into different phases of audiovisual industries (production, distribution, exhibition) and pay television. Also, companies with interests across key economic sectors were able to move into media industries.

Third, governments facilitated the transnationalization of media industries by removing limitations on foreign ownership and providing attractive incentives for external investors. Global capital responded favorably and moved across the region, primarily into the largest media markets. International flows of money rapidly shifted the media ownership landscape. In some cases, global financial capital partnered with leading companies such as Argentina's Clarín and Brazil's Globo (Mastrini & Becerra, 2009). Large companies needed fresh injection of large funding to move into cable and satellite business, update technological equipment in both newspaper and broadcasting, and expand operations across media sectors. In other cases, global media corporations, such as Spain-based PRISA, acquired media properties and/or formed joint ventures with major local companies. Latin America-based companies such as Televisa, TV Azteca, and the Gonzalez Group also took advantage of this process as they entered national markets in the region. Consequently, regional powerhouses were formed with extensive ownership and storing presence in television and radio throughout the region (Arango-Forero, Arango, Llaña & Serrano, 2010; Brunner & Catalán, 1995).

The combination of privatization, liberalization, and transnationalization consolidated multimedia and conglomerate concentration in Latin America. Even amidst the global process of media concentration, the depth and reach of this process is remarkable. Building upon oligopolistic markets, it strengthened the unmatched presence of a handful of media companies in each country. Becerra and Mastrini (2009) estimate that the four leading companies in both the media and telecommunication industries control between 77 percent and 82 percent of media revenues and audiences. These values far exceed the concentration standards of 75 percent considered high even for the first eight operators. Meanwhile, the dominance of the market by the main company added up to an average of 45 percent in 2004.

Oligopolistic markets characterize television systems in the region, including the pay-television industry (including over-the-air, cable, and satellite). Some national television markets are dominated by one company. For example, Angel González, a Mexican citizen who resides in Miami, has extensive interests throughout the region including Argentina, Ecuador, and Guatemala. The Esersky group controls leading television stations in El Salvador. Other markets are "imperfect duopolies" where two companies control the lion's share of audience and advertising such as Caracol and RCN in Colombia, and Televisa and TV Azteca in Mexico. Televisa controls 60 percent of television licenses and its networks generally command 70 percent of national audiences. Other markets have similar oligopolistic structure. Elsewhere in the region, it is typical that a handful of companies controls the majority of licenses and attract the bulk of media advertising (Buquet & Lanza, 2011), such as in Uruguay where the companies Romay-Salvo, Fontaina-De Feo and Cardozo-Pombo control the broadcasting industry (Kaplún, 2014).

Similar levels of concentration are also found in the newspaper industry. Despite the decline in the number of newspapers and readers, the industry continues to remain strong in terms of revenue and sales as well as politically influential. Whereas ownership used to be dispersed at the national level in past decades, a steady process of concentration has taken place. In countries such as Colombia and Ecuador, a handful of companies control the majority of newspapers, advertising revenues, and readers (Cerbino & Ramos Ávila, 2009). In Chile, the newspaper industry is controlled by two companies – the Grupo Edwards and the Grupo Saiegh (Jiménez & Muñoz, 2008). In Peru, the El Comercio group controls almost 80 percent of advertising investment and readership at the national level.

The structure of the radio market is more fragmented than television and newspapers. Radio licenses are scattered among hundreds of owners. Although generally a handful of media companies control a significant numbers of stations and national networks, ownership and revenues does not show similar levels of concentration (Ramírez Cáceres, 2010). Although private ownership is dominant, dozens of radio stations are owned by governments, universities, and churches. Yet the radio industry has significantly less economic weight than television or newspapers. On average, it attracts a smaller percentage of overall media advertising in the region. With variations across countries, radio advertising ranges between 8 and 10 percent compared to 60 to 70 percent for television and 20 to 30 percent for newspapers (Becerra & Mastrini, 2009).

Despite important continuities, contemporary media systems feature important changes in comparison to a few decades ago.

First, there has been a gradual transition from a model of family-owned media business to corporate ownership and management. Large conglomerates now dominate where family companies used to rule. Some are privately held companies (including companies where members of founding families control the majority of shares); others are controlled by public corporations with extensive industrial interests (Mastrini & Becerra, 2001).

Second, leading private media are owned by corporations that are branches of multi-industrial conglomerates in key economic sectors such as banking, agribusiness, real estate, construction, retail, and mining (Mastrini & Becerra, 2006; Checa-Godoy, 2012; Fox & Waisbord, 2002; Monckeberg, 2009). The number of leading media companies that are only media companies is far fewer than it used to be until a few decades ago. Instead, many are divisions of large corporate structures that control fundamental aspects of national and regional economies. This has happened in two ways. In some cases, family-owned newspaper and broadcasting companies eventually branched out into other media and industries. In other cases, major corporations in banking and retail acquired media companies. As result of a series of mergers and acquisitions during recent decades, they expanded onto the media business both domestically and internationally (Becerra & Mastrini, 2009).

Third, the editorial leanings of leading media companies have been unmistakably identified with conservative positions. Politically, dominant media companies have traditionally supported conservative parties and government and, in many cases, openly supported right-wing military dictatorships. An extensive literature has demonstrated that they have firmly opposed leftist causes and populist movements and governments. Given that newsrooms and content production lack strong buffers between editorial positions and content production, it is not surprising that the ideological politics of media corporations have been openly infused news coverage and programming. Editorial sympathies have tightly controlled opportunities for critical and progressive voices, which have been either distorted or simply invisible in the mainstream media.

Relations between media and organized political forces did not follow the conventional terms of "party/press parallelism." Although some media organizations were identified with political parties in the past, particularly in countries with a tradition of strong parties such as Colombia and Chile, most companies eventually adopted editorial positions identified with specific ideological camps more than "partisan" forces. Although publishers and media moguls memorably vowed to put their newsrooms in the service of specific political parties and presidencies, they also shifted political alliances according to circumstances in order to maximize business interest and political influence (Fox & Waisbord, 2002; Lugo-Ocando, 2009).

Public media

Given the early dominance of the private model in both print and broadcasting, public media never became the backbone of media systems in the region. The core principles of public broadcasting identified with the traditional Western European model did not steer the establishment of radio and television systems in the region. None of the ideals invoked elsewhere to justify state broadcasting monopolies gained significant political support. Neither the notion that public systems were necessary to safeguard educational standards nor concerns about national identity effectively articulated the embryonic development of broadcasting (Arroyo, Becerra, García Castillejo & Santamaría, 2012).

In the early decades of broadcasting, private owners dominated the introduction of technology and capital with government support. No clear and strong public alternatives ever materialized. Public broadcasting lacked a broad coalition that could have pushed for setting up strong foundations or preserving licenses dedicated to non-commercial pursuits. Nor did it have influential patrons worried about the cultural and educational implications of leaving content completely in the hands of the market. Nor did it have the backing of political elites concerned with the political implications of abrogating the public's right to control the airwaves. Since then, public media has remained intellectually inchoate and politically weak. In retrospect, it was a foregone conclusion that broadcasting would be anchored in market principles in all countries (Fuenzalida, 1998).

The idea of "public" remains protean. What conventionally have been called "public" media in the region were basically broadcasting licenses reserved and managed by national, provincial, and municipal governments with plenty of discretion. In some countries, governments controlled newspapers and other print publications run by executive offices and cabinet agencies as well as a small number of broadcasting licenses reserved for national, provincial, and city administrations. These media should not be called "public" for the simple reason that they have been operated strictly according to government interests rather than public considerations. They are public in terms of ownership, but not in regards to mission, management, or even funding. Nor should they be called "state" or "government" media as basically they were run by whoever occupied the executive office rather than by the state or governments as a whole (Becerra & Waisbord, 2015; del Bianco, Esch & Moreira, 2012; Martin Barbero, 2001; Moyses, Valente & Silva, 2009).

Whereas a full analysis of the historical path of public media in the region goes beyond the scope of this chapter, some key points need to be indicated. Some governments kept public media underfunded, which resulted in poor quality of programming and content. Military dictatorships that ruled most of the region in the 1960s and 1970s, instead, expanded production and financing of state-run media in order to strengthen their own propaganda capacity. Nor was there consensus on whether stations should be operated according to commercial criteria. Some stations essentially followed commercial principles, as they were expected to turn out profits, capture large number of audiences and advertisers, and achieve high ratings and market success. Other stations, instead, were not expected to compete with private media, as they were funded with public monies, typically assigned by governments (Pasquali, 1991, 1995).

A key problem is that the notion of public has been conflated with the government. Consequently, public media were not primarily imbued by visions of public service. None of the principles conventionally considered central to the mission of public media, such as citizenship, pluralism, accountability, and public service, actually underpinned the mission and the functioning of public systems. Nor were they designed to provide effective alternatives to commercial content or fill gaps left by market-oriented media. Instead, so-called "public media" have basically functioned as official megaphones for the presidency or specific cabinet offices. Public media were often mere communication appendices of political powers, particularly the executive office. Managers were generally directly appointed by cabinet members and/or the president (and governors and mayors). Non-partisan management structures and/or multipartisan mechanisms were indispensable to preserve public ideals and fend off commercial or partisan pressures. Nor were they regulated by independent regulatory agencies to monitor performance and recommend corrections. Obviously, such structural problems weren't the result of improvisation, forgetfulness, or bad planning. Rather, it was the expected outcome of deliberate strategies to maintain public media on a short leash. Even if state-run media fancied themselves to be public and even trumpeted their public mission in their name and branding, they were anything but.

All in all, public media in the region were subjected to mixed expectations, including following partisan lines, commercial standards, and, in some cases, artistic and cultural merit. Yet, without clear public, educational, or cultural missions, public media were basically relegated to a secondary place in media systems. State-owned media were largely relegated to another set of considerations: partisan calculations, commercial gain, and clientelism.

The historic problems of public media are grounded in the particular management structure that exacerbated its vulnerability to political pressures and corruption, the lack of financial models to sustain stability and autonomy, and erratic programming decisions. Without appropriate basic conditions, namely autonomous management and diversified funding mechanisms, they could not meet public principles. They lacked the necessary institutional architecture to foster independence and be protected from inevitable, persistent, and powerful influences.

This was done through the way funding was structured. Whether at the national, provincial, or municipal levels, public media have been financially tied directly to the executive office with limited, if any, oversight from other public bodies such as the city council or the state or the national congress. Certainly, no independent body existed during authoritarian regimes. Unsurprisingly, then, as long as the finances of public media depended on official sources managed with partisan criteria, they were expected to be conduits for official views. Although they remained publicly owned, they were operated by the party in government and directly depended on the executive at the national, regional, and municipal levels. Therefore, rather than serving "public" interests, they supported the partisan interests of political powers that assigned funding.

Some exemptions stand out amidst this bleak history of public media. Scholars have argued that other experiences came closer to fulfilling the ideas of public media. Among others, the cases of Venezuela's Radio Alegría, Argentina's Canal Encuentro and Canal Paka Paka, and Brazil's TV Cultura have been mentioned as interesting exceptions to the overall trajectory of public broadcasting for they successfully expanded content beyond commercial parameters by casting a wider net on social and cultural subjects and were able to stay sheltered from commercial and partisan pressures (Arroyo, Becerra, García Castillejo & Santamaría, 2012; Guerin, 2013; Lugo-Ocando, Cañizalez & Lohmeier, 2010). They aired dissident and socially marginalized voices, cultural expressions largely ignored by commercial media, the lives of myriad ethnic and linguistic groups. These have been, however, limited, small-scale experiences. In other cases, some public broadcasting stations were able to come closer to meeting public ideals as they opened up spaces to multiple publics and kept a distance from both market and government interests. They have been ephemeral, however, as they lacked the appropriate management and financial structures for long-term continuity. Unfortunately, they were subject to negative political dynamics that ultimately weakened their sustainability, such as intra-government bickering, instability, and policy reversals. These forces were ultimately responsible for why promising experiences failed to become institutionalized.

In summary, public media has lacked basic conditions to become a core component of media systems in the region. Its meaning and purpose has been ambiguous. It has lacked a common blueprint for the affirmation of state-owned media in the service of public interests. Even until today, the notion of "public" applied to media remains ambiguous. It is used interchangeably with "government," "cultural," and "official" media. The semantic confusion reflects the lack of a consensus about their mission. Further, without suitable institutional conditions that could have ensured minimal autonomy, public media were constantly vulnerable to partisan interests. There have not been political coalitions with a clear vision and sufficient influence to steer its development in ways that would have moderated, let alone prevented, official takeover of public media. Given these conditions, "public media" drifted in too many directions. They wavered in many directions: pushed by political pressures, they were only intermittently committed to diversifying content according to public ideals.

"Third sector" media

The label "third sector" media refers to a heterogeneous group of radio stations, film/video cooperatives, and publications connected to myriad social movements and organizations of workers, peasants and farmers, miners, indigenous peoples, human rights groups, unions, local churches, neighborhood associations, and the urban poor. The history of the "third sector" media goes back to the emergence of low-power radio stations associated with peasant organizations in Colombia, miners' unions in Bolivia, and grassroots churches in

Venezuela and other countries in the 1940s and 1950s. They are called popular, community, citizens', and alternative media.

What these media have in common is allegiance to the idea that they should prioritize citizens' voices and participation. They are conceived as channels for the public expression of ordinary citizens and the affirmation of social demands. By rejecting the propaganda principles of state-run media as well as the profit-seeking goals of the private media, they have sought to expand communicative spaces by giving access to issues and perspectives generally ignored by the mainstream media. This has positioned "third sector" media directly in opposition to the market and the state as spaces for both resisting private domination and governments, and fostering alternative views. They have vigorously opposed private media for shutting off their demands and prioritizing content that fails to reflect citizens' lives and concerns. They have confronted the state, particularly during military dictatorships, for silencing citizens and defending dominant interests.

Historically, the situation of "third sector" media has been paradoxical. Despite widespread and long-standing presence linked to neighborhood associations, social movements, and local activism, they have survived in clandestine and precarious conditions. This condition was not accidental. Community media have been deliberately marginalized by the state and market actors. Because legislation did not contemplate the existence of non-commercial, non-government media, they were relegated to existing in limbo. The political vibrancy of "third sector" media contrasted with the lack of legal recognition.

Because they operated without licenses, they have been frequent targets of judicial persecution as well as police raids and closures instigated by private owners and governments.

They have chronically operated on shoestring budgets. Because they existed outside legal frameworks, they could not have access to "legitimate" funds whether advertising or government support, which, in turn, perpetuated chronic economic difficulties. Consequently, even though many grassroots media remained active and strongly connected to local politics, they have confronted persistent economic difficulties. Existing amidst such difficult economic conditions has been a high-wire act for community media. Therefore, they confronted enormous difficulties to emerge as a distinctive and fully recognized sector of media systems.

Almost no country in the region had legislation recognizing non-profit or "third" sector media as legitimate service providers until 2004. In some countries, they were authorized with restrictions on areas of coverage and financing methods. Therefore, despite the remarkable proliferation of the sector, particularly radio stations, the majority of operators remain illegal and still await opportunities to apply for licenses. Furthermore, the chaotic situation and the absence of serious attempts to legalize stations produced a considerable information void about the sector. Largely due to this unusual situation, there are no precise, reliable numbers about the sector – the number and reach of operators, the quantity of staff members, the size of the audience, the characteristics of content, and other issues. It is estimated that between 10,000 and 15,000 community radio stations operate in the region (Gumucio Dragon, 2003).

Limited pluralism

In summary, the overwhelming presence of commercial interests and the lack of countervailing forces have historically limited pluralism of media systems in the region. Exacerbated commercialism pushed out content that was not favored by advertisers or demanded significant production investments. Concentrated ownership reduced the potential for market competition and the levelling of opportunities for public expression. The dominant position of far-flung business networks in media ownership has laid out limitations for content that questions dominant socio-economic structures and ruling interests. The interlocked system of media and business has reduced opportunities for giving voice to citizens and issues that governments and private cronies find uninteresting or inconvenient. It is hard to imagine that the media would show interest in exposing the negative consequence of the business practices of parent corporations or cover labor rights, environmental degradation, human rights, and financial mismanagement. The weakness and political manipulation of public media coupled with the illegality of "third sector" media added further limitations.

This media order was not monolithically opposed to any form of diversity and pluralism. To conclude that media systems were seamlessly closed to diverse public manifestations is misguided. There have been occasional opportunities for critical and diverse content, but they were limited by the constraints of runaway commercialism and intertwined political and economic interests (Waisbord, 2000).

In addition to the distorted structure of media systems, state performance has adversely affected pluralism, too. How states have tampered with pluralism needs to be analyzed by examining three key issues: the persistence of legal frameworks that discourage critical expression, poor governance that favors state opacity and favoritism, and the failure of states to guarantee the right to expression amidst violence.

One main feature of pluralist media systems is the ability of the public and journalists to scrutinize public officials. In Latin America, however, a range of press laws has discouraged pluralism, specifically, contempt, libel, and defamation laws that criminalize speech. Rather than providing robust constitutional protection for a diversity of perspectives, enduring press laws have punished criticism of government officials. This problem is compounded by the severity of criminal penalties for defamation offenses which have been disproportionate to the content and impact of the actual expression. Expectedly, gag laws and hefty penalties result in self-censorship as they discourage potential scrutiny of public officials, as studies in the region have shown. The presence of repressive defamation laws stifles public criticism of corruption and other forms of government wrongdoing.

Another deficit of state performance has been the absence of legislation allowing public access to government information. Only in the past two decades, such legislation was passed in some countries, a process discussed in depth in another chapter. Citizens' ability to request official information is a basic requirement of the democratic rule of law. International legislation defines it as "a basic human right, an instrument for citizen participation, an element to guarantee other rights, a mechanism for improving governance" (Organization of American States, 2013). The absence of or weak access to government information reflects a chronic problem of governance in the region, namely, the general weakness of oversight mechanisms of state performance. This has been put in evidence by the frailty of check-and-balance mechanisms and the manipulation of oversight agencies. The reluctance of governments to make its affairs public is symptomatic of the general opacity of the state.

Aside from its implications for the overall quality of democracy, the lack of government transparency and accountability has had particularly negative consequences for public expression and democratic media. Because the state plays critical functions in media systems, the deficit of state publicity undercuts media pluralism. It condones rampant arbitrariness in decisions affecting media economics and the overall structure of media systems.

This is why, despite the domination of the market, the economic power of the state cannot be underestimated in media systems in the region. As many case studies have demonstrated (see Waisbord, 2010), they have extended the duration of licenses, set up prices for biddings, manipulated the number of licenses to limit competition and benefit holders, and decided whether licensees complied with legal obligations, including content and investments obligations. Also, governments have discretionally enforced legislation, punishing selected media companies with fines for not complying with laws but ignoring blatant transgressions in other cases. Selective enforcement of media laws also affected media economies. In addition, governments also control decisions with important consequences for the business interests of parent corporations such as official contracts, subsidies, and other economic sectors. Governments have been able to wield influence through controlling key resources such as the distribution of official advertising without bids, the domestic production as well as the importation of newsprint, tax exemptions, permissions for importing technology and inputs, granting loans on state-owned banks, and other matters.

Obviously, these decisions affect key aspects of the media business. For example, official advertising remains a crucial source of media funding. Although advertising has historically been the lifeblood of media economics, the main sources of funding vary across countries. In countries with large economies such as Brazil, Colombia, and Mexico, the private sector is the main source of advertising, particularly for the metropolitan media. In contrast, the government is the largest advertiser as well as municipalities and provinces with low levels of private investment. In media markets where few newspapers and broadcasting stations draw revenue from commercial advertising, governments provide the lifeline for many media.

Also, it is not uncommon in such environments for local political families to own leading newspapers and broadcasting stations and hold interests in the main local advertisers. In these situations, political and economic powers as well as media elites are virtually undistinguishable. Such ties are grounded in common social backgrounds and even family ties. In some cases, political families and media corporations are intertwined.

The problem is not that states control substantial budgets that affect media finances. Public funding can eventually be used for levelling conditions and introducing positive, democratic measures in media systems. Also, official advertising could be deemed necessary, ideally, to publicize government acts and provide the public with important information. Certainly, such goals are different from typical propagandistic uses of state advertising devoid of any intention to duly inform the public. The problem is widespread discretion and lack of transparency in the management of public resources and decisions. Consequently, top officials enjoy virtually unrestricted power over decisions with huge economic implications for media companies. Presidents, prominent cabinet members, governors, and mayors have significant bargaining power vis-à-vis media companies. They control plenty of resources to pick winners, reward allies and punish critics in order to keep the media on a short leash and curb critical expression. Needless to say, media corporations with enormous stakes in official decisions are not seriously motivated to scrutinize government officials or challenge common practices. The power of governments lies not only on the significant economic impact their decisions have on media companies. It mainly lies on the fact that they operate in a political system rampant with arbitrariness and opacity.

Certainly, not all media companies have consistently benefitted from quid pro quo practices. Occasionally, there have been notable fissures between media companies and governments due to unsurmountable ideological, economic, and political differences in specific periods. Political contentiousness have driven high-profile battles between them that filled the airwaves and news pages. Typically, governments punished the opposition press by reducing or withdrawing advertising and/or declining to grant other economic benefits. Such decisions prompted companies to denounce governments for secrecy and arbitrariness and to call for strengthening public oversight. Some denunciations, albeit correct, were shamelessly opportunistic for they were the product of circumstantial antagonism. They conveniently ignored previous cases when media companies benefitted from government largesse. They generally condemned specific unfavorable decisions rather than the underlying system of mutual advantages.

Such a system is evidently contrary to democratic expression. Pervasive state opacity in decisions affecting media economics contradicts key international legislation stipulating that equitable and transparent official management is central to ensuring levelled conditions for public expression. Favoritism in the allocation of resources by the government threatens freedom of expression and should be prohibited by law according to Article 13 of the Declaration of Principles of Freedom of Expression of the Organization of American States.

Finally, the inability of the state to ensure democratic rights has also hampered citizens' expression. This failure is evident in large swaths of the region characterized by statelessness – that is, when the state neither controls the legitimate means of violence nor guarantees peaceful expression. These are areas controlled by rogue police and army officials, armed gangs, drug traffickers, and parastatal squads. For the past decades, press organizations have denounced scores of tragic episodes of citizens and reporters threatened and murdered by non-state groups. Although these circumstances are found across Latin America, they have been particularly sensitive in the hinterland of Brazil, Colombia, Guatemala, Honduras, and Mexico. Although ordinary citizens are habitually vulnerable to violence perpetrated by those groups, dissident news organizations and reporters have been consistently in the bullseye of armed groups. Considering the incredibly dangerous conditions, the persistent interest of journalists to denounce crimes and complicity between political power and parastatal forces is remarkable. They have been regularly subjected to verbal threats, kidnaps, intimidation, and murder. The region has a tragic record of journalists silenced for pushing to expand the boundaries of expression (Relly & Bustamante, 2014; Waisbord, 2007).

The state has contributed to limiting media pluralism primarily through jurisprudence legislation aimed at chilling speech, the arbitrary management of public resources in favor of pro-government companies, and the inability and reluctance to guarantee the basic right to expression.

A legacy of elite-captured policies

How should we explain the limitations of media pluralism in Latin American media systems?

The configuration of media systems in the region was not the preordained outcome of the unstoppable forces of the market. Nor was it the result of pure entrepreneurial ingenuity or abstract properties of media technologies. Accidental decisions did not result in media systems dominated by minority interests. Instead, the structures and practices analyzed were the culmination of a decades-long legacy of elite-capture policies. They resulted from the cumulative impact of policy decisions that overrepresented the interests of economic and political elites and failed to institutionalize a diversity of citizens' interests. Policy-making has not been a levelled field with equal opportunities for the participation of a broad range of interests. Indeed, when reviewing the history of media legislation in the region, one is struck by the continuation of back-door, sweet deals between officials and private companies, and the notorious absence of various publics.

This pattern reflects dominant media patrimonialism in policy-making (Guerrero, 2010; Picco, 2013; Waisbord, 2010). The notion of media patrimonialism draws from Max Weber's classic typology of political domination. It is characterized by relationships based on the principle of reciprocity. Rulers deliver goods in exchange for political support. Interactions between patrons and clients are based on reciprocity and voluntary compliance. Relations last as long as each party fulfills expected actions in a system of exchanges of goods and services. Patrimonialist politics feature administrative apparatuses controlled with discretion by leaders who delegate control to loyal followers. Patron–client relations organize the distribution of promotions, gifts, jobs, and placements. They are not regulated by impersonal laws or rules, as in the bureaucratic form of domination, but, instead, they are anchored on particularistic and private bonds.

The notion of patrimonialism for media policy-making is analytically valuable, for it directs attention to how states function and how state and market powers are intertwined. It essentially reflects the prevalence of personal ties and particularistic interests over the rule of law and public good. Certainly, specific aspects of media systems cannot be only explained by patrimonialism. Typologies, as Weber argued, identify some elements not every component of existing phenomena of particular cases. Not absolutely everything that belongs to "the media" in the region – news and entertainment content, journalistic practices, laws – can be solely explained by patrimonialism. Yet, addressing patrimonialism is fundamental to explaining essential characteristics of media systems in the region.

Media patrimonialism is characterized by the particularistic use of public power to obtain media favor, reward loyal media owners and companies, punish opponents, and draw political and personal benefits. Patronage dynamics underpin structural relations between governments and media companies, particularly in small markets where governments are the largest advertisers and are able to affect the economics of media companies in various ways. Weak government accountability makes it possible for officials to make decisions affecting media economies with weak oversight. Virtually any business affected by state policies can be affected by the dispensation of favors and personal loyalties. In return, owners of news business and/or parent companies promise supportive coverage and silence on sensitive matters affecting governments. Clientelistic relations exist between officials and media owners who regularly engage in favorable exchanges based on personal trust and loyalty.

Patrimonalism underlies Brazil's dominant *coronelismo electrônico*, a system in which politicians and family members own a large number of broadcasting licenses and news organizations throughout the country. The country's media system is rife with "client relations with a high degree of reciprocity" and "weak distinction between public and private interests" (Santos, 2013: 57). Although the constitution bans members of parliament from owning a public service, scores of representatives and senators own broadcasting licenses. In 2008, 271 elected representatives and officials were linked directly or indirectly to 324 media companies (Hailer, 2014). These linkages configure multileveled influence-peddling networks that closely tie politics and media ownership.

Media patrimonialism underscores the centrality of quid pro quo relationships in policy-making. In exchange for favors, public officials receive favorable coverage and other personal benefits plagued with illegalities such as shared ownership and kickbacks from media companies. Access to government resources and mechanisms confer officials and parties with tremendous capacity to continue or change the terms of engagement with media companies depending on specific alliances and circumstances. Not surprisingly, private media have constantly courted public officials, no matter their political sympathies, to gain economic advantages. Amidst weak or non-existent controls and obligations to publicize decisions, officials had significant leeway to reward allies and punish critics in return for docile news and kid-glove treatment. Officials and media companies developed links through reciprocal, often undisclosed arrangements that secured respective political and economic interests (Kitzberger, 2012).

Pervasive patrimonialism lays bare the absurdity of the "free-market competition" mantra endlessly repeated by national and regional media business associations. For decades, they have constantly pushed the timeworn shibboleth of the libertarian tradition of the press in the West: the defense of free enterprise and the condemnation of any state interference in the marketplace. History shows, however, that despite a discourse of "corporate libertarianism" (Pickard, 2013), leading media companies actually benefitted from close linkages to governments. Indeed, the remarkable expansion of contemporary media giants reflects the contradictions between their discursive hosannas to open markets and competition and actual behaviors. Their singular development and enormous success was hardly the outcome of a levelled, competitive marketplace but the result of close proximity to state officials. Corporations' exuberant love letters to freedom and competition sound hollow considering that media systems have not been exactly paragons of free-wheeling markets that rewarded entrepreneurial creativity or respect for the laws of competition. In fact, histories of major media corporations have amply demonstrated that the key to business expansion was collusion with governments, no matter political or ideological orientation (see Fernández & Paxman, 2000; Mastrini & Becerra, 2006; Sivak, 2013). Their phenomenal grip on media markets is grounded in their ability to exploit patrimonialist politics rather than to follow the supposed laws of free-market capitalism.

This is why "the best law is not law at all" line, another rhetorical evergreen deployed by media companies, reveals more than its champions actually mean. It unintendedly revealed the reality of media patrimonialism and private hostility to the rule of law. Private companies have vigorously opposed any attempts to regulate media markets, no matter their scope or content. As soon as governments mentioned the need for regulation or policy drafts circulated in congress, private trade associations rushed to condemn any decision that would restrict "open and competitive markets" and painted it simply as "censorship." What worried them was not necessarily or mainly the specifics of any form of regulation. Rather, they were alarmed about the prospect of rules organizing media markets. Just as they flatly rejected any law that would safeguard the public interest, they opposed any attempt to legislate. The rule of law is contrary to the personalist and particularistic dynamics of patrimonialism. Laws could do away with the standard modus operandi of backroom deals and pressures to prosper in media industries and other economic sectors. Private companies needed completely unregulated markets as well as arbitrary and non-existent law enforcement to succeed.

Governments doled out broadcasting licenses and other goods as giveaways, demanding little, if anything, in return. Media corporations had virtually no public obligations and made ludicrous payments in exchange for profiting from public resources. Failure to meet legal obligations was typically ignored or condoned, unless governments were politically motivated to castigate law infringement (as the quip goes, "a mis enemigos la ley" – "the law applies to my enemies"). Selective enforcement of the law clearly attests to the domination of patrimonialism.

Elite-captured policies essentially remained unchanged even after democratic governments replaced military dictatorships throughout the region in the 1980s. Unquestionably, the stability of democracy for over three decades has been a remarkable, unprecedented development in Latin American politics. Most government transitions have been relatively peaceful and conducted through free and fair elections. Conditions for public expression significantly improved with the consolidation of democratic rule, specifically the abolition of formal censorship and the end of official persecution of dissident media and journalists.

The consolidation of democratic rule, however, did alter the fundamental dynamics of media patrimonialism. The elimination of authoritarian laws and practices was not followed by a broad transformation in policy-making. The politics of personalism, discretionality, and spoils systems remained firmly in place. The persistent lack of accountability and transparency further facilitated these practices. Not only democratic governments in the past were uninterested in reversing the path dependency that shaped media systems. They also perpetuated established practices by deepening market principles and reinforcing government discretionary control over media operations. Collusion between government and media companies remained standard practices (Fox, 1988).

Why civilian administrations refused to undo the foundations of media systems can be attributed to three causes. Some governments subscribed (and benefitted from) the fundamental premises of patrimonialism and had no intention of changing the rules of the game as they came to power. Just as their predecessors, they sought to use existing practices and unwritten rules to their advantage by acquiescing to private demands in return for favorable news and content. Other governments were interested in the problems of media pluralism, but they were not interested in prioritizing progressive reforms. Realpolitik agendas meant that media reforms were sacrificed or forever postponed. Unfavorable political conditions made it unlikely that reforms would get passed. Concerns about the political fallout of regulatory policies, especially the reaction of media corporations, discouraged reformist spirits, too.

The shake-up of media systems demanded significant will and appropriate political alignments. Major legislative transformations were required to tackle fundamental problems: ownership concentration, the discretionary power of public officials, the disempowerment of regulatory agencies, and the situation of public media and third sector media. Taking action on any of these issues were not exactly easy political propositions. They demand resolute political will, broad support, careful strategizing, and the right balance of forces. Media reforms implied opening sensitive fronts with powerful media corporations and conservative political elites interested in preserving the status quo.

What democratic governments did, instead, was to perpetuate policies and practices that eventually further strengthened the power of media companies and public officials. Nor did they fundamentally change the way policies are made. Patrimonialist policy-making continued as official discretionalism remained common practice. By the early 2000s, it became clear that two decades of democratically elected governments did not spark progressive transformations in media systems to promote broad public expression.

Considering the prevalence of elite-capture policies, Latin American media systems are, in Guerrero and Márquez-Ramírez's (2014) notion, a "captured liberal market." This concept directs attention to two essential elements discussed here: ownership structure and policies. "Liberal" refers to the primacy of market principles in ownership, financing, and mission. "Capture" means that the same interests affected by policies, namely media owners and public officials, wield unduly influence in the policy-making process. Guerrero and Marquez's category underscores the fact that a particular style of policy-making spawned the particular "liberal" characteristic of media systems in the region – namely, elite-controlled and influenced process which excluded a range of public interests and actors. Asymmetric relations in the decision-making process have been standard. Political and economic elites wielded disproportionate influence over policy decisions that affected the public.

Therefore, Latin American media systems diverge from conventional models in the West (Hallin & Mancini, 2004). Although they were fundamentally anchored in market principles, they have not been replicas of the US media system. While it featured high levels of concentration and excessive commercialism as in the United States, chronic problems of governance meant that states retained ample and discretionary powers over media systems. Neither market forces nor governments had firm restrictions. Just as markets remained largely unregulated, governments retained significant discretionality in decisions affecting media performance and pluralism.

Nor did media systems exhibit key characteristics of the democratic-corporate model found in Northern Europe, namely, strong democratic interventions from the state in favor of pluralism with significant participation of political parties and other civic forces. The reason was simple: none of the principles that characterized this model ever became central. Market principles ruled unchallenged, public broadcasting never became the backbone of media systems, and unilateral and discretional government actions have been common.

Finally, Latin American media systems did not meet central criteria of the polarized-pluralist model of Southern Europe. Notwithstanding a similar tradition of clientelism, they generally lacked stable and strong political parallelism. Nor did they exhibit targeted state interventions in support of specific forms of pluralism.

Conclusion

Our argument is that the limited pluralism of media systems is grounded in market failures and problems of governance in the state. High ownership concentration coupled with the weakness of public media and the marginalization of community media has reduced the diversity of public expression. The domination of commercial principles and private ownership has been primarily concerned with delivering audiences and advertising, and expanding owners' business rather than reflecting the broad heterogeneity of Latin American societies. Media concentration narrows down the spectrum of issues and perspective in the media. Furthermore, the editorial agenda of dominant corporations is closely intertwined with dominant business interests both at national and regional level. The domination of commercial principles and private ownership leaves out a diversity of views, particularly the voices of ethnic minorities, local organizations, and progressive actors (Waisbord, 2011). Neither government officials nor private companies were particularly interested in strengthening alternatives to foster media pluralism. Whereas "public broadcasting" remained beset by chronic underfunding and official manipulation, the "third sector" sputtered along amidst legal persecution and economic troubles.

The particularities of media systems in the region are the result of the historical layering of elite-captured policies. Governments remained crucial actors because they are the unique actors that can guarantee communication rights. Instead, they have traditionally regulated media systems to favor public officials and private companies, thereby ignoring or suppressing public media and community media. The first wave of democratic administrations during the 1980s and 1990s failed to change this legacy. On the contrary, they basically continued long-standing practices and favored policies that further bolstered the power of media corporations and government discretionary practices. The emerging picture is obviously disturbing for democratic life. The region does not exactly have a luminous past in terms of media democracy. There is no glorious past to vindicate for the drawing of ideas for progressive media system reforms. Politics are severely hamstrung by media systems notoriously tilted in favor of economic and political elites. It is hard to imagine that the media provides room for the vast diversity of publics and perspectives in these conditions.

What is wrong with elite-captured media policy-making? Put simply, it is contrary to core democratic values – citizen participation, openness, and public scrutiny. Because policy-making should be a democratic communicative process, open to relevant stakeholders, the exclusion of affected citizens shuts down opportunities for deliberation and engagement. By excluding a diversity of political and social interests, policies have expectedly delivered benefits for particular interests. Regulations in support of the public good not only have been minimal; they have also consistently lacked strong political teeth. Public provisions have been flagrantly disregarded and small penalties have only occasionally been enforced in cases of violations. Given these conditions, it is not surprising that regulatory agencies have remained fragile, inefficient, or simply non-existent. Subjected to personal and partisan politics, they have lacked necessary autonomy to effectively control and enforce existing legislation.

Given that states have been responsible for shaping media systems through policies and decisions that heavily favored large private companies, the key question is not whether states intervene in media policies and decisions. Debating the relevance of the state on media policies does not lead to productive lines of inquiry to understand media policies and the prospects of progressive reforms. States are always present in media systems through multiple policy and legislative mechanisms and myriad decisions, as the history of Latin America media patently demonstrates. Even when they decide to refrain from any explicit intervention, favor light public interest legislation, or fail to enforce regulations, states wield significant, unmatched influence in setting basic structures and dynamics of media systems.

If we assume that states have to intervene in order to assure freedom of speech and information access, a different set of questions needs to be examined: How do states intervene? Who participates in debates and policy-making? How are policy battles decided? How does the particular structure and political balance of states affect media reforms? Who ultimately benefits from policy decisions?

The chapters that follow discuss recent experiences in citizen mobilization in support of policy innovations to promote media pluralism and communication rights. Reviewing these experiences is necessary to assess whether they have effectively reversed a tradition of elite-controlled media policies and policy-making processes.

2 | THE FIELD OF MEDIA ACTIVISM: ORGANIZATIONS AND DEMANDS

This chapter examines the field of media activism – the organizations and the demands of media movements in contemporary Latin America with particular attention to the case of Argentina, Uruguay, Ecuador, and Mexico. The focus is on civic society organizations (CSOs) that have worked on three issues: the reform of broadcasting systems, public access to government information, and press laws. Certainly, these cases do not exhaust the richness of civic participation on media and public communication issues in the region. Citizens have also mobilized around a host of other matters related to media policy and performance, such as the regulation of official advertising, stopping violence against journalists, strengthening public broadcasting, Internet regulation, equity in electoral coverage, telecommunications, audiovisual production, the transition to digital television, and media and journalistic quality, matters that have continued to attract attention from scholars (Rey, 2003; Sáez Baeza, 2008).

Why is it important to analyze the field of media activism? From the perspective that civil society is a vital space for the expression and inclusion of communication rights, organizations are a critical component of collective action and participatory politics. For activists and political strategists, organizations are solutions to collective action challenges – how citizens can be relevant, influential, trusted, and connected in democracies with considerable power asymmetries. Organizations are key institutional resources for channeling citizens' participation and form the building blocks of social movements (Haug, 2013; Fligstein & McAdam, 2011; McAdam, McCarthy & Zald, 1996). They are central to mobilizing demands on state authorities. This is why authoritarians fear organized citizens, and try to control, coopt, manage, diffuse, and defeat organizations. For democratic theorists, organizations are central to participatory politics. They are the linchpins of associational life, the social capital of democracy essential to cultivate networks of trust and solidarity (Putnam, 2001).

The field of media activism comprises organizations and networks that are essential to articulate citizens' demands, translate debates into proposals, and turn ideas into public policies. It is the institutional scaffolding for civic-driven media reforms. CSOs are necessary for the consolidation of citizens as rights-bearing actors and protagonists of policy-making processes. They lay out the institutional floorboard for media movements and bring expertise and capacity for continuous policy advocacy. CSOs exercise "social accountability" (Peruzzotti & Smulovitz, 2000) of media policies, articulate demands and proposals, and participate in the formulation and implementations of media policies.

Our argument is that the consolidation of an array of CSOs and policy coalitions strengthened the institutional density of media activism and bolstered the public presence of a rights-based vision of public communication. These developments reflect the coming of age of media activism in the region. They are positive insofar as policy transformations are unthinkable without bricks-and-mortar organizations with adequate technical capacity and political savvy. The number of organizations and the range of demands examined reflect unprecedented developments in the history of media activism in the region – the accumulation of institutions and expertise grounded in civil society. These are not only vital resources for civic life – the networks and associations democratic theorists believe are essential – they are also indispensable assets for strengthening citizen participation in media governance – the institutional moorings of activists.

The maturation of media activism reflects the heterogeneity of citizens' demands and the support for a common vision of the right to communication as the fundamental principle of public communication. Panels of organizations and democratic aspirations, as diverse as civil society, are sewn up in the quilt of media activism. The field is not a single, cohesive actor with shared demands, identical policy proposals, and common strategic priorities. It is not a common front of frontline organizations. Instead, it reflects the cacophony of civic life and features heterogeneous spaces for the formation of public will. This should come to no surprise to any observer or practitioner of the rough-and-tumble world of collective action and practical politics. Media activism speaks with different voices, is driven by myriad demands, and is concerned with particular policy reforms. It is not a harmonious realm of political will simply because civil society is not a monolithic bloc of common expressions and aspirations. Despite differences, progressive media activists share the notion that media policies should be grounded in the principle of the right to communication of all citizens.

Organizations

Contemporary media activism is at the point of confluence of different historical lines of participation and demands in Latin America.

One line of activism is embedded in long-standing struggles for the recognition of community, alternative, and indigenous media. The precursors were community broadcasting associations that pioneered demands for the reorganization of fundamental aspects of media ownership and policy to promote the diversity of production and content. They are the oldest media movements in the region with a tradition of grassroots activism in radio and television stations as well as film and video cooperatives. Their main demands have been the legal recognition of diverse forms of media ownership and ending the persecution of community media staff and supporters.

The origins of community broadcasting in the region go back to the foundation of peasants' and miners' radio in the 1940s in Bolivia and Colombia. These were radio stations linked to grassroots associations, unions, and the Catholic Church. The FM revolution rapidly transformed the community radio landscape as hundreds of stations emerged throughout the region during the 1970s and 1980s. Community radio became woven into citizen mobilization and social movements for the defense of human rights and the expansion of political rights (Darling, 2014; Hintz, 2011; López Vigil, 1995). With limited range and operating on shoestring budgets, stations became identified with pro-democracy movements and the emergence of alternative media and collective actors, particularly during military dictatorships.

In the 1980s, community television also gradually became part of the media landscape, largely aided by the boom of satellite and cable television and surging demand for content. However, community television never had similar relevance and impact in the region compared to radio due to its lower numbers and more limited public access to technologies (Vinelli, 2014).

Virtually in all countries of the region, associations mobilized to end political persecution of community and alternative media, achieve legal recognition, and reorganize media policies. The first national associations were founded in the 1960s and 1970s. The numbers grew in the 1980s and 1990s in the aftermath of military dictatorships. In Argentina, the Foro Argentino de Radios Comunitarias (FARCO) was formed in 1985, and represents ninety-one radio stations. In Ecuador, the Coordinadora de Radios Populares y Educativas del Ecuador (CORAPE) was formed in 1990 and has twenty-seven station members. Established in 2001, Ecos Coordinadora de Radios Comunitarias del Uruguay also represents community radio stations.

In Bolivia, Educación Radiofónica de Bolivia (ERBOL) was the first national association in Latin America established in 1967 to represent the interests of more than 170 stations. In Peru, the Coordinadora Nacional de Radio (CNR) was founded in 1978, and it represents forty-nine radio stations and twenty-seven educational and community communication centers. In Paraguay, three national networks have been active: Coordinadora Nacional de Radios Comunitarias del Paraguay, Red de Radios Populares del Paraguay, and Asociación Paraguaya de Radiodifusión Comunitaria Comunica. In Brazil, the Associação Brasileira de Radiodifusão Comunitária was formed in 1996, and it has around fifty affiliated stations.

Other associations were created in the 1990s and 2000s in the context of the promotion of alternative media by the *movimiento altermundista*, such as the Brazilian Centro de Estudos da Mídia Alternativa "Barão de Itararé," and Argentina's Red Nacional de Medios Alternativos (RNMA) and the Espacio Abierto de Televisoras Alternativas, Populares y Comunitarias. In some countries, indigenous media are organized in several associations, such as the Red de Comunicación Indígena created in Argentina in 2002 and Chile's Red de Comunicadores Mapuche (Doyle, 2015).

Two regional networks have played important roles by bringing attention to the situation of community media. The Asociación Latinoamericana de Educación Radiofónica (ALER) was established in 1972, and it originally represented radio stations affiliated with progressive groups within the Catholic Church. Although the stations had worked on distance learning, they became identified with leftist demands for anti-poverty policies and democratic expression during military dictatorships. The stations took a participatory approach to radio production that foregrounded local communities in terms of production and audience. ALER currently represents several community radio networks, including FARCO, CORAPE, CNR and ERBOL, and stations from sixteen Latin American countries.

The other network with extensive presence in the region is the Latin American and Caribbean branch of the World Association of Community Radio (known as AMARC in its Spanish acronym), which has national chapters in Argentina, Uruguay, Brazil, Chile, Guatemala, Mexico, and Peru. ALER, AMARC and other CSOs formed the Plataforma por los Derechos a la Comunicación in 1996, which set up the Campaña por los Derechos de la Comunicación en la Sociedad de la Información in 2001 as the Latin American chapter of the Communication Rights in the Information Society (CRIS) campaign.

Another line of media activism is grounded in the work of non-government organizations (NGOs) founded during military dictatorships and the subsequent constitutional governments to defend human rights and civil liberties, including the right to freedom of expression. They are staffed by lawyers, journalists, academics, political scientists, and other professionals. They are non-profit organizations with bureaucratic structures and paid staff, and are largely funded by foreign donors (governments, political parties, private corporations, or multilateral organisms). They function as think tanks that produce research and policy briefs, provide technical assistance to governments and international agencies, and they have also engaged in litigation.

In Argentina, several organizations have worked on a range of freedom of expression issues. In 1979, human rights activists founded the Centro de Estudios Legales y Sociales (CELS) to document and report human rights abuses during the authoritarian regime and to strengthen democratic institutions, including freedom of speech and communication rights. Central to its work has been demands to investigate crimes against humanity committed by the military government grounded in the public right to information. Other NGOs include Poder Ciudadano (the national chapter of Transparency International since 1993), the Asociación de Derechos Civiles (ADC), and the Centro de Implementación de Políticas Públicas para la Equidad y el Crecimiento (CIPPEC). These organizations have worked on a range of issues related to the quality of governance and problems of government performance, including arbitrary allocation of public advertising, the lack of national law granting public access to government information, the absence of public and non-governmental media, and inequalities in election media advertising. They have provided technical and legal assistance and conducted research and legal advocacy.

In Ecuador, a number of organizations working on freedom of expression issues have their regional offices. Leading organizations include: the Centro Internacional de Estudios para América Latina (CIESPAL), a research and teaching organization founded by UNESCO; ALER; the Agencia Latinoamericana de Información; the Organización Católica Latinoamericana y Caribeña de Comunicación; the local offices of UNESCO and UNIFEM (the United Nations Development Fund for Women); AMARC; and Radialistas Apasionados y Apasionadas; and Asociación para el Progreso de las Comunicaciones. They are similarly interested in policy advocacy, training, and research. Also, Fundación Andina para la Observación y Estudio de Medios (Fundamedios), founded in 2007, has monitored attacks on freedom of expression, supported training of reporters, and has been an outspoken critic of the Correa administration on matters of public expression.

In Mexico, the Asociación Mexicana por el Derecho a la Información (AMEDI) was founded in 2001 and it is integrated by academics, journalists, legislators, social leaders, writers, and artists. México Infórmate has done work on freedom of information legislation, transparency, and accountability. FUNDAR Centro de Análisis e Investigación was created in 1999 to promote citizen participation on a range of governance issues. Transparencia Mexicana has also been active on similar issues. The Mexican chapter of Article 19 has also worked on the protection of reporters, the elimination of censorship and violence, public access to government information, media concentration, the repeal of contempt laws, and the decriminalization of libel and slander.

In Uruguay, the Centro de Archivos y Acceso a la Información Pública (CAinfo) was created in 2009. After the passing of the 2008 law granting public access to government information, activists concluded a new organization was needed to support the implementation of the law. Although a coalition of CSOs had successfully advocated for the law (the GAIP described below), policy implementation demanded tasks that required the presence of an established organization (da Rosa Pírez, 2015). CAInfo was created, then, to monitor the use of the law and expand its use in various areas such as education and health.

CSOs with similar missions related to access to government information and freedom of speech also exist in other countries: Chile's ProAcceso and Observatorio de Medios FUCATEL, Peru's Suma Ciudadana, Guatemala's Fundación Myrna Mack, the Centro de Acción Legal en Derechos Humanos, Instituto de Estudios Comparados en Ciencias Penales and Acción Ciudadana, Colombia's Derecho Justicia y Sociedad, Fundación para la Libertad de Prensa (FLIP) and the Comisión Colombiana de Juristas, Costa Rica's Instituto de Prensa y Libertad de Expresión (IPLEX) and Instituto Interamericano de Derechos Humanos, El Salvador's Fundación Salvadoreña para el Desarrollo Económico y Social, Paraguay's Instituto de Derecho y Economía Ambiental (IDEA), República Dominicana's Participación Ciudadana, and the Brazil and Mexico offices of Article 19 (Lozano, 2015; Álvarez Ugarte, 2015; Bertoni, 2015). Brazil's Coletivo Intervozes and Peru's Asociación de Comunicadores Calandria are other leading CSOs working on media property concentration, community and indigenous media, public broadcasting, and other media issues.

Other organizations have primarily focused on issues pertaining to journalists' work, namely the safety of reporters, legal threats (e.g. disclosing sources, contempt, libel) and public access to government information.

Established in 2002, the Foro de Periodismo Argentino (FOPEA) aims to provide a forum for journalists to discuss matters of common interests such as ethics, training, and quality, and voice collective demands about freedom of expression. It has monitored and denounced attacks on journalists as well as multiple forms of violations of freedom of expression. Over time, it has expanded its agenda to include advocacy for an act to give access to public information, regulation of official advertising, and principles for public media. These demands were initially supported together with other NGOs. In addition, it has demanded that public officials hold open press conferences and promoted a "conscience clause" bill for journalists (Michi, 2015).

In Mexico, Periodistas de a Pie was founded by journalists in 2007 to promote quality reporting, the protection of journalists, and the defense of freedom of expression and the right to information.

In Peru, a group of lawyers, journalists, and editors established the Instituto de Prensa y Sociedad (IPyS) in 1993, during the escalation of attacks against the press perpetrated or condoned by the Fujimori administration. Since then, it has monitored and denounced attacks against the press, promoted access to information, supported investigative journalism, engaged in litigation in support of journalists and against government officials, and conducted training for reporters. IPyS is one of the four organizations of Proética, Peru's national chapter of Transparencia International. IPyS has affiliated associations in Colombia and Venezuela.

These examples demonstrate the consolidation of CSOs working on a range of issues related to public communication and freedom of expression. Many organizations originally emerged during the transition to democracy to promote the rule of law and human rights. Others emerged during democracy in reaction to specific problems or to represent common interests. Some associations represent community media and alternative groups with a tradition of grassroots activism in radio and television stations as well as film and video cooperatives. Some CSOs are think tanks that produce research and policy briefs, provide technical assistance to governments and international agencies, and engage in litigation. Other organizations are professional associations of journalists established to monitor and report physical attacks and legal threats.

Coalitions

An institutional innovation in the contemporary field of media activism is the formation of issue-specific, broad-based coalitions to promote media reforms. Coalitions are formed when "two or more social movement organizations work together on a common task" (Van Dyke & McCammon, 2010: xiv). Institutionally, they illustrate the notion of "bloc recruitment" (Oberschall, 1993) by which new media movements recruit and build on already existing organized groups and CSOs. The driving factor of coalition is activists' conviction that adding institutional resources, efforts, and expertise is strategically necessary to maximize political reach and the legitimacy of certain demands. Most coalitions resulted from grassroots processes and extensive discussions to build trust and reach common agreements among CSOs and media activists working on a range of public communication as well as civil, political, and social rights. Coalitions are intended to tap into the diverse expertise as well as the recognition of several organizations to strengthen institutional power and visibility. Whereas they aim to have a broad base of institutional support, coalitions are issue-centered formations focused on specific demands and proposals. Although coalitions had different impact, as we discuss later in the book, they were similarly premised on the conviction that they were necessary to bring together civic actors around two clusters of media reforms: broadcasting reforms and public access to government information

Broadcasting reforms Argentina's Coalición por una Radiodifusión Democrática represented a truly institutional innovation in the region. Established in 2004, it brought together myriad organizations that have long demanded policies to curb the power of market interests in media systems (regarding ownership concentration, runaway commercialism, and the presence of foreign capital and content) and the power of states regarding public and non-government media, and participatory agencies. It also promoted the legalization of community and indigenous media, and the protection of national, local, and independent content production. The Coalición was integrated by public universities, workers' unions, human rights organizations, associations representing indigenous peoples, community media associations, small and medium-sized business associations, women's groups, and other social and political organizations. After the passing of the 2009 law, the Coalición became inactive (Segura, 2011c; Álvarez Ugarte, 2013).

In Ecuador, CSOs failed to produce a unified coalition to mobilize behind a common agenda because of differences over relations with the Correa administration. As a consequence of divisions, three networks were formed to promote separate proposals for media reform. In 2007, during the debates about the constitutional reform, the Foro Ecuatoriano de la Comunicación produced fourteen points about the Right to Communication and drafted a bill to present to Congress. The Foro was convened by the Universidad Central de Ecuador and included journalists' unions and organizations (Federación Nacional de Periodistas), associations representing indigenous populations (Confederación de Nacionalidades Indígenas del Ecuador) and women's and youth movements. A second network was the Colectivo Ciudadano por los Derechos de Comunicación. This was convened by CIESPAL in 2009, after the 2008 constitutional reform, to propose a broadcasting bill, and brought together fourteen organizations. Community media organizations (ALER, CORAPE, ALAI, Radialistas Apasionados and El Churo Comunicación) formed a third network called the Autoconvocados de la Comunicación (Segura, 2012; Ramos, 2013).

In Mexico, the Frente Nacional por la Reforma de los Medios de Comunicación was a coalition formed in 2007 to represent CSOs that criticized the so-called "Televisa law," which granted benefits to the eponymous media corporation. The Frente, however, quickly broke up due to internal differences (Calleja, 2015). Later, many of its members formed the Coalición Ciudadana Democracia y Medios to express demands about media performance during the 2012 election campaign.

In Uruguay, the Foro de Comunicación y Participación Ciudadana was formed in 2004 as a coalition of several CSOs, but it failed to produce a common proposal for broadcasting reform. Many CSOs that were integrated into the Foro eventually participated in the Coalición por una Comunicación Democrática established in 2010. The Coalición agreed on sixteen points that were considered in the drafting of the 2014 Broadcasting Law.

Similar coalitions were formed in other countries, too. In Brazil, the Forum Nacional pela Democratização das Comunicações was formed in 1990. Originally, it was formed by press unions, students, and scholars, and eventually a wide array of CSOs were integrated into it. It brought together more than 120 CSOs working to represent community, alternative, public, and university media as well as workers' unions, university students, other unions, women's movements, cultural organizations, and municipal associations. It has worked on various aspects of public communication, including program content, journalists' rights, community media, and the regulation of pay television (Olivera Paulino, 2014; Valente, 2015).

In Peru, a landmark experience in media reform coalition was the Veeduría Ciudadana de Comunicación Social led by the Asociación de Comunicadores Sociales Calandria. The Veeduría was established to promote citizen participation in media criticism and public discussion and to articulate proposals for media reform during the Fujimori government (Asociación de Comunicadores Calandria, 2013; Castañeda Menacho, 2008). Calandria also had a leading role in public debates linked to the 2004 Radio and Television Law and public media. In Costa Rica, the Movimiento Social por el Derecho a la Comunicación presented a draft for broadcasting reform based on participatory principles.

Access to information In Argentina, several CSOs including ADC, CIPPEC, Poder Ciudadano, FOPEA and CELS have collaborated on various initiatives, including common proposals to regulate access to public information, government advertising, and public expression, as well as fundamental principles for public media (Segura, 2011d; Saba, 2015; Michi, 2015; Pochak, 2015).

In Ecuador, academic and civic organizations that worked on a range of social issues joined in the Coalición de Organizaciones Civiles por el Acceso a la Información Pública to demand freedom of information legislation. They obtained supported from the German foundations Konrad Adenauer and Friedrich Ebert and the American anti-corruption program ¡Sí se puede! The Coalición Acceso drafted a bill, conducted advocacy with legislators, and organized public debates (Navas Alvear, 2015; Navas Alvear & Villanueva, 2004).

In Mexico, a successful coalition was the Grupo Oaxaca established to promote a law to grant public access to public information in 2001. It brought together scholars, journalists, and business, including *El Universal, Reforma*, and *La Jornada*, the national newspapers with the largest circulation. The original meeting was funded by Article 19, Oxford University's Program for the Rights of the Media, and the Foundation Konrad Adenauer. The Grupo Oaxaca proposed key six points for a federal law. The Grupo Oaxaca played a significant role by advocating with members of Congress engaged in discussion of the draft of the bill. This was a pioneering experience because the Constitution doesn't allow the right for citizens' initiatives. Some members of the group participated in drafting the text of the bill that eventually was approved by Congress. The group disbanded after the law was passed. In late 2004, the Colectivo por la Transparencia was established to promote public access to information and related issues.

In Uruguay, the Grupo Archivos y Acceso a la Información Pública (GAIP) was formed shortly after the inauguration of Frente Amplio's President Tabaré Vázquez in 2005. It was a coalition of CSOs that included press, media, human rights, information, and academic organizations. The coalition reflected the conviction that they shared similar goals regarding the need for legislation about public access to government information, and that the coming to power of the Frente Amplio was a novel opportunity to pushing for reform. The GAIP disbanded soon after the freedom of access law was passed.

Similar issue coalitions were formed in other countries, too. In Paraguay, the Grupo Impulsor de Acceso a la Información Pública (GIAI), a coalition of twenty-two organizations, was formed to promote a bill to guarantee public access to government information. It drafted a proposal that was considered by legislators and eventually turned into law in 2014. Just like other regional civic coalitions, the draft was based on a model produced by the Organization of American states grounded on the principle of maximizing information – the state must prove that certain requested information cannot be made public due to public safety or privacy concerns when justifying decisions about what information to release.

In summary, the formation of policy coalitions reflects a growing awareness among CSOs and media activists about the need to strengthen the institutional presence of civic voices. Alliances are necessary to bring together efforts around common messages and actions with the hope of bolstering the visibility and credibility of demands for media reforms.

Demands and the right to communication

Aside from strengthening the institutional texture of media activism, CSOs and coalitions have also made another crucial contribution to collective action: They have diffused and bolstered the vision of communication as a human right of all citizens that should be guaranteed by states. This view posits that the central mission of media systems is to expand and protect opportunities for the expression of all citizens. Like any discursive framework, the rights-based vision of communication provides an interpretive schema to diagnose problems and propose policy solutions. It is the language used by media movements to make the reality of media systems and public communication intelligible. By doing this, they have accomplished what successful social movements have done – articulating a discursive frame that provides an understanding of conditions and identifies appropriate actions to address problems and promote social justice.

Citizens' demands can be clustered in two strategic foci: curbing the power of the market and limiting the discretionary power of the state in public communication and media systems. These two sets of demands direct attention to different problems. They reflect different philosophical perspectives about public communication. Whereas CSOs and movements share the views that civic society is at the core of democratic life and that public expression is a fundamental human right, differences are anchored in different models about the ideal relationship among state, market, and civil society in democracy. One position essentially believes that the oversized power of market forces in media systems is the overriding problem of public communication in the region. The other position is primarily worried about the discretionary power of the state, particularly the Executive, and government actions to silence critics and stamp out freedom of expression.

Embedded in postwar international legal standards and landmark documents on freedom of expression, the vision of communication as a human right underpins the work of associations worldwide on a range of issues related to public expression – from the cultural rights of minorities to the protection of the safety of reporters. It is articulated by the fundamental principles of the New World Information and Communication Order (NWICO) debates and the MacBride Report. Communication is envisioned as a fundamental, collective right like all other democratic rights. It is understood as a positive right that needs to be actively promoted rather than, as in the classic liberal model, a negative right that needs to be protected from an oppressive state. The democratization of communication is defined in relation to values such as access, participation, universal right, diversity, and equity. Therefore, policies are necessary to ensure that public communications are geared towards accomplishing central goals: broad access to use and produce diverse media and communication content; and civic involvement in the definition of broadcasting policies, the management of its institutions and broadcasting companies, and the production of broadcast programming. They also have to support the protection of national employment and industries;

promotion of cultural nationalism; media and content diversity; and equity in the distribution of information among nations, regions of a country, political powers, cultural communities, economic entities, and social groups. The right to communication endorses the diversification of the distribution of programs, the regionalization of broadcasting, and the decentralization of production. In terms of policy regulations, it espouses several actions to foster diversity in media systems: the decentralization of media ownership, the presence of new participants (governmental, community, and indigenous media), and the establishment of content quotas to reflect the cultural and political plurality and to decentralize the production of contents (Segura, 2013b, 2015b).

Rights-based ideals articulated demands for the democratization of public communication during the 1960s and 1970s in Latin America (Mattelart, 2007; Mastrini & Loreti, 2007). This conception of communication was traditionally found among grassroots activists pushing for the legalization of community media as well as in academic and legal quarters. In past decades, however, CSOs and coalitions have contributed to changing the social position of the rights-based framework as the latter gained visibility in public and legislative debates

Why is this important? Discursive frameworks anchor viewpoints and provide a blueprint for actions that are different from dominant approaches. The growing visibility and institutional embeddedness of the rights-based framework of public communication is important for social movements to perform key tasks: diagnose problems and causes, suggest solutions and courses of action, and motivate publics to action. It also reconfigures the discursive boundaries policy-making debates in the region by offering a "third way" alternative to market and statist discourses that have long dominated.

The rights-based view of communication diverges from free-market arguments in important ways. It flatly rejects the idea that the media should be primarily conceived as a business with minimal regulations (mostly dealing with technical and frequency matters that affect access and reception) or not regulated at all. It espouses the idea that the state needs to regulate media industries by making strategic interventions to guarantee the right to communication. This implies the existence of regulations to prevent private concentration, support public and non-government media, legalize and promote community media, and fill gaps left by the market, namely forms of public expression that are not supported by market forces. Just as states have historically assisted private companies in the region, particularly when in financial trouble, they need to intervene in media industries for the benefit of public interests. The difference lies in the goals and the procedures: whereas state interventionism was historically lopsided in favor of commercial and particular interests through methods fraught with opacity and corruption, state support for media pluralism is intended to serve the public good through fair, transparent, and accountable practices.

The rights-based position is also different from statist arguments about media democracy. It foregrounds the notion that the state needs to guarantee the right to communication for all citizens rather than to foster special interests. It champions the rights of citizens to know the functioning of the state in order to increase accountability and transparency of official actions rather than strengthen the ability of public officials to control information and be immune from public criticism. It foregrounds the notion of "public" as different from "state," and criticizes the application of statist policies in favor of particular interests rather than media pluralism. It conceives policy-making as a participatory and pluralist process rather than a matter exclusively reserved to political elites.

Embedded in the rights-based vision of communication, citizens' demands have focused on two sets of reforms.

One set of demands is based on the diagnosis that the excessive power of market interests is the main challenge for media democracy. Public communication is basically trampled by deep market inequalities. Private companies have hijacked media systems for their narrow benefits. Concentrated media markets, dominated by corporations with interests in various economic sectors, are the main threat to public expression (Segura, 2008a). They are contrary to the principle that citizens are the bearers of democratic rights and subjects of participation in the public sphere and matters of public expression. Commercial forces push the media to offer narrow views on social and cultural diversity. Dominant commercialism is contrary to the notion that the media need to provide content that serves the public interest of diverse populations. Absolute market domination is viewed as antithetical to the public good and plural media systems. As long as commercial goals are imperative and large corporations prioritize profit over public goals, media systems will be dominated by content produced to maximize the interests of media owners and advertisers. Reflecting and nurturing heterogeneous local and national cultures and artistic expressions is definitely relegated to a minor position.

Based on their critique of market-dominated media systems, CSOs and coalitions have demanded the implementation of policies to redistribute communication resources and opportunities and to foster socio-political and cultural pluralism. This goal underlies various proposals: the allocation of broadcasting licenses in three parts among public, private, and community/non-profit media; the promotion of ownership diversity by limiting vertically and horizontally integrated corporations and banning companies with interests in industries that provide public services (e.g. water, electricity) from owning media licenses; the legal recognition and promotion of community media as well as media representing indigenous populations, universities, unions, and other organizations; the restriction of the participation of foreign capital; and legislation to protect and stimulate production and distribution of domestic and independent audiovisual content.

They have demanded legislation to protect and stimulate production and distribution of domestic and independent audiovisual content. These demands are driven by the goal of protecting local and national production, promoting cultural nationalism and local jobs.

To be clear, the rights-based vision of communication does not propose the complete elimination of market-based media. While critical of market concentration, it does not propose the complete abolition of the private sector. Instead, it espouses the notion of regulated markets as necessary to bolster conditions for democratic communication.

These demands are integrated in calls to overhaul the role of the state in public communication and media systems. The state is viewed favorably as arbiter and guarantor of the right of expression for all citizens, as a potential and necessary ally to ensure that collective rights are legally supported and enforced. While it recognizes that the state has often been responsible for restrictions on public speech, it embraces a positive view of the state. It believes in its capacity to redress deep imbalances in the distribution of communication resources and opportunities. The state is indispensable to regulate media systems – it is the only institution capable of ensuring the universal right to communication for all citizens by passing legislation to strengthen community/non-profit media, curbing ownership concentration, and promoting the production and distribution of content that reflects the heterogeneity of Latin American societies.

Instead of rewarding large corporations and narrow political interests with favorable policies, the state should regulate media systems to ensure communication rights for all citizens (Segura, 2008a).

This shift in the performance of the state in favor of rights-based communication is possible as long as citizens are empowered in policy-making. Only when citizens become integral actors to policy-making can the historical pattern of an elite-captured policy-making be overturned. A regulatory state and protectionist legislation are necessary conditions to achieve media systems with strong public and citizen media, diverse content that reflects the needs and expectations of various populations, citizen participation in media production and management, and the creation and protection of media jobs (Badillo, Mastrini & Marenghi, 2015).

A second cluster of demands has dealt with problems for public expression grounded in chronic problems of government arbitrariness and opacity. Specifically, it has focused on the discretionary power of governments over public information, laws criminalizing public speech, and the opacity of official decisions related to media economics. These demands share a common diagnosis: the poor quality of democratic governance and state performance underlies persistent problems for public expression. Deep-seated governance problems include the reluctance of governments to make affairs open to public scrutiny; rampant abuses of public resources for personal benefit of public officials and media cronies; misuse of state institutions (including public broadcasting) and public resources to bolster the propaganda goals of particular administrations; and collusion between governments and private companies in the application of media legislation. This line of reasoning echoes arguments that identify profound problems of democratic governance in the region also rooted in the concentration and opacity of state power (Olvera, 2006; Peruzzotti, 2005).

These demands are grounded in a perspective concerned with the failings of the state on democratic expression. States should not have unchecked power in the use of public resources such as government advertising and other decisions that affect media economics. Opacity inevitably favors cronyism through which the particular interests of public officials and media companies draw benefits. Instead, states should use public resources and make decisions to serve the public good and address inequalities in public speech. Official information is a public good that governments should administer to increase citizens' knowledge about the workings of the state. Public broadcasting needs to be managed with democratic goals in mind rather than to spread narrow official views or lubricate clientelistic networks. Press laws should promote public communication rather than silence dissent and encourage self-censorship. As long as these problems persist, it is impossible for states to protect the communication rights of all citizens (Segura, 2008a).

These arguments are grounded in a progressive interpretation of philosophical liberalism. It is premised on liberalism's distrust of absolute authority. It reflects John Locke's conviction that the state inherently tends to secrecy and power concentration, James Madison's vision of society controlling the government, and John Stuart Mill's argument in favor of freedom of speech to combat state opacity and arbitrariness to allow the exercise of public reason. The individual right of speech should be protected given the state's penchant to stifle public expression in order to maintain privilege and power. A progressive view of liberalism champions civil society as the space for public deliberation. This demands that the state actively intervenes in media systems to guarantee the speech rights of all citizens. The state should not be simply rolled back or completely removed from matters of public expression. It has the obligation to ensure the right to communication of all citizens by taking actions to correct deep imbalances in public speech caused by the domination of market principles. The state needs to guarantee rights and bolster citizens' participation and monitoring power in democracy.

CSOs and coalitions have made several demands embedded in this conception of free speech. For example, they have demanded states to guarantee public access to government information through appropriate legislation and mechanisms to record and process official proceedings. Such legislation was virtually non-existent two decades ago in the region. Other CSOs have expanded the notion of access to information to include information of public interest controlled by private companies (Saba, 2015; Acosta, 2014; Abramovich & Courtis, 2000). They demanded information to hold governments accountable, that citizens be brought into policy-making decisions, and a host of social and public rights related to workplace discrimination, the environment, and consumer interests. Demands for access to information are also linked to movements demanding the right to truth in relation to human rights violations, access to personal data in public and private databases, and the right to investigate (Loreti, Lozano & Pochak, 2014; Solís Leree, 2015).

CSOs have demanded the repeal of laws criminalizing critical speech against public officials grounded in matters of honor and national security. They also demanded the reduction of civil penalties given that the persistence of severe legal and monetary penalties on reporters and news organizations has chilling effects on the reporting of government officials and other powerful actors, and promoted self-censorship (Loreti & Lozano, 2014).

CSOs and coalitions have also called for transparency and accountability in the assignation of official advertising, which has been historically rife with chronic abuses and collusion between officials and media owners. By arguing that government advertising is a public resource that needs to be assigned according to the public interest, CSOs have aimed to curb discretionary and opaque procedures. Some CSOs have also demanded the need to regulate state funding of media companies, including government advertising, tax exemptions, subsidies, extensions of expired licenses, and other instruments long used to favor private interests, and bolster citizen participation in decisions affecting media economics (Becerra, 2009; Lozano & de Charras, 2012).

CSOs have also demanded that states investigate and bring justice to attacks against reporters and to prevent such attacks. Throughout the region, citizens and journalists have been targets of verbal and physical violence at the hands of state and parastatal actors. In some countries, such as Honduras and Mexico, the situation has been particularly difficult in recent years. The continuation of violence and the failure of the state to ensure the right to free speech remain critical problems amid the spiral of violence perpetuated by state, parastate, and private actors such as gangs, drug-trafficking organizations, and para-police and military bands, and condoned by the state.

Finally, CSOs have also demanded major reforms in public broadcasting. Organizations have criticized governments for the chronic use of state-owned broadcasting stations and networks for partisan propaganda and clientelism. Instead, they have argued it is necessary to ground the functioning and management of public broadcasting on principles oriented to serve the public.

In summary, various demands made by CSOs and activists are intended to achieve two major objectives: curb the unregulated power of market forces in media systems and restrain the discretionary power of governments on information, freedom of speech, and media systems. Both goals are anchored in the rights-based vision of communication that places people, rather than markets or states, at the core of democratic communication. This vision not only advances the notion that media legislation should be oriented to maximize public expression of all human beings, it also promotes citizen participation in media policy-making as integral to the quality of democratic governance.

The field of media activism

The organizations, issue coalitions, and rights-based vision reviewed here characterize the field of media activism in the region. The gradual consolidation of the field is auspicious for two reasons: it solidifies the institutional backbone for citizen participation in matters concerning media pluralism and public speech, and it legitimizes the rights-based view of communication as the fundamental principle for organizing media systems and public communication.

The field of media activism represents the expansion of institutional opportunities for citizen participation and representation in media policy debates. Although its foundations were laid down in the 1940s, it came to fruition after the fall of military dictatorships in the 1980s. Democratic stability facilitated the emergence and the stability of CSOs dedicated to the promotion of reforms of media and information policies. Undoubtedly, the consolidation of media activism is enormously important considering the chronic weak position of civil society vis-à-vis the state and the market in policy-making. In no previous time in the history of the region do we find a similar situation: numerous CSOs expressly dedicated to channeling citizens' demands and influencing policy-makers and media policies by championing rights-based principles. This is truly a historical novelty.

The field of media activism did not flourish as a result of the decision of states to create spaces to encourage media activism. Certainly, as we discuss in the next chapter, civic organizations were able to capitalize on the gradual opening of state-sanctioned spaces such as participatory mechanisms and the courts. The field, however, grew out of the efforts of mobilized citizens to carve out spaces for public discourse, demands, and political engagement.

Although they are anchored in civil society, CSOs have constantly pushed to find opportunities to engage with state actors. They are not conceived as alternative spaces completely removed from the institutional architecture of democratic politics – state institutions and political parties and other forms of representation – nor are they interested in remaining peripheral to state politics. Instead, their view is to articulate citizens' demands and spearhead policy changes.

The institutionalization of media activism has contributed the mainstreaming of the social position of the rights-based vision of public communication in the public sphere and the state. Whereas it used to be chiefly a matter of concern to selected groups of media activists, this vision has gained newfound prominence. As we will show in the chapters that follow, rights-based principles are ubiquitous in the public sphere. They are woven into an array of media reform proposals and policies. They frequently appear in the news media, legislative debates, public audiences, and the courts.

Traditional forms of organized politics such as business organizations, political parties, unions, or religious institutions have not played central roles in the institutionalization of media activism. Nor did they become the institutional backbone of media movements. In fact, media activists' organizations have maintained relative autonomy vis-à-vis traditional forms of organized politics such as unions, churches, and political parties.

Instead, the field of media activism comprises organizational offspring of diverse traditions of citizen politics in Latin America. It is integrated by an array of NGOs and community groups that bring together the technical expertise of professional think tanks and the territorial presence of grassroots activists. CSOs come in different shapes. Some are organizations staffed and managed by small cadres of technical professionals; others have larger memberships with roots in journalism and media activism. Most organizations count on modest human and monetary resources.

Grassroots groups are organizational hybrids with different legal statuses, funding sources, operations, volunteer and paid work, and social presence. They represent a vast array of media workers, critics, and community residents from television and radio stations, film cooperatives, universities and schools, and workshops. NGOs, in contrast, are bureaucratic organizations with legal status, permanent staff, and funded by international donors, membership fees, and/or sympathizers. Coalitions are yet another different type of organization: they are conceived as temporary strategic instruments to unify demands among CSOs and activists and to achieve specific goals (Cruz, 2009). Although coalitions are generally short-lived, they are primarily sustained by organizations with bureaucratic structures, deep expertise, and extensive contacts in civil society, market, and the state.

One lesson from these experiences is that media activism requires organizations with track records and established connections. Organizations provide stable connective structures that mediate public will and engage with governments. They are institutional formations that result from the sedimentation of relations, experience, recognition, and previous efforts. They perform key functions in participatory politics, such as facilitate communication, articulate objectives, coordinate actions, and implement strategies. The "routinization" of organizations is essential to achieve policy reforms. Organizational trajectories and reputation certify the bona fides of activists in the eyes of other actors in civil society, the market, and the state. Organizations are needed to achieve stability and recognition as legitimate representatives of specific constituencies and valid interlocutors.

It is important to underline the significance of bricks-and-mortar organizations as the institutional infrastructure of media movements, particularly in light of rushed conclusions about the end of organizations and considerable enthusiasm about digital organizing in recent years. No question, the affordances of digital networks make online forms of activism possible, as shown by a growing literature in Latin America (Harlow & Harp, 2012; Treré, 2015) and elsewhere (Bennett & Segerberg, 2014; Milan, 2013). The consolidation of the field of media activism, however, suggests that "offline" organizations are still central. As the locus of policy mobilization, the field basically refers to formal organizations with established and recognized presence in society and politics.

Even though activists resort to online tactics or become digital foot soldiers, the field of media activism features an array of formal organizations as the institutional support of media movements. Formal organizations are necessary for citizens to be fully engaged in media policy-making. Media movements are not constituted by citizens interested in expressing positions about media policies only in specific moments or in response to government decisions. Rather, they aim to have sustained, long-lasting impact throughout the policy-making process. This is why short bursts of protests and demonstrations may be tactically necessary, but they are not sufficient to spearhead massive reforms in public communication. Ephemeral organizing is not always the best-suited instrument for scrutinizing governments, engaging citizens, or spearheading reform proposals. Policy-making is a long-term, zigzagging process that requires more than intermittent acts of contention and short-lived gatherings and actions. Media reforms demand considerable time and patience as well as formal organizations to sustain long-term strategic actions and keep citizens engaged in policy debates and decisions.

The consolidation of the field of media activism suggests that we are not in the "post-organization" era yet. As conduits for myriad citizens' interests, formal organizations remain important to promote social change. Because sustained attention and actions from activists are required to effectively influence policy-making, organizations with permanent presence may still be irreplaceable in strategic terms. They continue to provide platforms to keep citizens engaged in policy criticism, formulation, negotiation, and implementation, and the search for opportunities to have access and influence media policy-making.

3 | STRATEGIES

Our interest in this chapter is to examine the strategic playbook of media movements. Strategies refer to the tactics used by CSOs and issue coalitions to achieve specific objectives.

One aspect that has attracted significant scholarly attention is whether social movements are characterized by the use of specific strategies. Snow, Soule, and Kriesi (2004) affirm that the utilization of contentious tactics is a central characteristic of social movements. Studies on collective action have identified public protest as a preferred strategy for expressing grievances and making demands on dominant powers. Protest actions include demonstrations, strikes, marches, pickets, riots, and other forms of street theater. Other studies (see Giugni, 2008), instead, have argued that social movements use both institutional and non-institutional tactics to achieve social change. Although some movements have been identified with confrontational methods, others have shifted strategies as conditions, goals, and opportunities change. "The repertoire of collective action" (Tilly, 1986) is not limited to contentious strategies to demonstrate against authorities. Extra-institutional, disruptive tactics have been used in specific circumstances, yet they are not uniformly favored as the only tactic to achieve goals.

The choice of strategies chiefly reflects the condition of social movements vis-à-vis the state – the common target of citizens' demands. When they lack direct and fluid access to official decision-makers, movements utilize "weapons of the weak" (Scott, 1988) to voice expressions with the hope of attracting attention and influencing decisions. In cases of political exclusion, social movements have no option but to resort to protest strategies to make themselves heard. "Activism" is essentially protest directed to states, corporations and other powerful actors (Dauvergne & LeBaron, 2014). The use of these strategies differentiates movements from interest groups and other forms of association that generally use institutional channels to influence policy-making.

Media movements in Latin America offer an intriguing set of cases to discuss these arguments and analyze preferred strategies for policy reform. Without exception, as we show in this chapter, movements have used both "insider" and "outsider", institutional and non-institutional strategies. They have used traditional forms of protest such as public rallies as well as conventional institutional tactics including advocacy, technical advising, deliberation, and congressional and judicial testimonies.

It would be wrong, then, to classify media movements narrowly as "protest movements" or "interest groups" based on the choice of strategies. They don't neatly fit conventional arguments that offer a typology of categories of collective action according to the kind of strategies utilized. Nor do they fit the definition of "interest group" if this category refers to the exclusive use of institutional channels as a distinctive element, typically by established and well-funded groups with access to political power.

The experiences discussed here throw into question whether social movements should be characterized as forms of collective action uniquely defined by the use of certain strategies. Identifying social movements with specific strategies or classifying forms of collective action according to the use of certain strategies is misguided. It loses sight of the fact that social movements might use diverse strategies to promote social and political change according to context and political opportunities. Protest may be strategically smart in certain situations but unwise in other contexts. Institutional channels might offer chances to advance causes but they quickly shut off when political circumstances change. Indeed, the historical trajectory of prominent social movements in Latin America such as human rights, students, and women's groups precisely show strategic shifts (Almeida & Ulate, 2015).

Media movements seek to influence various actors, most notably the state, the media, the general public, potential allies, and opponents. To achieve this, they deploy various strategies across many public arenas such as public opinion, courts, legislature, the media, and elections. Consequently, they are not committed to a single form of action regardless of conditions, publics, or resources. Instead, they have proven to be quite flexible in terms of selecting strategies fitted to specific conditions and goals.

We find the strategic versatility of media movements remarkable, particularly given the strong tradition of protest in media activism in Latin America. A shift in strategies reflects changes both in the overall outlook of media movements as well as dramatic political changes that opened institutional opportunities to promote change.

We argue that the use of strategies beyond the "protest paradigm" reflects the political pragmatism and versatility of CSOs. The use of multiple strategies is indicative of their deliberate goal to set in motion profound policy changes, not only to use contentious tactics to oppose policy decisions. Anchored in civil society, CSOs intend to gather support and influence state decisions (namely, legislative and court decisions) to reform media systems. Strategies are aimed at cultivating public opinion and will inside civil society as well as articulating common interests with state actors.

With these goals in mind, both institutional and non-institutional channels are used. In fact, most organizations are not primarily interested in solely confronting the state; instead, they seek to reach minimal consensus with selected state actors to advance their causes and partner up behind common goals. The relations with the state, then, are more complex than in other cases of social movements that generally consider instances of protest against the state. Instead, the strategies used by media movements are aimed at promoting dialogue, negotiation, pressure, agreement, and collaboration throughout the three phases of policy-making: public debate, legislative definition, and implementation and monitoring of new policies.

In what follows, we review the strategies used by media movements: coalition-building, knowledge production and dissemination, voice and persuasion, advocacy, and state-sanctioned mechanisms.

Issue coalitions

As mentioned in the previous chapter, coalition-building has been a strategic priority of media movements in the region. Coalition-building lies at the core of the process of forming social movements and collective identities. It entails developing, accumulating, and maintaining links with organizations. It entails the creation and recognition of connections among people and organizations around shared interests and commitments to a cause (Diani & Bison, 2004). With these goals in mind, CSOs have reached out to others with shared goals and institutional make-up, including technical and professional associations as well as grassroots associations. Also, they have partnered with other associations specializing in social, civil, and political rights to promote media policy reforms.

Media movements are emblematic of the notion that contemporary movements are networks of interaction linking multiple organizations and activists. Coalitions are organization structures considered strategically necessary for successful collective action. They put in evidence actors' deliberate agency to create structures/fields and opportunities to generate and advance change. Coalitions are based on the recognition of diversity and respect for pluralism, and the belief that the establishment of a strong alliance structure broadly empowers movements by providing a locus of organizational interactions and supports. Coalitions foster the exchange of ideas, competence, and institutional capacity. Coalition-building is a process of mutual learning that expands the institutional network of specific organizations and bolsters their visibility and participation within a certain area of interest (Van Dyke & McCammon, 2010).

Unifying demands among diverse organizations is critical to avoiding dispersion and confusion about demands. Not surprisingly, a first task is to define common demands and principles for future legislation, as a recent document by a leading regional coalition on freedom of expression observes (Alianza Regional, 2013). For example, Mexico's Grupo Oaxaca brought together different actors (lawyers, activists, and academics, and representatives from the three newspapers with the largest circulation in the country) behind a common cause and course of action: passing legislation to ensure public access to government information. Similar dynamics drove the formation of Ecuador's Coalición Acceso, Uruguay's GAIP and a loose alliance of Argentine CSOs. Likewise, media reform coalitions such as Argentina's Coalición por una Radiodifusión para la Democracia, Uruguay's Coalición por una Comunicación Democrática, Mexico's Coalición Ciudadana Democracia y Medios, and Ecuador's Foro de la Comunicación, represented myriad interests and organizations and reached a consensus on common proposals.

Without basic agreements about principles, structures, and procedures, coalitions are not viable. Tensions can only be resolved when organizations find basic agreements on principles and courses of actions. Understandably, this is not easy matter. The uneven power and presence among various organizations, jockeying for positions, political sympathies, and personal and organizational ambitions generally make coalition-building a time-consuming process. Coalitions are viable only when differences are successfully bridged and partners build minimal trust. Only then are they able to express their demands in clear, unmistakable terms.

The diversity of organizations and missions has not always been successfully overcome and emerging coalitions have eventually unraveled. In Ecuador, for instance, wide disagreements among organizations that originally pushed for a new broadcasting law resulted in the formation of three groups. In Argentina, the coalition of several CSOs that promoted a common proposal for public access to government information fell apart due to disagreements about the specifics and the relationship vis-à-vis the Kirchner government (Acosta, 2014; Saba, 2015). In Mexico, the 2007 Frente Nacional por la Reforma de los Medios de Comunicación could not overcome disagreements among leading actors about common proposals (Calleja, 2015). This is hardly surprising: common opposition to certain policies does not guarantee agreements on alternative courses of action. As media scholar and activist Raul Trejo Delarbre (2015) observes, "It is more difficult to propose than to protest."

Argentina's Coalición sought to manage internal differences to avoid confrontations and contradictions in the overall plan of demands. Members deferred to organizations with experience in media issues to resolve disagreements, lead the process, and maintain the consensus around key issues which were reflected in its twenty-one points (Segura, 2011c). One source of constant tension was eminently partisan – differences between sympathizers and opponents of the Kirchner administration. Although they shared some demands and principles, disagreements became open, particularly at the time of the production of public documents, especially regarding issues sponsored and decisions made by the administration. Divisions reached a point of no return during the congressional debates of the bill that eventually culminated in the 2009 broadcasting law (Segura, 2011c; Álvarez Ugarte, 2013).

Most coalitions did not set up formal bureaucratic structures. For example, the Grupo Oaxaca was reluctant to establish a formal civil association; instead, it remained a loosely defined "collective space" – a network of scholars, media entrepreneurs, and journalists that shared the view that public access to government information is a human right, and it disbanded shortly after the information access law was passed (Acosta, 2014).

For coalitions, the main challenge has been balancing the heterogeneity of interests with potentially common objectives. Debates about the adequate organizational structure and procedures precisely reflected this permanent tension. Argentina's Coalición debated the adoption of a structure modelled after similar experiences in media activism elsewhere such as the Consejo Internacional del Foro Social Mundial, the Media Diversity Coalition in the United States (http://www.mediadiversity.org), the 2003 Coalition pour la diversité culturelle in Canada (http://www.cdc-ccd.org), and the Mesa de Diálogo para la Reforma Integral de la Legislación de Medios Electrónicos convened by the Mexican government.

Why did CSOs decide to participate in coalitions? One goal is to strengthen key institutional aspects of individual organizations as well as movements. Individual CSOs have participated in coalitions with the expectation that it might reap specific institutional benefits: raise the visibility of their mission and organizational profiles, open and renew opportunities for further work and funding, and consolidate their status within a certain area of work. Coalitions make it possible to build a more robust organizational structure with wider reach. Such a structure increases the chances of more effective advocacy (Alianza Regional, 2013). Also, international funders may favorably view coalitions at both the national and regional levels for similar reasons, as, in principle, they offer better opportunities to maximize expertise, resources, and impact (Behrens, 2015).

Some coalitions have represented CSOs working on a wide range of issues. Argentina's Coalición, for example, brought together organizations with different interests, areas of action, expertise, histories, structures, and degrees of institutionalization (Segura, 2011d). Most organizations have had virtually no experience working on media issues, let alone policy reforms, as they fell outside their mandate and traditional strategic focus. Similarly, Mexico's Frente Nacional por la Reforma de los Medios de Comunicación included more than 300 organizations that agreed that the lack of media pluralism not only affected freedom of expression, but also had negative effects for any progressive struggle (Calleja, 2015). Ecuador's 2004 Coalición Acceso and Uruguay's GAIP also included CSOs working on different issues (Navas Alvear, 2015). In contrast, other coalitions were basically integrated by CSOs focused on communication, journalism, and freedom of expression, such as Peru's Veeduría Ciudadana de Comunicación and the Foro de la Comunicación, Ecuador's Colectivo Ciudadano por los Derechos de Comunicación de Ecuador, Mexico's Grupo Oaxaca, and Argentina's alliance of CSOs pushing for public access to government information, independent public media, and the regulation of state advertising.

Broad-based coalitions are expected to raise the legitimacy of causes and supporters. Members hope to demonstrate that their demands are not circumscribed to a small number of organizations or associations focused on media issues. They expect to be recognized as stakeholders in public issues who need to be heard in public and policy discussions.

Coalitions capitalize on the prestige and expertise of recognized individuals, associations, and social movements with long-standing commitment to human rights, civil liberties, and the right of law. Partnerships with associations recognized in higher education, union activism, justice, and society at large are expected to further the recognition of specific demands. By elevating the visibility and prestige of the causes, coalitions are expected to make associations less vulnerable to being dismissed as "just a few" "unknown" actors by various publics. Argentina's Coalición tapped into the diversity and prestige of some members to legitimize its proposals. Undoubtedly, the participation of human rights organizations and universities recognized for their work on public communication reaffirmed its credentials as a pluralist body (Segura, 2011c).

Coalition-building requires streamlining demands and principles to reach a common political vision. Such vision needs to be recognized as legitimate by coalition members, and potentially by broad sectors of the public and legislators. Establishing ideological linkages with other causes and organizations is strategically smart to frame issues and position movements in the political landscape. Potential frameworks – the ideological repertoire of contention – to ground demands and principles are not endless. Specific discourses with recognizable language and narratives circulate in societies. They provide ready-made elements for media movements to frame issues and demands. They may be acceptable in particular historical conditions. Therefore, coalitions, especially if they are new, need to plug their demands and discourse to already established and legitimate frameworks that have resonance among citizens and policy-makers.

Organizations that are ideologically closer are more likely to form successful coalitions. Ideological proximity provides stronger ties to facilitate the harmonization of demands and principles. Ideology, including partisanship, provides a common vocabulary and shared worldview. It is the cultural glue that coalitions need to be successful. Ideational similarity underpins the "issue bricolage" process (Jung, King & Soule, 2014) by which movements strategically link themselves to past and present movements with similar discourse. New movements weave specific demands with social and political issues that already have public standing and prestige to raise their profile and legitimacy.

This process was noticeable in Argentina's Coalición twinning of demands for media reforms with human rights groups and other progressive groups widely respected in the country. The Coalición positioned itself and its demands as part of the broader struggle for the recognition of human rights. This framing positioned was further bolstered by the fact that the Mothers of Plaza de Mayo and other leading human rights organizations were members of the Coalición (Segura, 2011b). Media reform coalitions in Brazil also engaged in "issue bricolage" by which they connected their demands and actions to established social movements and CSOs working on human rights and labor issues (Valente, 2015).

Finally, coalitions are important to increase the geographical and political footprint of specific demands and organizations. Acting alone notably limits their reach and possibilities of making significant differences (Alianza Regional, 2013). Isolated, go-on-your-own actions are unlikely to build strong, broad-based support in civil society or help CSOs to make significant inroads into governments.

Knowledge management

Another tactic used by media movements is the production and dissemination of expert knowledge. Just like other social movements (Conway, 2006; Leach & Scoones, 2007; Parthasarathy, 2010), they consider the mobilization of specific expertise to advance policy reforms essential. It is a critical aspect of their work. The prospects of media reforms are contingent on producing knowledge documenting problems and solutions as well as persuading various actors about the merits and problems of specific policy proposals.

Media movements demonstrate that ideological convictions are not sufficient to accomplish tasks linked to policy reforms. Just the belief that the rights-based view of communication is normatively better than alternative frameworks and that it should be the foundational principle of media systems is not sufficient to achieve goals. The strategic politics of media reform demand more than upholding a specific view about democratic speech or clinging dogmatically to a given doctrine. Normative commitments need to guide the production and dissemination of fact-based knowledge articulated with advocacy objectives. Expert knowledge is not produced for its own sake or to advance social understanding of specific issues. Instead, it is essentially conceived as a valuable instrument for strategic purposes (Alianza Regional, 2013).

This is why several CSOs have set up knowledge-producing units, regularly commissioned position papers, and/or partnered with scholars and technical specialists. Several organizations are staffed by lawyers, academics, and activists with vast expertise in specific media legislation issues. Recognized national and regional specialists in information, media, and press laws are members of coalitions and associations. Experts' familiarity with legislation around the world on various matters – from public speech to community radio – have contributed to the production of proposals anchored in state-of-the-art debates and decisions. CSOs have created units to monitor the situation and gather data regularly on specific areas of media policies.

The constitution of media movements as "epistemic communities" (Haas, 1992) with recognized expertise and competence in media policy-making is remarkable considering the relative paucity of information produced by government agencies and the private sector. Most governments in the region lack the kind of accumulated knowledge and in-house expertise to closely monitor situations and produce technical reports and surveys about a range of media issues. Government information about specific media issues is not publicly available in forms that CSOs and citizens can read and use for various purposes. Nor do media business organizations fare much better in this regard.

Instead, CSOs are staffed with academics and experts who regularly produce reports on various issues related to public communication.

They have contributed to a significant body of knowledge that was almost non-existent decades ago – the "gray" literature on media policy, including policy briefs, surveys of community media and information access laws (CAInfo, 2014), reports on violence against the press, and regulation of state advertising (Asociación por los Derechos Civiles & Open Society Institute, 2005, 2008).

This wealth of information is deliberately produced as "actionable expertise" to inform multiple strategic considerations and objectives. Solid, fact-based technical arguments are aimed to bolster the credibility of CSOs and coalition in the eyes of the news media, legislators, citizens, and other experts. As long as they grounded in reliable data, positions are less likely to be flatly dismissed or countered with accusations of partisanship. At a time when getting news coverage is important to raise the visibility of problems and solutions, CSOs have deliberately produced information and develop media outreach activities to attract attention from media organizations and become regular sources for reporters (Waisbord, 2011).

Actionable expertise is also necessary to document problems, articulate demands, elaborate technical and policy proposals, survey advances and setbacks, and other tasks. This information helps to define strategic objectives, produce arguments and messages, and mobilize public opinion and political support. Technical documents are generally distilled to basic advocacy principles to be used with news organizations and legislators. In other cases, technical documents are central to engaging in litigation, as we show in the next pages.

Knowledge management gives CSOs opportunities to participate in the drafting of principles and proposals and present expert testimonies during the legislative debates about media bills.

Mexico's Grupo Oaxaca tasked a technical commission with producing basic principles for the Law of Transparency and Access to Public Information and also writing the draft of a bill. In Argentina, members of the Coalición contributed to drafting documents that were debated by Congress and included in the 2009 Law of Audiovisual Communication Services. Several CSOs published *Principios básicos sobre el funcionamiento de la radio y la televisión pública*, a document that reflected common agreements among social, professional, academic, and political actors (Segura, 2015a; Asociación por los Derechos Civiles & Open Society Institute, 2005; Saba, 2015). The

Asociación por los Derechos Civiles elaborated a proposal to regulate state advertising drawing from a comparative international study (Saba, 2015). In Ecuador, legislators presented media bills that were drafted by the Colectivo Ciudadano de Comunicación in the lead-up to the passing of the 2013 Communication Law. Ecuador's Coalición Acceso and Uruguay's GAIP also elaborated an access to information bill. In Peru, the Asociación de Comunicadores Sociales Calandria drafted a proposal for public media that was debated by Congress in 2004; the 2014 Foro produced eleven principles for media reform (Acevedo, 2015). In Brazil, the Forum Nacional produced a bill for "democratic media" to submit it to Congress as a popular initiative (Valente, 2015). In México, the Colectivo por la Transparencia and México Infórmate presented a proposal for a law of transparency and information access in 2014. Asociación Mexicana de Derecho a la Información (AMEDI) produced a bill on telecommunication and broadcasting, and the association Internet para Todos presented a proposal for internet access (Solís Leree, 2015; Meneses, 2015).

CSOs have also used technical data, experts' testimonies, citizens' views and other sources of information to rebuke arguments made by governments, political parties, and business organizations. They put their expertise in action "to speak truth to power," offering "counter-knowledge" that challenges the views of dominant actors.

Also, CSOs have produced reports based on their monitoring of congressional debates with the goal of providing easy-to-understand analysis about the functioning of Congress and technical aspects of bills. In Argentina, a handful of CSOs monitored progress of bills to provide access to public information (Acosta, 2014). The Coalición similarly followed and commented on technical aspects of the original bill to reform audiovisual legislation (Segura, 2011c, 2011d). In Uruguay, CAinfo created a dashboard to monitor the implementation of the 2009 freedom of information legislation, and promoted the use of new tools by providing advice and consultation to citizens, journalists, and other CSOs.

Finally, many CSOs have used knowledge management to strengthen citizens' understanding of media policies. They have deliberately used their expertise to broaden knowledge and support among key publics to spread knowledge and build political support beyond circles of experts and activists (Alianza Regional, 2013). CSOs have held workshops and open seminars in unions, universities,

Congress, and other forums. These activities reflect the view that knowledge management is not envisioned simply as an elite-targeted tactic to educate and persuade government officials, legislators, journalists, and experts. It is also premised on the notion that offering opportunities for popular literacy on media and policy matters is central to their mission. In Argentina, the Coalición has conducted activities in universities, social organizations, and unions (Segura, 2011c, 2011d). CSOs that integrated Ecuador's Coalición Acceso have organized various events to promote debate and learning about the right to access to public information (Navas Alvear & Villanueva, 2004).

The significance of knowledge management and leveraging information for strategic purposes for CSOs attests to the centrality of "the cultures of politics" (Alvarez, Dagnino & Escobar, 1998) in media activism. These developments reflect the realization among CSOs that discursive battles are essential to the success of their political strategy. Producing and systematizing knowledge is necessary to engage in the double process of articulating positions and demands, and re-signifying the purpose of public communication, media policies, and media systems. Ideology would not be sufficient to make progress if it is not grounded in information, and the information is not mobilized to persuade multiple publics. Building power and credibility is intrinsically linked to bolstering evidence-based arguments.

Voice and persuasion

Voice is a classic dimension of social movements. Traditionally, social movements and other forms of collective actions have been catalysts of the voice of ordinary citizens. Collective mobilization articulates the voice of those without powerful means to be heard, or that are typically ignored or whose voices are distorted by dominant politics and the media. Movements catapult the voice of marginalized actors to more visible social places, even momentarily or intermittently. As Albert Hirschman (1970) has argued, voice is the attempt to repair or improve the relationship between citizens and other actors through communication of complaints, grievances, or proposals for change.

Voice, however, is not simply public expression devoid of any purpose – a casual, neutral act of communication only intended to make public certain views, sentiments, and positions. Instead, voice is persuasion – a series of deliberate attempts to mobilize arguments to influence opinion and policies. They are public information campaigns aimed at "winning the argument" (Manheim, 2011) by persuading publics in different arenas. Key arenas are public opinion and policy-making circles. Media movements have aimed to persuade these publics that media reforms are necessary and to shape the debate about reform by mobilizing the rights-based frame. Although ideally they aim to persuade the public at large, they are primarily focused on "receptive social environments" (Campbell, Cornish, Gibbs & Scott, 2010) – actors who are more likely to be sympathetic and give support.

Street events are one tactic for voice and persuasion. In some cases, they were used to protest policies and demand specific reforms. The "Yo soy 132" movement resorted to street actions to voice demands. They held rallies outside the Televisa studios because they believe that the media company presented slanted coverage of a dispute between students of Universidad Iberoamericana and then-candidate Enrique Peña Nieto. They demanded policies to break up media concentration and promote media democracy (Trejo Delarbre, 2015; Meneses, 2015; Gómez García & Treré, 2014). The movement is credited with introducing the issue of news manipulation and media democracy in the election campaign and prompting candidates to state their position on media policy reform (Calleja, 2015). In 2004, Argentine media activists held rallies to demand that the Senate discuss the bill allowing public access to government information that had passed the lower chamber. Bolivian journalists marched in several cities to demand that Congress not pass a law that restricted public access to information in 2013. In Argentina, the RNMA and the Espacio Abierto de Televisoras Alternativas, Populares y Comunitarias held street rallies to demand the legalization of alternative media and the promotion of the sector.

Street events, however, have not been always tied to the logic of protest to level demands and complaints to state authorities. Instead, they were designed to achieve various objectives, such as demonstrating public support for advocacy and legislative actions and putting pressure on lawmakers. For example, Argentina's Coalición organized a massive rally to demand that Congress sanction the 2009 law. It also convened street mobilizations to defend the law and to persuade the Supreme Court to throw out petitions filled out by lawyers representing media giant Clarín to declare four articles of the law unconstitutional (Segura, 2011c).

Other media movements also resorted to demonstrations and other forms of street events to express support for legislative proposals and to reject government decisions. Here it is important to state that only coalitions that brought together an array of organizations with significant membership, such as unions, students' associations, and political parties, held public rallies. In Brazil, CSOs demonstrated in support of the government-convened Forum Nacional pela Democratização das Comunicações. Likewise, organizations close to the governments staged public events in support of the introduction of media bills in Congress in Ecuador and Venezuela. In Mexico, citizens' groups opposed to the government's proposal for a new telecommunication law held public rallies in 2014 (Meneses, 2015). The ten-kilometer human chain linking Televisa's studios to the presidential palace that they organized was packed with symbolism and significance (Trejo Delarbre, 2015; Calleja, 2015; Animal Político, 2014). In Argentina, CSOs pushing for a national legislation on freedom of access to government information staged sit-ins and mock-ups in Congress to show disapproval of legislators' reluctance to consider a bill.

Media movements also used news advocacy for voice and persuasion (Bertoni, 2012). News advocacy refers to efforts to shape news content by professionalizing approaches to news-making. This involves generating newsworthy events and material deliberately produced to attract media attention and working with reporters to find opportunities and educate newsrooms about the issues. Making news has become a strategic priority for civic organizations and media movements amid the mediatization of Latin American democracies. Organizations widely assume that visibility in the public sphere, particularly in the media, is a critical resource for political success. It is necessary to appeal to various actors and show presence (Alianza Regional, 2013).

Convinced that news appearances are instrumental for effective persuasion, many CSOs have developed professionalized units tasked with securing steady news coverage from the mainstream media and maintaining their own media through online and offline presence (Waisbord, 2011). News advocacy is deemed necessary to bring awareness and shape attitudes about specific media and information issues. It is deemed important particularly among organizations critical of large media corporations and pushing for ownership reforms, whose demands are rarely covered or distorted by the mainstream media. In fact, studies have demonstrated that their demands as well as other forms of citizens' mobilization have received limited news coverage (Mata et al., 2005; Segura, Nicolino & Córdoba, 2005). Not surprisingly, news companies that are the target of citizens' groups typically ignore their demands in their coverage. Instead, the situation is different for organizations interested in other matters, such as public access to government information, official advertising, and speech laws (Becerra, 2008). These issues are politically less sensitive to the editorial positions of media giants. The exception is, as it happened in Argentina, when legislators introduced changes in the bill to broaden public access to information controlled by governments and private companies. CSOs lost initial support, including positive media coverage that they originally received from media companies (Acosta, 2014; Saba, 2015).

To make news, organizations have used various tactics. They draw materials from their reports and activities. They field in-house experts to provide commentary. They also generate news events by holding press conferences and organizing debates and presentations especially on selected dates commemorating issues close to their expertise, such as World's Press Freedom Day or anniversaries of media laws. Because the media are more likely to cover those issues on those days, they focus their efforts around specific dates. They also submit letters to the editor and commentary to newsrooms, particularly in light of news events such as attacks against reporters, elections, and announcements and testimonies from high-ranking government officials. Brazil's Article 19, for example, has regularly denounced the use of gag laws, demanded the decriminalization of insult and slander, and expressed its opposition to the reform of the Penal Code to penalize defamation.

Because reporters and staff from other NGOs are rarely well-versed in the specifics of media legislation, organizations have also conducted training workshops for journalists and students about covering media reform. Movements stepped up news advocacy efforts at the time when legislative bills were discussed in open sessions in Congress to publicize the issue and explain positions among different blocs.

Organizations have also held public debates with similar goals. Peru's IPyS has held the National Conference of Access to Public Information with the participation of civic organizations, government officials, and journalists. Participants present experiences in using the law and discuss problems and legal consequences. In Argentina, a group of organizations held regular debates about public access and public media sponsored by the British Embassy for several years (Asociación por los Derechos Civiles, 2004). Chile's FUCATEL has regularly organized public events about freedom of expression, public media, and other issues. In Argentina, the Coalición conducted dozens of open sessions to present and discuss its proposal throughout the country, particularly after President Fernandez de Kirchner announced that she would send a bill to Congress based on its twenty-one points (Segura, 2011c, 2011d).

Advocacy

CSOs and media movements have also resorted to advocacy with government officials. Advocacy refers to actions designed to influence attitudes and responses about a particular issue among political elites who are in a position to influence the policy-making process in various capacities. It is a strategy explicitly intended to bridge civil society concerns with the state in order to find support and influence policy-making processes, particularly in the Executive and Congress. It reflects the intention of media movements to extend actions beyond civil society and rally support from public officials who influence or participate in the policy-making process. It patently represents the conviction among media movements that engaging with policy-makers is critical to achieving media legislation reforms.

Media movements conduct advocacy to achieve various goals. It aims to create awareness about a problem among legislators and other policy-makers. In turn, it is expected that some of these may become key allies by becoming advocates themselves. Advocacy is also expected to contribute to developing a common language among civil society and state officials about problems and solutions. It is also hoped to identify appropriate political opportunities to bring up demands and proposals to Congress and the Executive (Alianza Regional, 2013)

Activists have resorted to raising awareness about specific issues and shifting perceptions and positions among key officials directly engaged in certain policy decisions. They expect that sympathetic officials might provide support in different ways, such as pushing for the establishment of specific committees to discuss and draft bills, becoming champions for their causes, attracting media and public attention, persuading officials and legislators, and linking activists to policy-makers.

Advocacy demands contacts with decision-makers and nuanced knowledge about domestic politics. Developing and maintaining fluid relations with specific officials has been critical to maximizing opportunities for advocacy. CSOs select "advocacy targets" on the basis of two factors. One is the institutional position of selected officials in government which determines their ability to help the cause and persuade others. The other is "perceived belief congruency" – the extent to which activists believe that certain officials might be inclined to support their demand based on shared political and ideological outlook. Understanding shared beliefs is important to defining issues of interest for specific officials that may overlap or fit with citizens' demands.

Institutional channels

CSOs have also used two types of institutional channels to advance reforms.

One strategy is the use of litigation. Like other social movements (Barclay, Jones & Marshall, 2011), media movements have a dynamic, interactive relationship with litigation. They resort to litigation to achieve two goals. On the one hand, they serve to translate claims into law. Judicial victories help to lay out the legal ground which can be used to change institutions. They signify small victories in long battles for legal changes. They are opportunities to build legal cases for why specific changes are necessary. On the other hand, litigation also contributes to cementing symbolic advances by raising attention to issues and crystallizing new understandings of media and public expression. By gaining public visibility during court proceedings and news reports, issues and movements become better known and gain legitimacy in the public sphere.

In some instances, legal cases have been important and successful steps to reform. For example, CSOs have presented requests for public information to force public officials to provide responses and explain reasons behind decisions. The intention was to expose inconsistencies as well as decisions that run against the spirit of information access laws. In Uruguay, for example, CAInfo has used this tactic since the implementation of the 2008 information access laws to expose problems and introduce the issues to the judicial system.

Another purpose of litigation is to achieve legal progress on specific matters. This so-called "strategic litigation" aims to identify and remove structural obstacles to public access to government information, community broadcasting, and freedom of expression. CSOs select cases that are potentially strategic to achieve significant advancements in terms of the recognition of specific rights (Alianza Regional, 2013). The main intention is not to litigate a particular case, but rather to litigate the "issue". Therefore, CSOs need to identify specific cases that could contribute to moving forward the overall cause by bringing them into national or international courts. Successful cases can become legal precedents and set parameters for subsequent decisions.

In Mexico, community media organizations have used litigation to demonstrate that several articles of the 2014 Telecommunications and Broadcasting law violated freedom of expression legislation and the unconstitutionality of public bids that explicitly excluded them from participating (Trejo Delarbre, 2015; Calleja, 2015).

In Argentina, the CELS used litigation to push for the derogation of contempt laws and the elimination of penalties to libel and slander. Together with the now-defunct Asociación Periodistas, the CELS presented the Verbitsky case to the Inter-American Commission on Human Rights (IACHR). In 1992, journalist Horacio Verbitsky was condemned for *desacato* (contempt) after criticizing Supreme Court Justice César Belluscio in a 1988 article. The decision by a lower court was confirmed by the Court of Appeals. The Supreme Court rejected the "extraordinary appeal" filed by Verbitsky. Together with Americas Watch and the Centro por la Justicia y el Derecho Internacional (CEJIL), the Argentine CSOs submitted the "Verbitsky case" to the Inter-American Commission on Human Rights in 1992. They presented supporting briefs arguing that libel laws violated the American Convention on Human Rights (ACHR). A friendly settlement, which called for the removal of contempt provisions from the Argentine criminal code, was reached in 1993. The same year the Argentine Congress revoked that law.

CSOs also played a key role during the Kimel case. A journalist and writer, Eduardo Kimel, published a book about San Patricio's

Massacre that criticized members of the justice system for mishandling the case and the investigation of the murder of five clergymen during the last military dictatorship. In 1999, Kimel was found guilty of insulting former judge Guillermo Rivarola in his 1989 book and received a one-year suspended sentence and a fine of 20,000 pesos (US$20,000). After the Supreme Court rejected an appeal, the CELS and the CEJIL filed the case with the IACHR in 2001. The case affirmed that the state "has violated the right of individuals to express their ideas through the press and to debate public issues." The Inter-American Court found that the conviction violated freedom of expression as established by the ACHR.

Besides litigation, CSOs have used participatory mechanisms sanctioned by national constitutions and specific laws as well as ad hoc initiatives to influence media policies. These mechanisms are relatively new innovations in Latin American democracies, and resulted largely from citizens' mobilization to petition consultative opportunities to participate in the discussion of new bills as well as the implementation and monitoring of new legislation.

CSOs have participated in public audiences in Congress and the courts, citizens' initiatives, participatory councils, presidential consultative rounds, and national conferences (Olivera Paulino, 2014; Segura, 2011a). Ad hoc mechanisms are forums about bills and policy implementation in Argentina, and civil society roundtables in Mexico. In Peru, CSOs such as Otra Mirada, Calandria, Ideele, Coordinadora Nacional de Radio, and the Asociación Nacional de Periodistas participated in public audiences held by representative Manuel Dammert to discuss a bill aimed to curb ownership concentration in 2014. In Paraguay, the Frente Guasú, which includes former President and Senator Fernando Lugo, also conducted public audiences to discuss a media reform bill.

In Mexico, CSOs participated in public audiences held by a congressional commission to discuss broadcasting reforms in 2007 and in public consultation about a broadcasting and telecommunication bill in 2014 (Meneses, 2015; Trejo Delarbre, 2015). Therefore, AMEDI used Iniciativa Ciudadana ("citizen initiatives") to present a thirty-point proposal for a new communication law to the government in 2014. The proposal that had been discussed and endorsed by numerous CSOs, and was supported by a public campaign called "No mas poder" ("No more power"), in reference to media giants

Televisa, TV Azteca and Telmex, to demand that Congress discuss the Iniciativa in communication policies (http://nomaspoder.amedi. org.mx/iniciativa-ciudadana).

Eclectic strategic toolkits

The review shows the abundant and diverse strategic repertoire of media movements: coalition-building, knowledge management, voice and persuasion, advocacy, and participation in state-sanctioned channels. How do we explain the eclecticism of the strategic toolkit?

Strategic action entails attempts to secure the cooperation of others and identify collective interests. In order to achieve these goals, CSOs have been open-minded about the selection of appropriate strategies to promote policy reforms. Media activists can be characterized as "pragmatic ideologues" or "principled instrumentalists" (Mitchell & Schmitz 2013) – they have a blueprint for democratic communication yet are political pragmatics searching for suitable opportunities to advance their causes.

The complex nature of media policy-making demands strategic flexibility. Policy-making is typically a drawn-out process at multiple levels in civil society, the market, and the state. It includes three phases – public debate and opinion formation, congressional debates, and policy implementation. Each phase has different characteristics and challenges as well as actors – ordinary citizens, political influencers, news media, and legislators. Policy-making comprises multiple institutional spaces – the media, courts, congressional committees and open sessions, presidential cabinet meetings, and the streets. The path to policy reform includes nestled institutions, unpredictable opportunities, and myriad actors.

Targeting myriad actors and institutional spaces throughout the convoluted process of policy-making requires openness to several strategic approaches. One-size-fits-all tactics are hardly suitable for making progress on many political fronts. Stubbornly clinging to certain tactics – whether protest or litigation – may not deliver necessary results or lay down the necessary stepping stones to move forward. Formal and informal channels of communication and participation are both equally needed depending on specific circumstances.

Strategic flexibility is also necessary given the unpredictable course of policy processes. As Marshall Ganz (2010) writes, "strategic action is ... an ongoing creative process of understanding and adapting new conditions to one's goals." Because political and policy scenarios are dynamic, depositing all hopes in one tactic may cause strategic mistakes or cause CSOs to miss opportunities for change. Civic society should neither prioritize protest nor solely cultivate the politics of counter public spheres to spur reforms. Protest may be helpful to voice demands and to show that activists are, in Charles Tilly's (2005) phrase, "worthy, united, numerous, and committed."

Contentious politics, however, does not always pay off nor is it strategically wise. It would be similar to justifying the need to litigate cases because CSOs have legal expertise or holding street mobilizations because CSOs have the capacity to mobilize a significant number of people. These are poor reasons to justify specific tactics. The merits of strategic options need to be weighed in the context of prevalent political winds. Contentious strategies may be necessary to step up pressure and demonstrate broad support for reforms. Voice and litigation may be the only viable strategic options when governments refuse to listen to demands or, worse, persecute activists. In other cases, policy advocacy is strategically smart for CSOs to seize opportunities when political elites are willing to listen, are sympathetic to demands, and/or are interested in reforms. The participation of civil society in media governance, or for that matter any type of governance (Jobert & Kohler-Koch, 2008) demands different kinds of citizen engagement.

An eclectic strategic toolkit and political dexterity are necessary because media movements envision that both civil society and the state are crucial for policy reform. Different tactics are appropriate depending on the sphere of action. Specific tactics are important to promote public debates, educate citizens, and build broad-based support for proposals in civil society. Needless to say, policy reforms do not happen only because civil society mobilizes. It is often insufficient to spearhead long-term media reforms. Commitment from political elites is equally necessary. To achieve commitment from government officials, various strategies can be deployed. When officials refuse to listen to demands, changing policies requires street protest, critical documents, news advocacy, and litigation. Instead, when political elites are receptive, persuasion, advocacy, and engagement in participatory mechanisms can be used to promote changes.

Underpinning the pragmatic position of media movements is the notion that states can and should be mobilized for change. Media activists don't envision the state as monolithically opposed to their demands. They are not dogmatically "anti-state" forces like other movements in the region that have consistently confronted the state around a host of issues such as human rights, mining projects, social rights, and others (Stahler-Sholk, Vanden & Becker, 2014; Zibechi, 2010). Unlike their radical brethren, progressive media activists do not conclude that the state is beyond hope or that taking it by assault is the only viable tactic to bring about policy changes. Rather, they believe that substantive rights-based reforms in media governance are possible in the context of contemporary democratic states. Recent innovations in participatory politics, legal mechanisms, and partisan and ideological diversity among political elites offer opportunities for important reforms.

In closing, media movements are strategic omnivores. They are neither hard-headed protesters who inevitably default to street actions nor optimist institutionalists who believe that formal mechanisms and dialogue are the only possible avenues to promote change or that contemporary democracies are perfectly pluralist. They have circumstantially resorted to protest when the politics of resistance was considered necessary to express grievances and raise awareness, yet they also espoused institutional methods and participatory advocacy when they deemed that conditions were appropriate. This is why CSOs and coalitions need to be politically savvy to interpret political dynamics in public opinion and in the political sphere in order to identify political allies and suitable moments for various strategies.

4 | POLICY REFORMS

What have media movements accomplished? How do we determine the success of media movements? What policies have changed as the consequence of the mobilization of media activists?

Needless to say, these are difficult questions to answer. Just like for social movements in general, it is not easy to determine the impact of media movements or, specifically, their contributions to policy-making. The outcomes of social movements are opaque rather than self-evident or easy to pinpoint. Burstein and Sausner (2005: 417) perceptively observe: "We believe that collective action plays a critical role in democratic politics; we also believe that we know less about this role than customarily assumed and that changes in our research agenda must occur before we can make much progress." This assertion reflects a widespread sentiment in the literature about the impact of social movements and citizen participation. Explaining whether and how they contribute to policy changes is necessary, yet it is fraught with analytical and methodological challenges. It demands outlining causal linkages between collective action and policy outcomes, and specifying ways in which changes can be attributed to the actions of mobilized citizens (Kriesi, 1995; Tilly, 1999). To be persuasive, any explanation requires establishing a clear, reasonable causal pathway demonstrating how actions successfully contribute to policies.

It is hard to find parsimonious conclusions about the impact of collective action on policy-making. This problem is partially the consequence that early studies on collective action were concerned chiefly with understanding the causes of mobilization rather than outcomes. Studies were focused on teasing out the reasons why collective action emerges and the conditions that make it possible. Questions about why people mobilize, what conditions facilitate mobilization, as well as institutional and non-institutional tactics were central. Only recently, more systematic reflection has been done on the question of impact. As recently as the late 1990s, scholars lamented the neglect of the study of the consequence of social movements (Giugni, McAdam & Tilly, 1999).

Although a considerable amount of research and debate on the impact of collective action has been produced in recent years, disagreements and contradictions exist about the impact of social movements (Amenta, 2014; Burstein, 1999, Meyer, 2004, 2005). Whereas some observers conclude that social movements have had significant impact by forcing governments to concede to progressive demands and promote new policies (Amenta, 2006; Piven, 2006), others are more skeptical about their impact (Skocpol, 2003; Giugni & Yamasaki, 2009; Kolb, 2007). Despite some successes, it is questionable whether most movements effectively achieved their objectives and had significant gains. Conclusions are largely drawn from specific cases rather than based on a comprehensive overview of numerous cases. Because for every successful case one also finds other examples with null outcomes or uncertain impact, it is impossible to reach conclusions about outcomes that apply to all forms of collective action.

Likewise, studies about citizen participation have not reached straightforward conclusions about impact (Gaventa & Barrett, 2013). While assuming that participation in policy-making is desirable, there are no unanimous, synthetic conclusions about what difference citizens make when they take part in public debates, parliamentary discussions and procedures, and policy implementation and monitoring. Whereas some participatory policies have had positive consequences, others have not rendered significant, long-lasting, positive outcomes (Casey, 2004). Mixed results across dozens of experiences make it difficult to produce succinct and comprehensive statements. The fact that participatory processes have been implemented fully or partially across very different political settings, with dissimilar objectives (from environmental to health policies), and resorting to multiple mechanisms (from public consultation to citizens' testimonies in parliamentary hearings), makes it impossible to draw concise conclusions. Empirical cases are affected by too many variables to draw succinct conclusions.

In summary, the diversity of goals, strategies, resources, and contexts across social movements and citizen participation makes it exceedingly difficult to reach categorical conclusions. Because too many variables influence outcomes, it is hard to produce succinct answers to whether, when, how, and why collective action contributes to change. Instead of assuming or overestimating impact, it is necessary to take a nuanced approach to assess strengths and limitations (Woodford & Preston, 2013). Given a mixed record of numerous experiences, it is necessary to interrogate when and why specific cases succeeded or failed in diverse contexts (Cornwall, Robins & Von Lieres, 2011).

Part of the problem is that there is still no unanimity about what constitutes the success of social movements. As sociologist Bill Gamson (1975) observed, success is an elusive idea. For decades, scholars have tried to figure out various ways to determine how to evaluate the success of social movements. Are there solid and consistent indicators of success applicable across movements? Should impact be assessed exclusively in terms of the immediate objectives set out by activists? What is the timeline for determining outcomes? If states continue pursuing policies and decisions criticized by movements, should it be simply considered a failure for mobilized citizens? What if collective actions fail to achieve policy objectives, but they contribute to other dimensions of democratic citizenship? What if temporary defeats eventually lead to future successes? How do we determine the wide spectrum of possible changes caused by movements and draw relatively persuasive linkages between strategies and outcomes? The fact that these questions continue to be endemic in the literature suggest that they do not have simple answers.

With these questions in mind, we decided to analyze the impact of media movements in Latin America, with emphasis in the cases of Argentina, Uruguay, Mexico and Ecuador on the passing of new legislation. Because media movements targeted the state to change policy frameworks, we consider policy change that reflected citizens' demands grounded in the rights-based vision of communication as the main indicator of success. Media movements have had a noticeable impact on policy reforms grounded in the notion of communication as a human right in three areas: broadcasting, public access to government information, and speech laws.

Broadcasting reforms

Major laws aimed at reforming the radio and television industries and regulating the convergence between broadcasting and telecommunications were passed in several countries in recent years. This includes: Argentina's 2009 Law of Audiovisual Communication Services and 2014 Law Digital Argentina; Bolivia's 2011 General

Law of Telecommunications and Information and Communication Technologies; Ecuador's 2013 Organic Law of Communication; Uruguay's 2007 Law of Community Broadcasting and 2014 Law of Audiovisual Communication Services; Venezuela's 2004 Law of Social Responsibility of Radio and Television and 2010 Law of Social Responsibility of Radio and Television and Electronic Media; Brazil's 2011 Law of Pay Television; Mexico's 2006 Law of Radio and Television and Law of Telecommunications, and 2014 Law of Telecommunications and Broadcasting; Peru's 2005 Law of Radio and Television; Colombia's 2009 Law of Information and Communication Technologies; and Chile's 2014 Digital Television Law. Also, the Constitutions of Ecuador and Bolivia, passed in 2008 and 2009 respectively, acknowledge the right to communication.

Argentina's 2009 broadcasting law became a point of reference in the region and globally. It is based on the Coalición por una Radiodifusión Democrática's twenty-one point proposal. Except for its proposal to regulate official advertising, all Coalición's twenty-one points are reflected in the law. The original bill submitted to Congress by President Fernandez de Kirchner was based on Coalición's proposal, and recommendations by UNESCO and Freedom of Expression Special Rapporteurs of the Organization of American States (OAS) and the United Nations (UN).

The 2009 law features many demands from progressive activists. It introduces the right to communication as a public and social good. It recognizes the right of private actors, the state, and the "third sector" to provide audiovisual services in line with the Declaration of Broadcasting Diversity (United Nations, Organization of American States, Organization for Security and Cooperation in Europe & African Commission on Human and Peoples' Rights, 2007). It stipulates limitations of media ownership to curb concentration. It draws from UNESCO's 2008 Media Development Indicators by establishing a mechanism for undoing media concentration without expropriating or eliminating broadcasting licenses. Instead, it mandates companies to propose a plan to "de-concentrate" and to lead and administer the process within a specific timeline (Baranchuk & Rodríguez Usé, 2011; Mauersberger, 2012).

The 2009 law also recognizes community and non-profit media as part of the media system, the first time that all non-commercial, non-state stations have been recognized by broadcasting legislation in the country. It assigns a third of the broadcasting spectrum to the sector. It states that community and non-profit media should not be limited in terms of technical reach or geographical location, and have the right to economic sustainability and autonomy by obtaining funding from public and private sources. The law also stipulates that the sector should receive 10 percent of the annual revenues of the regulatory agency. The law also considers indigenous communities as people with public rights and recipients of licenses without having to participate in public bidding.

The law establishes principles for the strengthening of public broadcasting by setting up a state agency to manage, operate, and develop national state broadcasting services – radio and television stations. It reserves frequencies to provincial and municipal governments and national universities and other educational institutions. It also establishes that state media should broadcast a minimum of 60 percent of in-house production and 20 percent of independent production. The law also features other demands from civil society, including the promotion of national culture, diversity, and jobs through screen quotas for national, local, independent, and in-house productions.

Another distinctive feature was the process that culminated in the passing of the 2009 law. The official draft of the bill was discussed with the participation of organizations and citizens in forums around the country held by the presidency. The Coalición also hosted participative meetings and citizens' debates that produced a considerable number of suggestions and proposals to modify the original bill (Bulla, 2011). The National Congress also conducted four public audiences to receive input on different aspects of the bill.

The bill passed with support from legislators of the ruling Peronist Frente para la Victoria and other parties in Congress. International organizations such as the Freedom of Expression Rapporteurs of the UN and the OAS, the International Federation of Journalists, and Reporters without Borders supported the bill.

The democracy and human rights framework of the Coalición's proposal shaped the discursive boundaries of the debate of the bill regarding the need to reform broadcasting according to rights-based principles. Even legislators from the opposition who questioned the purpose of the official bill and/or were critical of several articles, shared the philosophical framework of the Coalición's vision and presented objections because the bill failed to reflect essential points included in the Coalición's proposal (Segura, 2011a). CSOs that were not part of the Coalición, such as the Red Nacional de Medios Alternativos, endorsed the 2009 law although they presented objections, such as the broad definition of private non-profit media, which includes community, alternative, cooperative, union, and religious media. Whereas the Coalición believed that the 2009 law reflected official commitment to addressing fundamental problems in public communication and opened a unique opportunity to bolster media pluralism, other CSOs remained suspicious of the political intentions of the administration (Saba, 2015; Michi, 2015).

Uruguay's 2007 Law of Community Broadcasting also reflects citizens' demands (Light, 2013). The law defines community media as "service of public interest independently from the State and offered by non-profit associations." The law reserves a third of broadcasting licenses to community media. It establishes the need for an open bidding process, transparent procedures in the granting of licenses, and public audiences for assigning and renewing licenses. It determines that community broadcasting should not be limited by geographic reach and that it is defined by its social and public goals. It bans community media from political, partisan, or religion propaganda and discrimination based on race, ethnicity, gender, sexual orientation, religion, age, or any other reason. It allows community media to draw funding from various sources, including advertising and donations (Kaplún, 2010).

The participation during the debate of the law was also remarkable. CSOs played critical roles during the process that culminated in the passing of the law in December 2007. The national chapter of World Association of Community Radio, the workers' union Plenario Intersindical de Trabajadores, and the Asociación de la Prensa Uruguaya conducted advocacy with political elites, presented testimonies in congressional sessions, and collaborated with members of Congress in drafting various versions of the bill. They frequently endorsed the position of the Frente Amplio administration on matters related to community media.

Leading regional and global organizations such as Reporters without Borders, Article 19 and the World Association of Community Radio hailed the 2007 law as a model of democratic legislation oriented towards the promotion of pluralism and the diversity of voices and called other countries to consider a model of inspiration. Article 19 (2007) Executive Director Agnés Callamard affirmed that the law "will be a crucial precedent for Latin America, a model to be emulated by other countries in the region." Reporters without Borders's Benoît Hervieu (Gómez, 2007) observed that Uruguay's community media law "should inspire the American continent."

Uruguay's 2014 Law of Audiovisual Communication Services shares many similarities with Argentina's 2009 law. It also guarantees freedom of expression of all citizens, stipulates limits on media ownership, promotes national production and media jobs, defends the rights of children and adolescents, and establishes the office of the "public's ombudsman." Just like in Argentina, CSOs played a leading role during the public and legislative process that culminated in the passing of the law. The law received unanimous praise from the UN and OAS Special Rapporteur (Lanza, 2015), Article 19, the Committee to Protect Journalists, and Reporters without Borders.

In Ecuador, the 2013 Organic Communication Law features inconsistent principles and regulations. Whereas some articles are in line with international standards and citizens' demands, other articles contradict democratic global norms of public speech. The law includes several demands from mobilized activists, including the notion of communication as a public service, the right of commercial, state, and community media, the division of broadcasting licenses in three equal thirds among state, private, and community media, the establishment of the five-member Council of Regulation (including a citizen representative), and the figure of the "audience ombudsman." At the same time, it introduces regulations contrary to pluralism, access, and participation that bolster the power of the government to control public speech. Article 22 establishes the right of the public to receive "truthful information" that is "verified, contrasted, precise, and contextualized." Obviously, how these requirements are defined and who defines the meaning of these concepts sets up conditions for government officials to determine content. Article 26 bans "media lynching," defined as information produced in a "concerted manner" by media or third parties "to destroy the prestige of a natural or juridical person, or reducing their public credibility." Again, this article leaves plenty of room for the government to determine what speech is deliberately produced to cause harm. Article 73 establishes that media companies should hire and pay an "audience ombudsman" appointed in a process controlled by a government agency, a measure that raises the potential of official censorship in newsrooms rather than the defense of the rights of the public.

CSOs also played important roles in the process previous to the passing of the law by participating in debates and presenting proposals. Not all CSOs held similar views about the bill. Some categorically rejected it, convinced that the law would worsen chronic problems for freedom of expression given articles that legitimized government censorship and the checkered record of the Correa administration on matters of public communication. Other CSOs endorsed the official bill, even if they had misgivings and disapproved specific articles that allowed government discretionality. Originally, they had endorsed the Correa administration's decision to introduce legislative reforms to promote the tripartite division of broadcasting licenses and to legalize the situation of community and indigenous media. These have long been their key demands for legislation reforms. José Ignacio López Vigil (2013), a leading figure in the community media movement in the region, observes that the law included regulations that were not discussed with CSOs: the creation of a government agency tasked with monitoring and sanctioning violations, the understanding of public as "official" media, and the requirement that all journalists should have a degree in communication. CSOs considered that these aspects were contrary to freedom of expression. Furthermore, López Vigil (2015) observes that controversial articles were inserted right before the bill was approved without the knowledge of CSOs and many legislators.

In Mexico, the 2014 Constitutional Reform of Telecommunications and Broadcasting reflects various civic demands (Calleja, 2015). It recognizes both sectors as a public service; limits ownership concentration; recognizes community and indigenous media; creates a national system of public media with autonomy from the government; fosters open access television by stipulating the assignation of new channels on the basis of competence and quality; promotes ownership diversification of the cable television industry; establishes that licenses are government concessions; and creates an autonomous regulatory mechanism (Dorcé et al., 2014).

CSOs held positive views about the 2014 Constitutional Reform of Telecommunications and Broadcasting. Many CSOs participated in the process that led to policy reforms. They participated in public audiences, submitted ideas to introduce modifications to the official bill, and met with legislators and public officials. The AMEDI produced a proposal that included various reforms and was presented to Congress in 2008. The proposal was eventually revised and became a source for the final text of the 2013 constitutional reform and the 2014 law (Trejo Delarbre, 2015).

Civic hopes about the prospects of progressive changes, however, became mixed expectations after the passing of the 2014 Secondary Law of Telecommunication and Broadcasting. Media activists criticized many aspects of the law. It exempts existing media corporations from paying for licenses but it imposes payments on new licensees. It restricts the ability of community and indigenous media to draw economic resources by stipulating that they are allowed to receive 1 percent of state advertising and no private advertising. The law limits the autonomy of the regulatory agency in favor of the presidency (Karam Cárdenas, 2014/15). Still, CSOs concluded that the law was a step forward even though it includes articles that contradict their demands. As Trejo Delarbre (2015) observes, "we did not achieve all the changes we wanted, but we achieved objectives we never thought we could."

Participatory mechanisms in broadcasting policies

One of the most innovative aspects of the broadcasting laws in Argentina, Ecuador, Mexico, and Uruguay is the creation of participatory mechanisms for defining, implementing, and controlling media policies. They institutionalize citizen inclusion in media policy-making by establishing consultative bodies integrated by representatives of CSOs and calling for public audiences for discussing license applications.

In Argentina, the 2009 law created the Administración Federal de Servicios de Comunicación Audivisual (AFSCA), the agency responsible for implementing and monitoring the new legislation. The AFSCA has a seven-member board: a president and a director appointed by the President, three directors appointed by a congressional commissions (one by the majority, one by the first minority, and another by the second minority), and two directors proposed by the Consejo Federal de Comunicación Audiovisual.

The AFSCA includes two participatory agencies: the Consejo Federal de Comunicación Audiovisual (Federal Council of Audiovisual Communication or COFECA) and the Consejo Asesor de la Comunicación Audiovisual y la Infancia (the Advisor Council of Audiovisual Communication and Childhood). Additionally, the law creates the Consejo Honorario de Medios Públicos (Honorary Consultative Council of Public Media) as advisor of Radio y Televisión Argentina, the oldest component of the national public media system. The 2009 law also established other participatory mechanisms: the Defensoría del Público (the Office of the Ombudsman for Audiences) tasked with receiving and processing demands from citizens.

The COFECA is an advisory body with the ability to propose two board members (out a total of seven) and control and remove members. It is obligated to inform to Congress about the progress of the law, receives reports from the AFSCA, and participates in the selection of proposals submitted to the Fondo de Fomento Concursable para Medios de Comunicación Audiovisual (FOMECA). The COFECA has thirty-nine members: three representing commercial media, three from community media, one from a university with a Department of Communication, one from public media, three from unions, one from human rights associations, and one from indigenous groups, twenty-four from provinces and the city of Buenos Aires, and two from rights-advocacy organizations. Members of the COFECA are selected appointed by the Executive from the names presented by the organizations.

The Consejo Honorario de Medios Públicos is composed of two representatives of national universities with a Department of Communication or Journalism, six from regions of the country, one from original communities, one from the Federal Council of Education, and one from the Advisor Council of Audiovisual Communication and Childhood. It is responsible for ensuring that the law is effectively applied regarding public media. It has the power to call public audiences to evaluate programming content and the functioning of public broadcasting, make proposals, establish channels for direct communication with citizens, request information from the national state public broadcasting company (Radio y Televisión Argentina Sociedad del Estado), and denounce problems and present conclusions to a special congressional commission tasked with promoting and monitoring the law.

In Ecuador, the Consejo Ecuatoriano de Regulación y Desarrollo de la Información y Comunicación (CORDICOM), which oversees various issues, from allocating licenses to establishing rules for content, includes a member of the Consejo de Participación Ciudadana y Control Social. This Council is established by the Constitution to control all areas of state. Additionally, the law establishes a consultative council in the CORDICOM including representatives of audiovisual producers, citizens' organizations, and universities. All members must be selected by electoral colleges designated by the National Electoral Council.

In Mexico, the 2014 Constitutional Reform of Telecommunications and Broadcasting stipulates that the Instituto Federal de Telecomunicaciones (IFETEL) must have a consultative council including experts from civil society, hold public audiences, and post deliberations online. The law also creates a similar consultative council for public media (Solís Leree, 2015).

In Uruguay, the 2007 Community Media Law also stipulates the participation of civic society in the implementation process. An important innovation was the inclusion of citizen participation in an advisory group to monitor the performance of state agencies as well as a consultative council that participates in the bidding process. The law establishes two mechanisms, the Consejo Honorario Asesor de Radiodifusión Comunitaria (CHARC) and the Comisión Honoraria Asesora Independiente (CHAI). The CHARC was created by law and was intended to ensure transparency in the assignation of licenses. It includes representatives from three ministries (Culture, Education, and Industry), Congress, community media, public and private universities, and NGOs focused on human rights.

Freedom of information laws

Media movements have also made significant contributions to the passing of laws granting access to public information (Risley, 2006, 2015). Between 2002 and 2014, seventeen Latin American countries passed such laws: Jamaica, Mexico, Panama, and Peru in 2002; San Vicente and the Grenadines in 2003; Dominican Republic, Ecuador, and Antigua and Barbuda in 2004; Honduras in 2006; Nicaragua in 2007; Chile, Uruguay, and Guatemala in 2008; Brazil and El Salvador in 2011; Guyana in 2013, and Paraguay in 2014 (UNESCO, 2014). Three countries already had laws: Colombia (1985), Belize (1994), and Trinidad y Tobago (1999). In Argentina, a 2003 presidential decree provides public access to information controlled by the presidency.

In a region with chronic problems of government opacity and corruption coupled with weak or non-existent mechanisms for citizen access to government affairs, this legislation is undoubtedly a promising and unprecedented development. Certainly, the wave of new laws is symptomatic of a global trend towards more government accountability and transparency as many countries passed similar legislation around the world (Berliner, 2014; Michener, 2011).

CSOs played leading roles in the processes that resulted in the passing new laws by holding debates, drafting bills, conducting advocacy with legislators and other stakeholders, and participating in congressional debates. Civic coalitions of associations of journalists and lawyers, human rights groups, and news companies were the drivers of the processes that culminated in new laws (Bertoni, 2012).

For example, Mexico's 2002 Ley Federal de Transparencia y Acceso a la Información Pública Gubernamental is unthinkable without the work of civil society. The Grupo Oaxaca has been widely credited for its leadership during the process that culminated in the new law (Michener, 2011). The Grupo Oaxaca offered a critical response to the Vicente Fox administration draft bill granting the right to information by counteroffering a different set of basic principles. Its members met with key government officials, both in the opposition and the ruling Partido Acción Nacional, to raise awareness about the need to have a law and discuss specifics and principles. They also participated in legislative debates. The Grupo's principles were eventually discussed in consultation with members of Congress, presented in parliamentary debates, and integrated into the final text submitted in 2001. Simultaneously, the Grupo used news coverage to raise public awareness about the legal vacuum and the need for new legislation. The fact that three leading newspapers were members certainly helped the public profile of their demands and proposals. Counting on the support of major news organizations was a major asset to push demands to public prominence. Also, the Grupo Oaxaca called for participation and held open meetings to discuss the bill.

Unquestionably, the Ley Federal de Transparencia y Acceso a la Información Pública Gubermental echoed key elements of the original proposal by the Grupo Oaxaca such as the definitions of government information, the principle of disclosure, clear exemptions, and the oversight of the Federal Institute for Access to Public Information

(Michener, 2011). The 2014 law also states that political parties, unions, and private companies that receive public money are obliged to provide information to public requests. It also establishes common norms for all states and updates the use of mechanisms to solicit information regarding human rights abuses (Solís Leree, 2015).

In Uruguay, too, civic mobilization was central to the passing of the 2008 Ley de Acceso a la Información Pública. Although Uruguay contemplates the possibility of citizens' introducing a bill in Congress, the GAIP coalition of CSOs decided to work with influential legislators to introduce a bill to grant public access to public information. The GAIP advocated, drafted, and shared versions of a bill among members of Congress from various parties. They also collaborated on a bill about public archives and data. This process demanded extensive contacts and conversations with lawmakers, many of whom were not familiar with international standards and freedom of information issues (Lanza, 2015). The coalition invited experts from other countries to discuss legislation and raise awareness about the situation in the region and the world. The GAIP also counted on significant support from leading news organizations that offered regular and positive coverage of the initiative. The bill was finally introduced in 2005. In November 2008, Congress passed a law that regulated both public access to government information and the protection of personal data (see Cruz, 2009).

The law was positively received by the GAIP as well as other CSOs. It largely reflected their demands and language. Article 2 features an extensive understanding of public information: It defines it as information produced or controlled by any public entity, including non-state entities, with the exception of specific issues indicated by the law as well as reserved and confidential information (Güida, 2015). It states that government officials have to justify why information is considered "reserved" and that they need to demonstrate evidence showing that the public interest would be damaged if certain information is divulged. It obligates officials to show that the damage to the State is larger than the harm to public interest when officials reject requests. It mandates that all government agencies have to disseminate and update information on their websites, and to appoint specific officials to receive public requests and deliver the information. Another important aspect of the law is that it grants citizens the possibility of using judicial mechanisms in cases when the government rejects or partially responds to petitions.

One contentious issue was that the law created the Unidad para el Acceso a la Información Pública to protect the right to information and to advise the government. CSOs criticized the inclusion of the Unidad under the presidency, specifically within the unit responsible for e-government (the Agencia para el Desarrollo del Gobierno de Gestión Electrónica y la Sociedad de la Información y del Conocimiento). Members of the GAIP believed that the position of the Unidad within the administrative structure of the Executive could potentially compromise its autonomy. Still, they supported the law for they believed that it was the best opportunity to make significant legal advances (Lanza, 2015).

In Ecuador, the Coalición Acceso played an important role pushing for freedom of information legislation. Although its members did not agree on several aspects, it was able to produce a shared document that was discussed with legislators and became the basis for the law. The Coalición held public debates and counted on support from the country's leading association of newspapers. The proposals received endorsement from prominent politicians at a time of strong public demands for transparency and accountability (Navas Alvear, 2015). The proposal drew from international standards, similar legislation elsewhere in the region, and recommendations from Special Freedom of Expression Rapporteurs for the UN and the OAS as well as global organizations like Article 19 (Navas Alvear & Villanueva, 2004). The 2004 law was based on the Coalición proposal, including citizens as rights-bearing subjects to demand information and free access, and the obligation of state and private organizations that control public resources to provide information. Yet some CSOs were critical of two key aspects of the law: the lack of specifics about who must provide information and the definition of public information in terms of source rather than content of public interest.

The repeal of contempt laws

A third set of policy reforms showing the impact of media movements is the repeal of contempt laws and the elimination of penal sanctions for public speech in numerous countries: Argentina in 1993; Paraguay in 1998; Costa Rica in 2002; Peru in 2003; Honduras, El Salvador, and Panama in 2004; Chile in 2005;

Guatemala in 2006; Uruguay in 2009; and Bolivia in 2012 (Loreti & Lozano, 2014). Undoubtedly, these have been unprecedented positive changes in a region where gag laws had discouraged critical news and fostered self-censorship among reporters.

It is not analytical overreach to also suggest that CSOs have played central roles in the repeal of contempt laws. For example, the derogation of contempt law and the decriminalization of libel in Argentina can be directly attributed to the work of CSOs. As mentioned in the previous chapter, CSOs presented the cases of journalists Horacio Verbitsky and Eduardo Kimel, who had been sentenced by the Argentine justice system, to the IACHR. The IACHR mediated the process that eventually resulted in a friendly agreement between the parties in the Verbistky case, and accepted the petition to repeal the *desacato* (contempt) law in concordance with Article 2 of the American Convention on Human Rights (ACHR) that Argentina signed in 1984. The government agreed to the proposal and repealed the contempt law in 1993. In the Kimel case, the IACHR concluded that criminal libel convictions violated freedom of expression and that the Argentine state violated the ACHR.

In 2009, the Argentine Congress approved the decriminalization of the libel and slander law related to public interests. These decisions were significant: it was the first time that the IACHR made decisions against the Argentine state on matters of freedom of expression, and it also set a legal precedent in a region with a long history of legal criminalization of speech. In the Kimel case, the IACHR concluded that criminal defamation convictions violated freedom of expression and that the Argentine state violated the ACHR. Nonetheless, Argentine CSOs have not been able to reduce civil penalties for libel and slander applied to journalists despite efforts to persuade legislators to move forward (Loreti & Lozano, 2014).

It is also reasonable to attribute to CSOs important changes in speech laws in Mexico. Defamation, libel, and slander were decriminalized at the federal level in 2007 after demands from CSOs. Problems persist, however, given that the majority of states in the country still have similar laws and that individuals can use civil law to bring lawsuits with potentially high economic sanctions (Méndez, 2011). CSOs also mobilized to demand the federalization of crimes against reporters and human rights activists and the creation of mechanisms to protect media staff (Meneses, 2015). In

2012, the national congress passed a law that creates a mechanism to protect individuals and the office of the prosecutor for crimes against freedom of expression.

Failures, compromises, and setbacks

Whereas the cases hitherto analyzed showed achievements, media movements have not always been successful in persuading legislators to produce bills that partially or completely reflected their demands. Citizen mobilization has been important but insufficient to catalyze policy reforms.

Despite long-standing civic mobilization, Argentina still has no national law granting public access to government information. Brazil and Peru, for example, do not have rights-based broadcasting legislation notwithstanding the long presence of media activism. In spite of persistent demands and civic advocacy, community media legislation in Chile, Paraguay, and Colombia still has significant limitations that undermine the sector.

The different impact of media movements across issues in the region is not unexpected. It would have been surprising, actually, if they had a perfect record considering persistent power inequalities in media governance, and the fact that the convergence of multiple factors is necessary for the passing of progressive legislation, as we discuss in Chapter 6.

Also, as previously discussed, media movements have supported laws even though the final text did not perfectly match their expectations. The cases analyzed reflect that CSOs endorsed laws not because they were flawless or completely embodied their objectives. Rather, they supported new legislation because they believed they represented a golden opportunity to take major steps towards media reform. Policy reforms even through flawed laws were better than no reforms at all. Political pragmatism trumped aspirations for impeccable laws.

These cases are also indicative of the fact that not all laws are consistent with all progressive principles and demands, but some have contradictions. Whereas some legislation incorporates the principles of a democratic communication outlined by the MacBride Report and the international legal framework of human rights, some laws also contain specific articles that directly oppose international standards of freedom of expression. The most obvious cases are

Ecuador's 2013 and Venezuela's 2004 broadcasting laws which, although they recognize progressive demands, also flagrantly contradict fundamental international principles.

In some countries, the contradictions and limitations of many laws not only prompted vigorous debates in civil society. They also divided CSOs about whether laws effectively advanced progressive causes. Even if they shared the principle of rights-based communication, they held dissimilar opinions about the laws and the intentions of governments. Whereas some activists applauded official initiatives, others emphatically criticized bills and laws.

These debates and fissures are rich in implications for the analysis of media movements and participatory politics.

Civil society encompasses widely heterogeneous perspectives and proposals about media pluralism and policy reforms. Even when citizens and organizations embrace the notion of rights-based communication as the foundational principle of media systems, they are divided by many factors – partisanship, ideology, political loyalties, and strategic priorities. These differences make it unlikely that any proposal or law would obtain unanimous support from CSOs, even if it is grounded in progressive principles.

Nor do media activists hold similar views about the necessary relations between civil society and the state. Some believe that citizens need to be consistently vigilant of the state, no matter the partisan orientation of governments. CSOs should keep healthy degrees of autonomy from the state in order to raise skeptical voices, ask tough questions, and hold the government's feet to the fire. Without separation from the state, the ability to be critical is compromised. CSOs can be strategically pragmatic in terms of finding interlocutors and allies in the state to promote policy reforms while retaining independence. Only then can they function effectively as a counter public sphere of the state and the market.

Some CSOs do not view the relationship between civil society and the state as necessarily and irreversibly antagonistic, however. They believe that CSOs should be close to governments when specific administrations offer options for progressive media reforms. Civil society should not be construed as a space (or series of spaces) inherently critical of and independent from the state. Positions and actions vary according to the particular agenda of administrations. When governments offer auspicious opportunities, absolute detachment and relentless criticism of the state actually undercuts progressive reforms.

Why media movements matter

It is undeniable that the media policy landscape in the region presents important differences compared to two decades ago. Notwithstanding the persistence of considerable threats to media pluralism, significant advances have been made. New legislation in many countries recognizes the right to communication as the fundamental principle and sets up conditions that, in principle, favor media diversity.

The cases reviewed here show that media movements have contributed to passing rights-based legislation and to overturning laws antithetical to freedom of expression. None of the major policy reforms analyzed were top-down affairs initiated by political elites. It is hard to imagine that political elites, generally content with "business as usual" arrangements with private media owners, would have enthusiastically jump-started the processes that culminated in progressive legislation. Nor is it conceivable that political elites had prioritized participatory mechanisms in new laws to strengthen the citizens' voice or that they were eager to derogate draconian laws designed to shelter government officials from critical speech. Instead, progressive reforms largely originated in collective actions. Media movements should be credited with prompting, shaping, and overseeing processes that culminated in important reforms. Certainly, as we discuss in Chapter 7, reforms are still incipient and policy implementation has fallen short of the expectations of media activists.

How have media movements contributed to reshaping media policies? They have done it by practicing deliberate politics – the kind of dialogic, reasoned, and engaged politics at the core of participatory democracy. Media movements have raised public awareness about pluralism deficits of media and speech legislation that needs to be addressed. They have mobilized citizens to express opinion and debate problems and solutions. Policy change invariably demands the expression of alternative, dissident voices unsatisfied and/or opposed to the current order. As Todd Gitlin (2003: 6) writes, "no noise, no improvement." Indubitably, CSOs have made "noise" by denouncing aspects of media systems that limit pluralism and criticizing legislation and decisions contrary to freedom of speech and international standards.

All these actions are at the core of participatory politics. They were aimed not only at shifting the fundamental principles of the legislation and foregrounding a rights-based vision long excluded from policy-making debates. They also tried to integrate citizens within the policy-making process in various capacities rather than simply ensuring that specific demands become legislation. Altogether, the strategies reflect a conception of participatory advocacy that differs from the practices of interest groups narrowly focused on affecting specific policies. Nor was citizen participation symbolic, limited, or controlled by political elites. CSOs have tried to become participants in policy-making processes rather than decorative figures rubber-stamping elites' decisions.

Certainly, not all media movements have achieved similar results. Their record is mixed in terms of succeeding to persuade governments to pass rights-based reforms. Just as some movements show significant accomplishments, others made limited inroads and/or failed to achieve policy reforms. Yet media movements need to be credited for pushing "the limits of the possible" (Gramsci, 1971) in media governance. Recent reforms reflect the ferment of media activism and the maturation of media movements and CSOs as legitimate actors in media governance. They are no longer systematically marginalized, but, rather, they have made significant inroads in policy-making.

Despite the persistence of myriad problems for public communication, media movements have achieved important goals, namely, passing legislation grounded in rights-based principles, repealing laws that stifle dissent and perpetuate inequalities in public communication, and integrating citizen participation in policy-making. These significant successes should be chalked up in the tally of media movements. They are particularly noteworthy achievements considering the legacy of elite-capture media policy-making and anti-democratic legislation on matters of public communication in the region.

5 | POLITICAL OPPORTUNITIES

Why did some media movements succeed while others failed? What explains their different outcomes considering that civil society organizations and coalitions have made similar demands and used similar strategies across countries?

To answer these questions, it is necessary to address issues at the core of the complex relations between collective action and policy outcomes (Tarrow, 2012). One line of argument suggests that the chances of success of collective action are contingent on political opportunities (Kriesi, 1995). Political opportunities refer to "the degree of openness of the formal political structure to advocacy efforts, the nature of alignments between powerful 'elites,' actual alliances between movements and these elites, and the state's ability and inclination to repress a movement" (McAdam, McCarthy & Zald, 1996: 8). Such opportunities are a "necessary prerequisite" for the success of mobilized citizens. As Sidney Tarrow (1994: 19) writes, "The most salient changes in opportunity structure result from the opening up of access to power, from shifts in ruling alignments, from the availability of influential allies and from cleavages within and among elites." Specifically, political opportunities are shaped by elite divisions and the presence of powerful political allies sympathetic to citizens' demand. These conditions may not guarantee success, but when present they offer propitious conditions for social movements to achieve policy goals. Instead, when such political conditions are absent, namely political elites are unified against public demands and movements don't find powerful supporters, the prospects of success are significantly dimmer.

Political opportunities explain not only the emergence and maturation of social movements (McAdam & Boudet, 2012; Tarrow, 1994). They are conducive to the success of organized publics, too. Amenta and colleagues (2010) have proposed that social movements lead to successful policy changes when they are situated in a favorable political context. Giugni and Yamasaki (2009) conclude that "the policy impact of social movements is conditioned by the presence of powerful allies within the institutional arenas, by the presence of a favorable public opinion, and/or by both factors simultaneously." In summary, movements are more like to achieve policy changes when the political opportunities are right.

These conclusions set the ground for the analysis of when and why media movements effectively achieve policy reforms. It is reasonable to expect that elite divisions and powerful allies contributed to the success of several media movements in Latin America. That is, media movements were not single-handedly responsible for policy reforms, but they had to find and partner with influential allies in government who could broker the legislative process. One can also hypothesize that the presence of powerful allies, albeit important, may not be sufficient for the success of media movements. Political opportunities also require other conditions besides elite support, namely, specific political junctures that open particular and appropriate situations for media reforms. Political junctures are unique political moments shaped by short-term conditions. The conjunction of elite allies and unique political junctures form political opportunities that influence the successes and failures of media movements.

To discuss these ideas, we think that a comparative analysis of the political opportunities that media movements confronted in various countries is appropriate to understand successes and setbacks. As Marco Giugni (1999: xxiv) rightly observes, "By comparing similar movements in different contexts or different movements in similar contexts, we can improve our chances of finding a relationship between movement activities and outcomes." Because the movements we have examined are similar in terms of strategies and goals, it is possible to examine the influence of national political opportunities on the prospects of policy reforms. By doing so, we hope to overcome the limitations of conclusions based on the idiosyncrasies of a single case and refine the argument about why media movements succeed and fail.

Our analysis basically confirms the conclusions from the literature on social movements: divisions among political and economic elites, the availability of powerful allies among officials and legislators, and specific political circumstances were crucial for the success of citizens' demands. Without these conditions, it is hard to envision how demands and proposals for reform could have advanced. When these conditions were absent, movements were not able to achieve reforms as they faced enormous obstacles to translate mobilization efforts into effective policy changes. Progressive polices resulted from the combination of citizen mobilization and favorable national political opportunities.

The Left in power

At first glance, the coming to power of political parties and political coalitions broadly identified with the Left since the early 2000s in the region appears to offer political opportunities for media movements to shape policy reforms. It could be reasonably suggested that the coming of leftist administrations signaled fissures among political and economic elites that opened up opportunities for reform, including media policies. The fact that leftist administrations also shared the same "ideological frequency" with media movements also ushered in favorable conditions for progressive reforms. Demands for curbing ownership concentration, promoting citizen participation, bolstering domestic production, and strengthening "third sector" media have long been central to a range of leftist parties and social movements in the region. Therefore, the ascent of the Left represented, in principle, an unprecedented political opportunity for media policy reforms identified with popular mobilization.

Although much has been debated about the ideological identity of governments and the presence of "two Lefts" in the region, it is undeniable that administrations broadly identified with leftist causes have dominated national politics in several countries (Boersner, 2005; Panizza, 2005; Philip & Panizza, 2011).

In Venezuela, President Hugo Chávez was elected in 1999 and died in office during his second term in 2013. Chávez was succeeded by President Nicolás Maduro. In Chile, the governments of the Concertación de Partidos por la Democracia were headed by Ricardo Lagos in 2000 and by Michelle Bachelet in 2006, who was reelected in 2014. Brazil's Partido dos Trabalhadores has controlled the presidency since 2003, first with Luiz Inácio (Lula) Da Silva's back-to-back terms, and then Dilma Rousseff was elected in 2011 and reelected in 2014. In Argentina, Peronist Néstor Kirchner was elected president in 2003 and was succeeded in 2007 by his spouse Cristina Fernández de Kirchner, who was reelected for a second four-year term in 2011. Uruguay's Frente Amplio came to power with Tabaré Vázquez in 2005, who was succeeded by José Mujica in

2010. Vázquez returned to the presidency in 2014. In Bolivia, Evo Morales of the Movimiento al Socialismo was elected in 2006 and reelected in 2010 and 2014. Ecuador's Rafael Correa was elected president in 2008 and was reelected for a third term in 2013. In Nicaragua, Daniel Ortega of the Frente Sandinista de Liberación Nacional (FSLN) was returned to the presidency in 2007 and reelected in 2012. Paraguay's Fernando Lugo was elected president in 2008 as head of the Alianza Patriótica para el Cambio and deposed in 2012. In El Salvador, Mauricio Funes of the Frente de Liberación Nacional Farabundo Martí (FMLN) won the presidency in 2009 and was succeeded by Salvador Sánchez Cerén in 2014.

Discussing why those administrations have been characterized as "leftist" goes beyond the scope of the analysis. It is a complex matter dealing with various issues – ideological inspiration, political discourse, and public policies – that deserves separate and extensive attention (Cameron & Herschberg, 2010; Ellner, 2013). For the purpose of our analysis, suffice to mention two key issues that ideologically peg those governments to leftist traditions in the region: the political structures that carried and sustained them in power as well as rhetoric and policy actions conventionally identified with leftist ideology and politics.

These governments represented political parties, social movements, and electoral coalitions long identified with the Left in each country. Also, they vindicated various causes broadly associated with progressive politics including issues related to the economy (the critique of market economics, capitalism, and imperialism, support for social policies and state interventionism in the economy), society (the defense of human rights, the championing of the rights of minorities and indigenous groups, the denunciation of poverty and social exclusion), and politics (support for citizen participation, government accountability and transparency) (Etchemendy, 2008; Nazareno, 2010).

Not all administrations, however, have consistently and uniformly subscribed to the many causes and policies traditionally identified with the Left. In fact, the diversity of experiences has prompted extensive debates about different types of leftist administrations in contemporary Latin America. These debates have produced an enormously rich reflection about the meaning of "the Left" in the region and churned out a slew of conceptual categories (e.g.

populist, moderate, social-democratic, center-left) to capture many characteristics and options/models of leftist politics.

Considering that the ideological orientation of government increases opportunities for media policy reform (Freedman, 2008), does ideological affinity with parties in power account for the different fortunes of media movements? Has the coming of leftist governments offered unique historical opportunities for media movements by supporting reforms targeting both market and government interests?

By addressing these questions, we hope to provide nuanced explanations about the linkages between national politics and media movements and to explore whether the ideological allegiances of governments drive forward the demands and proposals of media movements.

Activists recall significant enthusiasm among media activists after the electoral victories of leftist parties and coalitions because they ushered in unprecedented opportunities for change (Lanza, 2015). After years of grassroots organizing, they positively viewed the coming of leftist governments because they believed that it would give them a better chance to influence policy-making. Their hopes were grounded on sharing ideological principles and positions on a broad range of political issues with the governments rather than electoral promises or the past record of media policies (Segura, 2011d).

The rhetoric of some presidents against media concentration and the manipulation of information by private companies also reinforced hopes about policy reforms. Presidents like Rafael Correa, Hugo Chávez, Daniel Ortega, and Cristina Fernández de Kirchner adopted a combative discourse against selected media companies. They characterized companies as "media monopolies," "enemies of the nation," "agents of imperialist powers," and other similar accusations steeped in traditional populist tropes (Waisbord, 2013). Government officials questioned the claims to independence and impartiality of media opponents and accused them of representing the political and economic interests of the oligarchy, the upper classes, foreign capital, and powerful corporations. They argued that the fierce opposition by leading media companies transparently reflected the interests of "the powers that be" – they embodied the resistance to major changes promoted by leftist governments (Kitzberger, 2012). Such rhetoric, however, was not indiscriminately used to refer to the private sector as a whole. In fact, governments maintained cordial relations with media corporations that largely offered favorable coverage of their policies and strategically lobbed criticisms at major corporations that ostensibly adopted oppositional positions. In turn, media companies made consistent negative coverage, denounced verbal attacks, and criticized official proposals to reform media legislation as attacks against "freedom of the press." Because media corporations wielded significant, unchecked power on public opinion and politics, it was necessary to restructure media systems to bolster "the voice of the people."

It is reasonable to assume, then, that leftist administrations would put the political tailwinds behind progressive media movements (Natanson, 2010). Not only were they receptive to their demands. They also brokered the legislative process and advocated among lawmakers. Therefore, one could claim that leftist governments and media movements had an "elective affinity" that helps to explain why certain citizens' demands eventually became legislation. Official support thrusted civic demands into the political spotlight and paved the way for citizens into the policy-making process.

The complex relationship between media movements and leftist governments

Although it is tempting to draw a causal line between the ascendancy of leftist governments and the policy success of media movements, the association between them is more complex than it might seem. As we demonstrate in this chapter, the evidence is not compelling to suggest that leftist governments across the board have consistently contributed to a broad range of progressive demands. Some bills did not fully capture citizens' proposals and others contradicted some principles and demands. Therefore, ideology or partisanship is not a consistent predictor of the achievements (and failures) of media movements.

Below we analyze three scenarios to probe the argument that progressive media reforms were linked to the coming of leftist governments: the reforms that did not happen, the content of reforms sponsored, and policy reforms during conservative administrations.

The reforms that did not happen Not all leftist governments passed progressive reforms. Some administrations conventionally identified with the Latin American Left did not decidedly champion the restructuring of media systems upon rights-based principles. Not all have been similarly enthusiastic or uniformly supportive of progressive demands. In some cases, the political conditions were not right to pass reforms because they did not control the Congress. In other cases, leftist governments did not push to restrict concentration or curb government discretional control of public communication.

Some emblematic center-left administrations have not shown major commitment or urgency to introduce major changes to curb the power of market companies and strengthen the position of community and alternative media. In Brazil, the administrations of the Partido dos Trabalhadores did not push for major legislative reforms to reduce, let alone overturn, the grip that a few corporations have in Brazil's media system or to break up clientelistic networks in the media system. Neither former President Lula da Silva (2003–2011) nor his successor Dilma Rousseff (2011–present) showed clear commitment to major policy reforms (de Lima, 2011). In 2009, after CSOs had demanded it for two years, the da Silva administration invited government agencies, business and civic movements to organize the First National Conference of Communication (CONFECOM) and to debate potential reforms. This was part of broad government initiatives to hold public conferences to debate and draft proposals on a range of issues with the participation of civil society (Pogrebinschi & Samuels, 2014). The CONFECOM held debates at the state and national levels, and concluded with more than 600 proposals endorsed by civic organizations. Although the government created a commission to draft a bill to reform broadcasting in 2010, the administration of Dilma Rousseff shelved the project in 2011 and refused to engage with media movements (Valente, 2015; Olivera Paulino, 2014). In fact, the Executive Secretary of the Minister of Communications of Rousseff's government publicly announced she was not going to propel any reform because it was a pre-electoral year.

Other leftist governments, such as the administrations of Ricardo Lagos (2000–2006) and Michelle Bachelet (2006–2010, 2014—present) of the Concertación in Chile did not push for comprehensive, progressive media reforms. On the contrary, a few changes to the General Law of Telecommunications made on the initiative of the Bachelet government in 2008 favored media concentration (AMARC Uruguay, 2013).

In Nicaragua, President Daniel Ortega has not embarked in rights-based policy reforms since coming back to power in 2007. Notwithstanding his frequent tirades against the "capitalist" and "counterrevolutionary" media, his government did not introduce legislation to limit media conglomerates or foreign investments. His government did not overhaul chronic problems of the media system such as restricting ownership concentration, or bolstering the position of community media. Rather, it has secured favorable media through cronyism and nepotism as friends and relatives of the president control the leading media companies.

The administration of Mauricio Funes in El Salvador (2009–2014) did not promote reforms of the broadcasting system, but it supported legislation granting public access to government information that had been championed by CSOs (Álvarez Ugarte, 2013; Badillo, Mastrini & Marenghi, 2015).

Nor were major reforms passed during the Fernando Lugo administration (2008–2012) in Paraguay. President Lugo failed to reverse anti-progressive decisions passed by Congress, namely the modification of the Ley General de Telecomunicaciones which established restrictions for community media in terms of reach and sources of financing. Not only did Lugo lack a congressional majority to promote reforms, but he also faced opposition inside the government bureaucracy to push reforms forward (Uranga, 2010).

Progressive reforms? It is mistaken to suggest that leftist administrations are unequivocally committed to progressive reforms. Consider the presidencies of Rafael Correa in Ecuador and Hugo Chávez in Venezuela. As we discussed in Chapter 4, although they supported legislative changes along key civic demands, they also sponsored legislation that flagrantly contradicts fundamental international principles of public expression championed by progressive activists. Whereas legislation that they sponsored included articles to reduce the power of media corporations and bolster the presence of community media, other aspects and laws are contrary to rights-based principles. They promoted laws that stifle critical speech and impose severe legal penalties on dissident expression by leaving plenty of room for governments to control public speech. They pushed for broadcasting policies that directly curbed public expression. They have persecuted dissidents and have been reluctant to strengthen mechanisms for public access to government information (Conaghan, 2015; de la Torre & Lemos, 2015; Espacio Público, 2015; Hernández, 2006; Ramírez Alvarado, 2005).

Soaked in authoritarian visions of a state without public surveillance and the glorification of the voice of the presidency (Waisbord, 2013), these policies are plainly incongruous with the right to communication. Official proclamations in favor of progressive causes fly in the face of aggressive policies that perpetuate chronic problems for public expression. No truly progressive administration sets up myriad legal and economic obstacles to stifle public expression, persecute dissenters, and shelter the government and allies from public scrutiny.

Media reforms during conservative governments Some conservative administrations were amenable to demands from progressive media movements, especially laws regulating public access to government information. Certainly, no conservative government has endorsed proposals to organize media systems on the basis of the principle of communication as a human right, restrain media concentration, and level the playing field for non-profit media vis-à-vis commercial interests. However, some conservative administrations endorsed proposals to limited media concentration, promote media market competition, and legalize community media (although with restrictions).

In Mexico, the Grupo Oaxaca succeeded in its efforts to pass federal legislation authorizing public access to information during the presidency of Vicente Fox of the Partido de Acción Nacional (PAN). Positioned on the right of the Mexican political spectrum, the Fox administration had proposed a bill to guarantee public information access that was widely criticized (Acosta, 2014). Instead, the bill drafted by the Grupo Oaxaca received support from the main parties of the opposition, the Partido de la Revolución Institucional and the Partido de la Revolución Democrática, which had congressional majority. The final bill passed in 2002 was the product of negotiations in Congress.

In Paraguay, Congress passed a freedom of information law in 2014 during the first year of the conservative administration of Horacio Cartes of the Partido Colorado. Although CSOs had mobilized in support of the reform for several years, little progress was made. The situation suddenly changed when the Supreme Court of Justice published for the first time the salaries of judicial staff in response to demands from citizens and reporters. President Cartes followed with a similar decision, and Congress, after initially refusing to do so, eventually decided to pass the law amid press criticisms and street demonstrations (ABC Color, 2014).

In Chile, the law of Community Broadcasting was passed in 2010 during the administration of Sebastián Piñera. Although the law recognizes community media, it establishes restrictions in terms of reach and sources of funding. The law of digital television was passed in 2013, also during the Piñera administration. It features progressive aspects such as limits on media ownership, the recognition of community media, and subsidies for educational and cultural content, and reserves airtime for cultural and public information programs (Subtel, 2013; Biblioteca del Congreso Nacional de Chile, 2014).

In Mexico, the Enrique Peña Nieto administration of the Partido Revolucionario Institucional successfully pushed for the 2014 Constitutional Reform of Telecommunication and Broadcasting in agreement with the other major political parties. CSOs praised the reform, mainly because it featured several of their proposals for freedom of expression (Calleja, 2015).

What lessons should be learned from these scenarios? Not all leftist administrations were entirely receptive to all progressive demands from media activists or unconditional, ready-to-work allies for media reforms. Shared ideological leanings with the ruling party provided political opportunities in some, not all, cases. Given the heterogeneity of citizens' demands and the priorities of leftist administrations, not all media movements found unconditional political allies in governments. Whereas most leftist governments were receptive to specific demands, such as the legalization and promotion of the "third sector" and limiting media ownership concentration, others did not try or were not able to pass reforms.

Although most leftist and right-wing Latin American governments passed access to public information laws and eliminated restrictions to public speech, they continuously clashed with activists demanding other changes, namely accountability and transparency in the management of official advertising and public media. Considering the variety of leftist and conservative experiences and media movements, it is misguided to suggest that ideological allegiances inevitably lead to favorable political junctures for media activists. Factors other than ideological communion need to be addressed to provide a fuller explanation of why media movements occasionally found government support for media reforms.

When movements find supporting elites

While the cases previously examined challenge the notion that all leftist governments have consistently championed a broad range of progressive proposals and that conservative administrations have not, they underscore the fact that elite support is a key condition for rights-based reforms. The cases demonstrate that elite support offered critical opportunities for media movements. Policies do not change only because media movements demand transformations. Media activists need governments permeable to their demands and influential elites receptive to their proposals. Without the commitment of political elites, it is impossible to envision who and what will push progressive initiatives through Congress and receive the presidential signature.

In all successful cases of media reforms, influential elites threw their support behind civic demands and proposals. In Mexico, the push for public access to government information led by the Grupo Oaxaca found receptive political elites in opposition parties amid the transition from one-party authoritarianism to a competitive political system. In 2006, during the debates about what became the Ley de Radio y Televisión (derisively known as *Ley Televisa*) CSOs found a key ally in PAN Senator Javier Corral. As chair of the Broadcasting and Film committee, Corral had originally supported the citizens' initiative to introduce modifications to the law. With other legislators, he filed a legal action in the Supreme Court challenging the constitutionality of the law. Media activists credited the lawsuit for the elimination of key articles in the 2006 law. Beatriz Solís Leree, founder director of the Mexican Association for the Right to Information, recalls that Corral was "the bridge" to CSOs (Segura, 2008a).

Similar cases are found in other countries. In Uruguay, the governments of Tabaré Vasquez and José Mujica of the center-left coalition Frente Amplio endorsed citizens' initiatives grounded in a rights-based conception of public communication. In Ecuador, the Correa administration tapped into long-standing demands for recognition of community media and indigenous media activists. In Argentina, the Fernández de Kirchner administration embraced key demands for media reforms championed by myriad CSOs.

Also, personal connections with public officials in the administrations and parliaments as well as the appointment of media activists in government positions reinforce the opportunities of civil society to impact on communication policy reforms. They ease access to key legislators during the deliberation and the drafting of new bills. In Argentina, members of the Coalición por una Radiodifusión Democrática were also on the staff of the Executive power and Congress. In Ecuador, a legal advisor to the Colectivo Ciudadano de Comunicación became advisor of the National Assembly during the discussion of the communication bill. In Uruguay, a member of the Coalición por una Comunicación Democrática, and lead promoter of the community broadcasting law, became Director of Telecomunications and Broadcasting in the Mujica administration during the drafting of the broadcasting bill passed in 2014. In Mexico, a member and former president of AMEDI were advisors to Senator Corral who played leading roles during debates about media reforms. In Paraguay, the Communication for Development secretary of the Lugo government had long been a known activist in social movements and community radio associations (*Página/12*, 2010). In Brazil, a close advisor to President Lula da Silva had "good dialogue" with media movements when the administration called for a national conference on communication (Valente, 2015).

Why were political elites interested in specific reforms? It is difficult to provide a comprehensive and nuanced explanation applicable to all cases. The unique political context is of utmost importance in terms of shaping how administrations and influential officials react to citizens' demands and proposals. So, too, are the particular calculations of administration within multi-layered political scenarios.

Freedom of information laws In his explanation of political opportunities to pass public information access laws, Michener (2011) states that elite interest is stronger when presidents do not control the Congress. Information laws are tools for political maneuvering and exercise eventual pressure and control. Even if politicians may eventually be subjected to those laws when in power, they endorse them to strengthen their position when they are in opposition. Along the same lines, Berliner and Erlich (2015) have argued that interest in legislative reforms among Mexican political elites is symptomatic of new conditions for political competition. They want to secure forms of control of political competitors when they are not in power. Commitment to transparency is a function of self-interested incentives. Having access to government information and other accountability mechanisms in place is reassurance for wielding oversight over other parties. This is why elites in more competitive states were more willing to pass access to information laws.

For President Vicente Fox and his PAN, the support for public access to government information legislation was not only the fulfillment of electoral promises of democratic accountability and transparency. It was also a tactic to put pressure on the parliament and government bureaucracy that largely sympathized with the Partido Revolucionario Institutional (PRI). At the same time, the two major opposition parties, the PRI and the Partido de la Revolución Democrática, viewed the law as a means to control the Fox administration.

In Ecuador, the Coalición Acceso integrated by academics and CSOs has pushed for freedom of information legislation for several years. The right opportunity opened up after a string of corruption scandals and public demonstrations in the late 1990s. Political elites and media companies supported a law to respond to demands for government accountability and transparency, which was passed in 2004 (Navas Alvear, 2015).

Broadcasting laws What about the decisions to endorse reforms to curb ownership concentration? Although some presidents, like Fernández de Kirchner, came to power with the promise of reforming broadcasting laws, decisions were grounded in particular political contexts, specifically the deepening of elite divisions and particular political junctures. Presidents promoted substantial reforms in media markets in the aftermath of profound conflicts with political and economic elites, including leading media corporations. In these cases, the relationship between ruling administrations and selected media companies unraveled in the context of political crisis unleashed by coup d'etat (Venezuela), police insurrections (Bolivia), demonstrations and road blockades (Argentina and Mexico), and the erosion of political legitimacy.

In Argentina, although the Néstor Kirchner administration had maintained the alliance with leading media companies, political opportunities changed after the conflict between President Fernández de Kirchner and Grupo Clarín. In 2007, the government established a new taxation system on exports that stipulated a tax hike and tax relief on agricultural exports. The official proposal met strong opposition from the four leading associations of agricultural producers who ordered locking out production and staged roadblocks throughout the country. During the months-long battle between the government and the producers, the Grupo Clarín openly criticized the government and offered sympathetic coverage of its opponents. Reportedly, Clarín's unfavorable coverage angered President Fernández de Kirchner. Other analysts have suggested that the origin of the conflict were differences over the future of the telecommunications industry between former President Néstor Kirchner and Clarín (Becerra, 2015). Regardless of the true reason why their relationship rapidly deteriorated, it is undeniable that the government pushed for a broadcasting law after the rift with Clarín became wide open. At the beginning of the conflict, the administration decided to sponsor a bill that incorporated demands from the Coalición of media activists, including limits to media ownership. Although the bill effectively challenged the interests of more than a dozen media corporations by imposing limitations on media ownership and the role of foreign companies, it was evident that Clarín was a prime target.

In Ecuador, the debate over a new media law took place amid confrontations between the Correa administration and commercial and indigenous media, which resulted in the former imposing severe penalties, including censorship, lawsuits, and temporal upholding and termination of broadcasting licenses (Segura, 2012). A similar rift between administrations and leading media corporations also took place in Venezuela, as expressed by the 2002 coup d'état actively supported by several media companies (Organization of American States, 2002b; Ramírez Alvarado, 2007; O'Briain & Bartley, 2003).

In Mexico, the 2014 Reforma de Telecomunicaciones y Radiodifusión was passed amid tensions between the Peña Nieto administration and the powerful telecommunication company Telmex as well as popular demonstrations against the new government. Political elites had become worried about the unmatched power of Telmex in national politics and the economy. A key issue was the country's inadequate network and expensive services, which was basically due to the quasi-monopolistic position of Telmex (it controls 85 percent of the market). The reform, then, was aimed at curbing the power of Telmex and promoting the entrance of new companies, including broadcasting giant Televisa (Calleja, 2015; Meneses, 2015; Solís Leree, 2015; Trejo Delarbre, 2015).

These cases illustrate similar dynamics: presidents decided to sponsor media reforms to restrict ownership concentration after specific events opened rifts with certain media companies. The conflicts became the political springboard for policy reforms. They were historical switches when governments and major media corporations parted ways. Once the relationship reached a point of no return, governments rushed the legislative process to pass new media bills as score-settling decisions against political rivals. Simultaneously, governments encouraged citizen participation to submit and debate policy proposals. Activists found allies in powerful positions. Political crisis and confrontations between governments and media companies laid out ripe political opportunities for sweeping changes in media legislation (Lázzaro, 2010; Padilla, 2010; Ramonet, 2009; Waisbord, 2011).

When movements lack influential allies

In contrast, chances of success are slim when media movements do not find support among influential elites. The lack of fluid contacts with public officials undermines any possibility of real policy success, observes the former Director of Colombia's Fundación para la Libertad de Prensa (Cortés Castillo, 2015). A former director of Argentina's Poder Ciudadano points out, "legislative approval [of media reforms] largely depends on who is on government" (March, 2015).

No shortage of examples illustrates situations when the prospects for media reforms floundered or reforms were limited because movements were not able to find influential political allies.

In Argentina, the Kirchner administration initially continued long-standing practices in media politics by cultivating close relationships with media corporations, including the Clarín Group. In fact, President Kirchner granted the media giant important benefits (Segura, 2011d). This largely explains why media activists initially met official disinterest in their progressive proposals. In 2004, media activists had requested a meeting with President Kirchner to discuss ideas for media reform, including introducing legislation to limit media concentration. They met a chilly response from the government. According to two leading media activists, they were told by the general secretary of the presidency and the media secretary that media reforms "were not in the government agenda" (cited in Segura, 2011d: 192). Nor did they have much success when they presented their proposal to the House Committee of Communications. As we previously discussed, opportunities for media reform drastically changed after the Fernández de Kirchner suddenly broke up friendly relations with Clarín Group.

In Argentina, the opposition of the political parties in Congress to a federal law granting public access to government information has been a major obstacle for CSOs. The bill initially received support from the lower chamber in Congress. CSOs' hopes were dashed when the Senate controlled by the official Frente para la Victoria approved a different version of the bill with the changes suggested by the Commission of Constitutional Affairs, presided over by then-Senator Cristina Fernández de Kirchner, in 2004. The bill introduced many exemptions and ambiguous language that contradicted demands from CSOs and international standards. Surprised at the ambiguous position of the Kirchners who supported changes and passed an agreed Executive decree of Access to Information but endorsed a bill that restricted access, CSOs continued to push for changes. Since then, however, the relationship has drastically changed. Several organizations (including Poder Ciudadano, Asociación por los Derechos Civiles, and the Centro de Implementación de Políticas Públicas para la Equidad y el Crecimiento) became vocal critics of the Kirchner administrations on free speech and other matters.

Other cases similarly illustrate that the absence of political opportunities undercuts progressive reforms. As in most countries of the region, Argentine CSOs pushing to reduce civil penalties for libel were not able to garner significant support from the leading political parties.

Political moments

Just as elite divisions and influential allies opened political opportunities for media movements, specific political moments have also played significant roles.

Political moments are short-term circumstances that might be critical for the success of long-term processes and policy outcomes. Time is a critical dimension for the analysis of collective action (McAdam & Sewell, 2001) and policy-making processes. Just as they are shaped by cumulative developments, policy decisions are also bounded by considerations grounded in momentary, unique contingencies. Whereas some circumstances are favorable to promoting legislative changes, others close off opportunities and make success unlikely. Specific events may quickly alter political scenarios and calculations. These are unpredictable and unexpected "interventions" that determine political *fortuna*, as classically understood by Machiavelli. Politics is filled with temporarily contingent and unstable events that shape the course of decisions and outcomes. They not only affect the actions of rulers; they affect the political life of organized movements, too, insofar as they put constraints on the path of potential reforms or, conversely, ease the way for policy changes. The right political moments are precipitating conditions – the necessary catalyst for driving legislative processes ahead. Instead, bad *fortuna* make specific decisions less likely and block opportunities for policy changes.

Unpredictable factors are unplanned events that change political dynamics and the calculations of political actors. Unexpected conflicts between administrations and media corporations, as it happened in Argentina and Ecuador, opened up opportunities for citizens' demands to curb media concentration and the promotion of the third sector. Corruption scandals may push administrations to support legislation for public access to government information to bolster transparency credentials, as happened in Chile in 2008 (Sánchez, 2015). In Mexico, the succession of high-profile murders of journalists prompted the Fox administration to promote the federalization of the investigation into and legal process for anti-press violence in 2012. In Mexico, the 2014 visit of presidential candidate Enrique Peña Nieto to the Universidad Iberoamericana triggered an angry reaction from students that eventually turned into the social movement *Yosoy132*, which pushed for media reform. In Peru, the scandal triggered by scores of videos revealing pervasive spying, corruption, and the complicity of major news organizations with the Fujimori presidency opened up the opportunity for debates about a new broadcasting law, especially after the downfall of the government in November 2000.

Predictable factors also shape political moments. They refer to considerations that can be reasonably anticipated ahead of time and affect political opportunities for policy reforms (Burstein, 1999; Burstein, Einwohen & Holla, 1995). These include the balance of forces in parliament, the prospects for congressional coalitions behind legislation, presidential priorities, and other issues competing for public and legislative attention.

Again, political timing matters. Legislators have limited ability to pay attention to many issues simultaneously. If demands for legislative reforms compete with other issues considered more urgent or strategically important, they are more likely to be shelved. Political elites are keenly mindful of appropriate timing in deciding whether to support specific bills. When they believe that they could secure sufficient votes, they are more likely to move forward. Congressional majorities offer suitable conditions; uncertainty about electoral results and their impact on the size of favorable votes may discourage postponing the process. Bringing up bills for congressional consideration and voting has definite opportunity and political costs. Because legislators are mindful of potential political gains and losses linked to supporting specific policy proposals or misusing certain windows of opportunity, they are careful to pick appropriate moments to move forward. Political elites are unlikely to bring bills to the floor of Congress without securing necessary votes.

Counting on party majorities or the ability to assemble voting coalitions behind specific bills is necessary to advance the legislative process. When political elites are skeptical that they will gather sufficient votes, they are reluctant to initiate action or move a bill throughout the legislative maze. Uruguay's governing Frente Amplio as well as Ecuador's Alianza Pais had congressional majorities to be able pass landmark media legislation.

When ruling parties do not have sufficient votes in their own bloc and coalitions and need to secure support from other parties, the text of specific bills needs to be adjusted as a result of legislative horse-trading and compromises. For example, the original bill submitted by the Fernández de Kirchner administrations to Congress was adjusted to meet demands from legislators from other parties. In Mexico, the Fox administration had to negotiate modifications to the bill for freedom of information access because it lacked congressional majority. Paraguayan President Lugo's party did not have sufficient votes in Congress to avoid the inclusion of restrictions to community media in the legislation promoted by opposition parties.

Critical junctures

To understand the successes and setbacks of media movements, it is necessary to examine political opportunities. They affect the prospects for citizen-driven policy reforms and help to explain, in Marshall Ganz's (2010) phrase, "why David sometimes wins."

Attention to political opportunities is necessary to comprehend the prospects of particular policy proposals pushed by media movements. While we recognize that progressive policy reforms represent the culmination of long-term processes largely driven by organized citizens, it is also necessary to highlight the importance of "political opportunities" in media policy-making.

Political opportunities form "critical junctures" – periods when the convergence of media activism and political opportunities result in policy changes (Capoccia & Kelemen, 2007; Pickard, 2010). Critical junctures condense developments that lay out favorable conditions for reforms. The interests of media movements and political elites are aligned within specific political moments. Media movements as well as their demands and proposals are more likely to be accepted by some influential political elites. When citizen mobilization intersects with elite allies willing to move into action and favorable political situations, policy transformation becomes possible. Critical junctures represent the completion of the long arc of media movements: from occupying relatively marginalized positions in media policy-making to becoming critical for media reforms in the context of institutionalized democratic politics.

To be clear, we are not suggesting that critical junctures are simply created by developments or forces completely external to supposedly "passive" media movements. Opportunities are not just gently given. On the contrary, media activists permanently strive to find political opportunities. They step up efforts when they believe that certain developments such as elections or unexpected events provoke political shifts and offer better shots at spearheading policy changes. The coming of sympathetic administrations and/or elite divisions (re)ignites hopes and reenergizes mobilization. Personal contacts with influential allies in government open doors for sharing proposals and discussing strategies. Unpredicted events such as crisis, scandals, and conflicts potentially inject new dynamics in national politics that change conditions and calculations. It is then that there are reasonable chances of success, and media activists and allied elites capitalize on long-term efforts to drive changes.

Media movements, then, are "strategic opportunists" (Goodwin, 2011) who seize opportunities created by the presence of influential allies. They are constantly searching for potential allies to partner with. Media movements need to find allies – what Tarrow (2012) calls "well-placed reformists" – with the skills and entrepreneurship to turn civic demands and ideas into viable proposals to successfully navigate the political process.

The dynamics of political junctures amply demonstrate that state support is indispensable for citizen-initiated policy reforms. The success of efforts to mobilize citizens and persuade key government allies is ultimately dependent on state politics – the dynamics of legislative politics and factors that influence elite calculations and decisions. Therefore, we believe that the analysis of media movements needs to go beyond the conditions and dynamics of civil society and integrate the articulation (or lack of) with broad political conditions and actors.

By calling attention to the importance of state politics, we do not assume or suggest that states are necessarily and consistently permeable to citizens' demands. Ours is not a vision of pluralist democratic politics completely receptive to all kinds of demands for media reforms. The pluralism of democratic politics and the fluidity of the state to citizens' demands should not be exaggerated. The fact that many causes have yet to find receptive elites in most countries in the region – curbing the power of media corporations, the regulation of official advertising, and the strengthening of the "third sector" to name a few – attests to the considerable obstacles that continue to shut off opportunities. Numerous causes and media movements have confronted unsurmountable obstacles, namely, unresponsive political elites and state politics stubbornly against progressive reforms.

Our point is different: because states are the center of gravity in the policy process, state politics need to be closely examined to understand when and why media activists succeed. As long as deep power asymmetries between elites and citizens exist in the context of representative democracies, the nexus between media movements and political junctures is crucial to explaining the policy outcomes of collective action.

The cases here analyzed suggest that "the state" is not uniformly supportive or contrary to citizens' reforms. Democratic states in Latin America are neither completely accessible nor bullet-proof to myriad demands from media movements. The shifting and convoluted dynamics of democracy and media governance in the region challenge oversimplified arguments that view contemporary states as open and pluralistic or closed and inflexible to citizens' demands for media reforms. Neither vision of the relationship between states and media movements captures the complex and changing dynamics of the past two decades.

The prospects for media policy reforms can rapidly change as political junctures fluctuate. The experiences of media movements in Latin America show the sinuous path of change, with plenty of turns and twist that reflect changing junctures. Fault lines among governing elites coupled with the volatility of politics can suddenly open doors for citizens' demands and reforms. Elite positions about citizens' demands as well as relations between media movements and elites are not permanently settled. Elite insiders are the necessary nexus to shepherd citizens' initiatives through the legislative process. In contrast, the absence of elite supporters blocks the chances of legislative changes. Citizens' access to state politics becomes difficult when political and economic elites oppose demands for media pluralism. Because political opportunities wax and wane, the analysis needs to be sensitive to political junctures in order to comprehend the triumphs and setbacks of media movements.

6 | WHY TRANSNATIONAL ACTIVISM MATTERS

In this chapter, our interest is twofold: we want to examine the linkages between local activism with regional and global actions and organizations, and the consequences of transnational activism on media policy reforms. These are important dimensions for assessing whether and how transnational activism contributes to the work of local media activists. Several questions guide our analysis. How are domestic media movements networked with transnational forms of media activism? What is the relevance of global networks for understanding media reforms? How do global actors intervene and influence domestic changes? How do local activists combine state-centric and global mobilization?

The ascendancy of global activism and organizations across a range of issues at the local, regional, and global levels issues has attracted significant attention. In Keck and Sikkink's (1998: 2) well-known definition, transnational advocacy networks (TANs) are "bound together by shared values, a common discourse, and dense exchanges of information and services … [that] help create news issues and categories to persuade, pressure and gain leverage over much more powerful organizations and governments." Scholars have been generally hopeful about the prospects and impact of TANs on global social change. Many have praised them, for they represent new forms of activism and policy-making (Bennett, 2004; Edwards & Gaventa, 2014; Gilson, 2011; Heller, 2013). Their conviction is premised on the notion that transitional activism expands the thematic focus as well as the political horizons of democratic participation by superseding the boundaries of the nation-state as both power center and container of democratic participation.

On the one hand, the formation of a global public sphere is critical to deal with planetary challenges that cannot be addressed by national institutions and mobilization. The traditional boundaries of the "nation-state" are too limited to conceptualize and act upon global shared interests and problems that affect humanity (Anheier, Kaldor

& Glasius, 2006; Fraser, 2014). Against state-centric views of world politics and social movements, it is necessary to direct our attention to trans-border forms of activism. At a time of myriad borderless problems such as global poverty, war and conflict, security, and climate change, global civil society is necessary to redefine problems and solutions. It provides new spaces for tackling fundamentally different social problems that demand both transnational vision and actions. Given the inability and/or reluctance of states to attend to problems that extend beyond the conventional limits of national sovereignty, global activism is necessary.

On the other hand, transnational participation introduces new ways of linking local and global change. Just as global actors affect local change by supporting domestic movements and pressuring governments to adopt international legislation, they are also nurtured by local participation. The formation of global networks of activists transforms the conditions, resources, and opportunities for social change. Cross-national engagement, then, opens up novel ways of conceptualizing both social problems and participation.

Recent studies have focused on assessing the impact and contributions of transnational activism. The consolidation of the presence of global activism in international organizations, forums, and bodies patently demonstrates that transnational mobilization has made remarkable strides. It is difficult, however, to draw categorical conclusions about the impact of transnational activism (Rodrigues, 2011). Neither optimistic expectations nor pessimistic predictions about global civil society are solidly confirmed. Just as selected evidence demonstrates positive contributions to global governance, other findings suggest that transnational activism has limited effects on specific issues (Scholte, 2014).

One issue that makes it difficult to reach categorical conclusions about the impact of TANs is the diversity of organizations, structures, and capacities. Consider the case of global media movements. It features networks of civil society organizations, inter-government organizations, international NGOs with national chapters, and bilateral and multilateral donors with different funding structures and mechanisms.

Also, "impact" is not a simple concept, as we mentioned earlier in connection with assessing the success of social movements. It refers to myriad actions and goals. Analysts have already observed the continuous difficulties of assessing the impact of global organizations on issues pertaining to media democracy (Abraham-Dowsing, Godfrey & Khor, 2014). One can assess the impact of global activism on several issues, including policy proposals, actual legislation, law enforcement, public debates, news coverage, public awareness and opinion, funding, and organizational structures. Positive impact on raising awareness about issues among citizens and policy-makers does not necessarily lead to the adoption of new positive legislation or ensuring that progressive laws are effectively implemented.

Moreover, not all networks of activists define similar goals or have comparable expectations about eventual effects. They work at different levels and, consequently, identify multiple goals and indicators of success. Furthermore, assessing impact is not an easy matter, for it carries complex issues related to measurement such as the definition of proper indicators and methodologies used to determine impact. Nor is it obvious that impact refers to the same time horizon, namely short-term and/or long-term consequences.

In summary, producing cross-cutting and conclusive statements about impact are exceedingly difficult because every issue includes multiple dimensions, and global civil society comprises wide-ranging interests and experiences. By understanding the linkages between global activism and domestic media activism in Latin America, we hope to contribute to a better understanding about how global activism supports change.

Our argument is as follows: global activism helps to solidify the organizational infrastructure and the strategic goals of local activism. As discussed in Chapter 2, on-the-ground organizations and coalitions are critical for effective social mobilization and advocacy. Because policy-making demands constant, long-term actions, participation and collaboration with global actors helps local media activists in five ways: linking up with transnational communities of practice, obtaining funding, raising the legitimacy and visibility of local activists, strengthening the rights-based framework of public communication, and recruiting international organizations with "moral persuasion" power.

Transnational communities of practice

Participation in transnational networks helps connect local activists to transnational communities of practice with shared interests, goals, and expertise.

Just like other social movements in the region (Alvarez, 2014; Cabezas, 2014; Chartock, 2011), media activism in Latin America has long maintained linkages with transnational civic and governmental organizations, and participated in transnational forms of activism. Long before the notion of "rooted cosmopolitanism" (Tarrow, 2005) gained currency in the academic literature, Latin American media movements recognized that transnational activism was critical to pushing for media reforms.

Since the 1960s, media activism has displayed a cosmopolitan consciousness that conceived policy reforms as part of broad transnational efforts (Burch, 2014). Grounded in Marxist and nationalist views that underpinned then-dominant media dependency ideas in political and academic circles, media activism has been envisioned as a transnational endeavor. The conviction that virtually any question about the media needs to consider the context of international flows of media capital, production, content, and reception runs through media activism in the region. Likewise, the diagnosis that global developments had historically shaped negative and dominant aspects of media systems, namely commercialization and the limited presence of local content, is widely found among scholars and media activism (Fox & Waisbord, 2002).

Solutions were considered global, too. Because the challenges were grounded in global patterns of media development, domestic struggles for freedom of expression and media pluralism demanded transnational activism. This vision appears in the foundational documents of regional associations of media workers established in the 1970s, such as the Asociación Latinoamericana de Educación Radiofónicas in 1972 and the Federación Latinoamericana de Periodistas in 1976, as well as regional academic associations such as the Asociación Latinoamericana de Investigadores en Comunicación formed in 1978 and the Federación Latinoamericana de Facultades de Comunicación Social in 1979 (Beltrán, 1993).

Not surprisingly, then, the 1970s debates about the NWICO sponsored by UNESCO generated considerable enthusiasm among media activists, policy-makers and scholars in the region. The debates were primarily concerned with issues that were already present in policy and academic debates, namely, the one-way flow of communication dominated by Western countries and particularly the United States, and policy options to curb the power of transnational and domestic private companies in media systems. The NWICO ideals and goals eventually became articulated in the 1980 MacBride Report, yet they lost ground in global debates about media and communication. This shift was caused by changes in geo-political conditions, specifically the weakening of the Non-Aligned Movement that had promoted the NWICO debates (Buchanan, 2015; Exeni, 2003).

Progressive Latin American organizations continued to participate in global networks and conferences. Many organizations participated in the Right to Communication roundtables and other meetings inspired by similar principles and objectives – the promotion of alternative and community media and the critique of media concentration and commercialism under capitalism (Capriles, 1976; Fisher, 1982). Overall, however, regional activism waned in the late 1970s amid the consolidation of military dictatorships and, as the late communication scholar Luis Ramiro Beltrán (2007) observed, "the disillusionment with the failure of struggles for communication policies and a new world communication and information order."

Transnational media activism around the demand for right to communication gradually reemerged as demonstrated by the participation of Latin American representatives in meetings and forums, including the creation of the Platform for the Rights to Communication in 1996, which launched the "Communication Rights in the Information Society" (CRIS) campaign in 2001 aimed at articulating civil society demands to participate and influence the UN World Summit on the Information Society (WSIS) in Geneva in 2003 and Tunisia in 2005 (Raboy & Landry, 2005; Burch, León & Tamayo, 2004).

The CRIS campaign has been credited with reviving and reinforcing regional and national media movements (Mattelart, 2005). It included international NGOs with long-standing presence in Latin America such as ALAI, the Asociación para el Progreso de las Comunicaciones (APC), ALER, AMARC and Inter Press Service (IPS). The campaign has various goals: to expand the network with civic actors, to ensure that WSIS includes "civil society" as an actor as well as states and companies in its debates, and to foreground a human rights perspective in those debates. The campaign included the production of policy papers, holding events, and advocacy with governments.

In 2003, the first World Forum on the Right to Communicate

was held simultaneously with the first stage of the WSIS. This meeting helped organizations to agree on human rights as the overall framework for information and communication matters (Mastrini & de Charras, 2005; Frau-Meigs et al., 2007). Observers concluded that the participation of civil society at a global level has been one of the most important achievements of this process (Burch, León & Tamayo, 2004).

Beginning in 2002, the Latin American Communication Networks headed the WSIS activities in the region with the CRIS campaign. The ALAI held a meeting in Quito with support from UNESCO, the World Association of Christian Communication, and the Friedrich Ebert Foundation. More than 100 participants agreed on the need to defend the right to communication, the value of participation and communication, criticized media concentration, and agreed on the need to promote a human rights approach as an alternative to both economicist and technological approaches to communication. The meeting produced a document called "Otra comunicación es possible," which urged the democratization of communication, demanded a legal framework to ensure communication rights, established the need for public media and support for alternative and independent media, urged for pressure to be put on private media to foster social responsibility, and stated the importance of educating citizens in critical media literacy and opening up public debate on communication rights (Segura, 2010).

Although the WSIS emphasized the transfer of knowledge and information structures and technologies from wealthy to poor countries and from well-off to poor populations (Mastrini & de Charras, 2005; Calabrese, 2004), an approach identified with the Right to Communication and the democratization of communication resources also gained visibility. Civic organizations produced an alternative, non-official declaration that emphasized the need to put human rights and needs at the center of the information society. Also, they recommended that information technologies be seen as instruments for human development, and that the digital gap be understood as a reflection of social gaps that required a broad analysis of political, economic, social, education, and gender dimensions and could not be solved by addressing technical obstacles.

A range of organizations also came together around the World Social Forum held in Porto Alegre, Brazil, in January 2001 in support of new forms of media monitoring and legal reforms, and the launch of the CRIS campaign and the World Forum on the Right to Communication (Segura, 2010). Since then, a network of social movements, the Comunidad Web de Movimientos Sociales and Minga Informativa de Movimientos Sociales, has functioned with the participation of several local and national organizations (León, Burch & Tamayo, 2005). Communication was incorporated as a thematic focus of the 2003 World Social Forum. It led to the creation of Media Watch Global tasked with the promotion of the rights of all citizens to be properly informed, and with chapters in many countries, including Brazil and Venezuela.

These declarations were based on the recognition that the right to communication is a long-standing, historical vindication that originally started with the acceptance of the right of media owners, then media workers, and eventually became accepted as a universal right for all people. This vision demanded the kind of public policies recommended by contemporary media movements in Latin America: the promotion of citizens' media, the limitation of media concentration, the critique of the commodification of information, and the development of pluralist media systems that reflect social diversity, including gender, age, race, ethnicity, and religion (Segura, 2010).

Simultaneously, media activists formed regional coalitions grounded in the consolidation of the field of media activism at the national level. For example, the Alianza Regional por la Libertad de Expresión y el Derecho a la Información is a network of non-partisan NGOs. In 2005, the Trust for the Americas Foundation based in the OAS proposed to CSOs based in Mexico and Central America that they form a network to articulate and represent common interests. The initiative brought together organizations that had been working on combating anti-press violence and libel laws and demanding journalists' rights, justice, and transparency. Eventually, more than twenty organizations from the region joined in, convinced that the Alianza was an appropriate instrument for exchanging ideas, increasing visibility, and achieving "power in numbers" (Sánchez, 2015). Early on, the Alianza decided it needed to focus on a single issue, public access to government information, to avoid competition and duplication with other existing organizations working on freedom of expression. Although the Alianza circumstantially participated in other initiatives, it basically supported the work spearheaded by other organizations such AMARC on community radio and Transparency International (as well as its local chapters or partners).

The case of the Alianza Regional (2013) illustrates the belief that regional networks perform valuable roles in support of local activists. The Alianza was established to provide a mechanism to connect governments, inter-government organizations (like the OAS), and civil society in matters of freedom of expression. It was envisioned as a forum for civic organizations to make collective demands on governments at the regional level. It was seen as necessary to achieve several goals: unify common demands, strengthen organizational presence, bolster the presence of civil society vis-à-vis governments and international organizations, share knowledge and technical expertise, and accumulate experiences. Today, it brings together more than twenty CSOs from throughout the region. Since 2006, it has supported initiatives to promote public access to government information in El Salvador, Guatemala, Nicaragua, Honduras, Bolivia, Paraguay, and Colombia by helping local CSOs to elaborate proposals and advocacy training (Alianza Regional, 2013).

Other cases similarly demonstrate that transnational networks facilitate the sharing of experiences across the region. For example, Mexico's 2002 information access legislation, Uruguay's 2007 community media, and Argentina's 2009 broadcasting law became lead cases widely discussed in the region. UN and OAS Freedom of Speech Rapporteurs and leading international NGOs praised the content of these laws as well as civic participation during the process. These reforms eventually became sources of references. Members of Argentina's Coalición as well as Uruguay's CSOs were invited to collaborate with civic coalitions and governments interested in similar reforms in other countries such as Brazil, Chile, Colombia, Ecuador, and Peru (Gómez, 2014).

Certainly, such traffic of ideas was facilitated by the fact that media activists in Latin America share a common language. Certainly, the virtual absence of language barriers has facilitated cross-border communication and institution-building. Not only is Spanish the lingua franca, among activists even for those fluent in Portuguese and indigenous languages; equally important is the fact that media activism has embraced the same discursive framework already analyzed: international standards of human rights of the OAS and the

UN, and specific policy recommendations such as the legalization of community media and the tripartite conception of broadcasting.

In summary, Latin American networks have offered vehicles for the dissemination and discussion of national experiences among local activists and experts. Belonging to issue coalitions and networks and participation in global forums has offered opportunities to participate in "communities of practice" that help not only to strengthen technical and policy knowledge but also to enlarge the scope and presence of specific CSOs.

Funding

Funding is another important contribution of transnational networks to strengthening local organizations in the context of "international media assistance" and "media development" programs.

Several organizations have relied on international funding for operations and activities. Local activists believe that many CSOs working on community media, public access to government information, and press laws would have a difficult time without the support of international donors. Consequently, many associations are financially dependent on grants, consultancies, and other forms of funding offered by international donors. Typically, funding is available for specific projects rather than for institutional expenses. International funding is particularly significant considering that local funds, whether from governments or philanthropic institutions, are limited to initiatives related to media policies and freedom of speech. Also, many organizations have been reluctant to rely on official funding for their activities to preserve autonomy.

Donors have generally channeled funds through NGOs and coalitions. In addition to overhead funding for basic expenses, they have financed a wide range of programs linked to information policies, press laws, journalism training, and media structures.

International donors include the cooperation agencies of the governments of the United States (United States Agency for International Development, National Endowment for Democracy), Canada (Department of Foreign Affairs and International Trade), United Kingdom (Department for International Development), Germany, and the Scandinavian countries. They also include multilateral donors such as the United Nations Democracy Fund, UNESCO, the Inter-American Development Bank, and the

World Bank. Local CSOs have also relied on the support from philanthropic organizations such as the Ford Foundation, Tinker Foundation, Hewlett Foundation, Open Society Foundations, Adessium Foundation, Carter Center, and Freedom House, which have supported a diversity of projects related to media legislation reforms. Other prominent funders have been the Konrad Adenauer, Friedrich Ebert, and Friedrich Naumann foundations affiliated with major political parties in Germany. All three foundations have had a long-standing presence in Latin America and supported a range of media activities – from debates on media legislation to journalism and academic training.

Constant interaction and financial dependence on global donors has encouraged organizations to adopt bureaucratized procedures. They need to meet donors' requirements, such as being a legal entity, financial plan, accounting structure, reporting system, and other conditions. Such expectations have prompted local CSOs to develop procedures and structures. Also, they had to develop fundraising skills, understand donors' priorities, and become conversant with the language and dynamics of international cooperation. Global funding does not have the same significance for media activists uninterested in developing organizations that follow "bureaucratic" procedures or reject so-called "insider strategies" to promote change (Fogarty, 2011).

One challenge for media activists is the influence of donors' priorities on their work (Russell, 2011). Donors don't have similar levels of interest across issues and countries, and their priorities are subject to change. At times, dependence on foreign funding creates problems. The volatility of donors' priorities has tremendous impact on the financial situation and the survival of local organizations. From cycles of interest in specific issues in international aid among donors to changing and unpredictable local situations, a host of factors affect their agenda on freedom of expression. The worsening of conditions for freedom of expression in some countries drives interest in specific issues, such as anti-press violence in Mexico and Colombia, and legislation criminalizing public speech and dissident reporting in Ecuador and Venezuela in the past decade (Balbi, 2015). However, particular political conditions also affect donors' calculations. Notoriously difficult situations for freedom of expression coupled with the lack of trusted and fluid communication with administrations has led donors to shut down operations, as the Adenauer Foundation (Behrens, 2015) did in Ecuador in 2014, and the Carter Center also did in Venezuela in 2015 (*El Nacional*, 2015).

Another sensitive issue is the level of support that international funders provide to different media reforms issues. Not all citizens' demands have similar resonance with funders' priorities. Because donor programs are generally focused on specific issues, opportunities for addressing various problems of public communication vary widely. There has been more funding support for the promotion of "independent" journalism, the elimination of contempt laws, the decriminalization of libel and slander, the regulation of official advertising, and public access to government information than for tackling market concentration or the legalization of community media (Vaca Villareal, 2015).

Donor priorities do not always match local interests and perceptions about key issues. Neither are all programmatic directions set and funded by headquarters equally perceived as critical by local partners. Interviewees observe that donors and local organizations frequently negotiate priority programs, although not all CSOs have similar bargaining power to shape program priorities (Bertoni, 2015; Saba, 2015). Because a wide range of issues fall under the umbrella of freedom of expression and media reforms, the priorities of international donors and local activists are not always aligned. For example, donors may consider Internet content policies and digital rights as central programmatic priorities in their global plans, but those issues are not necessarily central to the work of Latin American media activists. Instead, they contend that priorities are different given the characteristics of the media landscape in the region, namely, the continuing popularity of radio and television, rampant anti-press violence, legal threats to public expression, and persistent problems for basic digital connectivity. Negotiations about programmatic priorities are inevitable given mismatched expectations and priorities. Negotiations do not always take place on a levelled ground. Not all donors solicit input from potential grantees and partners when defining their priorities. In fact, many global and regional donors generally have pre-established objectives and preferred courses of actions.

Finally, not all CSOs hold similar views about partnering with all foreign donors. CSOs and activists identified with the Left have been reluctant, if not completely opposed, to working with US funders. In a region where US governments and philanthropic organizations have supported military coups and dictatorships, antipathy persists towards a range of funders identified with US interests. Several organizations have either shunned foreign funding altogether or only worked with selected European donors (Wolfson, 2013).

Visibility and legitimacy

Global organizations and networks also bring visibility and legitimacy to local activists and demands in the eyes of domestic actors, particularly governments.

Local CSOs usually confront difficulties in gaining visibility and recognition in domestic politics. Only in exceptional circumstances, as discussed in Chapter 5, are governments interested in prioritizing media reforms. Private media corporations are either skeptical or simply opposed to core demands from media activists. News organizations, especially those owned by leading media giants, flatly ignore or distort citizens' demands that challenge their power. Therefore, media activists often have a hard time gaining recognition from key policy stakeholders and remaining visible in the media and legislatures.

Ties with global organizations offer local activists opportunities to coordinate actions and solidify their stature both locally and internationally. Cooperation with transnational networks and organizations, with well-coordinated actions and specific demands and messages, are critical to increasing the chances of gaining prominence and respectability – conditions that are essential for successful policy advocacy (Shawk, 2011).

In this regard, the offices of the Freedom of Expression Rapporteurs of the UN and the OAS have played important roles. The UN Rapporteur for Freedom of Opinion and Expression has the ability to introduce information from local associations about conditions and problems in the Universal Periodic Review (UPR) of the human rights records of UN member states. The UN General Assembly created the UPR on March 2006 to review the human rights records of member states.

Likewise, the Office of the Special Rapporteur for Freedom of Expression of the OAS has played a critical role. The Office was created during the Second Summit of the Americas held in Santiago, Chile in 1998, and it is housed in the OAS IACHR. It defines and systematizes principles espoused by local organizations which might eventually inform court decisions, and produces reports that assess the state of freedom of expression in the region.

Changes in the range of issues that the Office has covered for the past few years tellingly reflect the expansion of the agenda of freedom of expression in the region as well as the ascendancy of CSOs. Whereas the Office originally focused on bringing attention to the persistence of libel laws and anti-press violence, it gradually incorporated a new set of issues. The expansion of the thematic foci in its annual reports patently illustrates these changes. Recent reports include the analysis and denunciation of indirect forms of censorship, discretionary practices of official advertising, concentration of media ownership, and the need for the protection of the right to expression of all citizens and specific communities. None of these issues are found in early reports.

Former Rapporteurs (Bertoni, 2015, Botero, 2015, Cantón, 2015) credit the close relationship between the Office with civil society organizations for this change. As organizations began to see the Office as a potential supporter for their causes at the national level, they continuously contacted it to collaborate in specific issues and strategies. Gradually, a "virtuous circle" of mutual collaboration and comparative strengths developed. With close knowledge of local developments, civil society brought up new issues that needed to be addressed. The Rapporteur, in turn, benefited from their work identifying needs, learning from local experiences, and systematically elevating principles to the regional level.

Also, the bully pulpit of international organizations is particularly valuable for raising awareness among governments and the public. Inter-state agencies, such as the Office of Freedom of Expression Rapporteurs of the UN and the OAS, command a great deal of respect and visibility. Their annual reports as well as country visits generally attract substantial news coverage. Rapporteurs are able to bring up issues that are sensitive to national governments or that directly take issue with official policies as well as demands that are contrary to the interests of media corporations.

Annual reports on the state of freedom of expression produced by the UN and OAS Rapporteurs as well as other international organizations such as the Committee to Protect Journalists (CPJ) receive media attention, especially if they address issues close to journalists' interests such as the state of the press, violence, and legislation. Reports are also used by local and international organizations to inform debates and policies and to discuss specific issues with relevant parties – presidents, cabinet members, diplomatic corps, and other international organizations.

Also, meetings between representatives of inter-state organizations and key legislators and other government officials help to raise awareness about issues and CSOs. These are important opportunities to meet with key government actors in public forums and to bring up the public profile of specific demands and policies. Presidents and prominent legislators are less likely to refuse requests for meetings with international envoys out of fear of negative repercussions. Unlike the cooperation agencies of foreign governments, they are not hamstrung by institutional reluctance to engage in domestic politics to address matters of freedom of expression. Whereas the latter tend to remain above the political fray and refrain from confronting administrations (Bush, 2015), other organizations, including inter-government organizations and some donors, have reached out to prominent officials. They carefully waded into domestic politics, knowing that their participation and/or sponsorship of specific events and documents commands respect in certain political quarters but also sensitive to not meddling with domestic affairs (Behrens, 2015; Rincón, 2015).

Certainly, not all transnational networks and global organizations bring legitimacy to local activists in the eyes of national governments. In many cases, they have been entangled in high-profile, drawn-out debates with national governments opposed to their agendas and recommendations. In the past decade, several conflicts pitted governments against local and international associations critical of official positions on issues related to freedom of expression. For example, the Correa administration negatively reacted to critical reports produced by the OAS Freedom of Expression Rapporteur and actively sought to weaken the financial capacity and autonomy of the Office. Besides, strident cases have been the confrontations between the governments of Bolivia and Venezuela and US-based and US-funded organizations. In 2008, the Chavez government detained and expelled representatives of Human Rights Watch after the release of a report documenting violation of human rights norms by the government, and accused the National Endowment for Democracy (as well as its domestic grantees) of interfering with domestic affairs and being "funded by CIA." According to Human Rights Watch (2013), in 2010, "the Venezuelan Supreme Court ruled that individuals or organizations receiving foreign funding could be prosecuted for "treason." The National Assembly passed legislation prohibiting organizations that "defend political rights" or "monitor the performance of public bodies" from receiving international funding. It also imposed stiff fines on organizations that "invite" foreigners who express opinions that "offend" government institutions" to Venezuela. The Morales government accused USAID-funded NGOs of working in "the service of foreign powers." US diplomatic cables leaked in 2010 revealed funding linkages between the US government and some CSOs in those countries (Becerra & Lacunza, 2012).

Exceptions aside, international agencies and transnational networks bring recognition to the work of local CSOs and provide invaluable strategic support. Working with transnational organizations and belonging to networks enhance the visibility and legitimacy of the demands of local activists. Arguing that principles and demands reflect the interests of dozens of organizations in the region (and the world) and that they are included in documents by prestigious NGOs carries more persuasive punch. It is harder for government officials and market actors to dismiss demands and proposals as marginal ideas of a local organization. The legitimacy of international actors is grounded in the perception that they are impartial and technical agencies committed to public goals. Unlike specific governments or foundations, they are less likely to be suspected of promoting partisan agendas or private interests. Association with prestigious international agencies has positive spillover effects.

It is also important to mention the significance of regional actors such as the Alianza and AMARC with vast expertise in specific media policy reforms. They bring credibility in support of local initiatives by showing that similar debates and policy goals took place in neighboring countries. Rather than pointing at experiences in Europe or countries in the global South, activists can direct attention to actions and achievements in Latin America. This is why CSOs invited experts from other countries in the region to provide testimony to local audiences, especially policy-makers, about their experiences and success in passing legislation (Gómez, 2014). By doing so, local activists intend to bring legitimacy to their struggles as part of broad movements for change in the region.

Strategic frames

Linkages to transnational networks and organizations also contribute to bolstering the rights-based policy frames underpinning the demands and proposals of local media activists. Just as global agencies and coalitions bolster their visibility and legitimacy, they also give credibility to policy proposals grounded in the right to communication.

The mobilization of the human rights "interpretative package" (Gamson & Modigliani, 1989) by transnational actors not only contributes to legitimizing the positions of local activists; it also helps to shift the way freedom of the press and freedom of expression have traditionally been understood in the region. When international agencies make public pronouncements that endorse the vision of public communication grounded in the 1948 Declaration of Human Rights, the 1980 MacBride Report, and other documents, they reaffirm a vision that essentially differs from the dominant market and statist perspectives.

As previously discussed, foregrounding communication as a human right contradicts market-based perspectives that narrowly identify freedom of expression with ownership rights and unregulated markets. It also clashes with the position of governments who fear public and critical expression by invoking the protection of national security and/or the honor of public officials. In a region where these positions have long dominated public debates, international endorsement of human rights as the normative frame to understand freedom of expression is quite innovative. It underscores the need to embrace a positive conception of freedom as the ability of all citizens to express in public. It calls for public policies to ensure a range of citizens' rights to speech and to promote pluralism.

Support for a human rights frame is laid out by international organizations in myriad ways: press conferences, advocacy meetings, and annual reports documenting national and regional situations produced by Reporters without Borders, the CPJ, and the OAS and the UN freedom of expression Special Rapporteurs.

The fact that the Special Rapporteurs for the UN and the OAS are embedded in human rights agencies within inter-government organizations has been, undoubtedly, important. It is indicative of the ongoing shift in the conceptualization of freedom of expression as a human right. This has helped to framing freedom of expression as a matter of human rights rather than an issue linked to national security or economic development. In fact, many national courts and legislatures have invoked human rights principles in international treaties and they have been endorsed by regional and global agencies in their decisions to abolish contempt laws, decriminalize libel, and promote public access to government information.

Indeed, the growing expansion of the thematic agenda of annual reports produced by OAS and UN Freedom of Expression Rapporteurs is symptomatic of the gradual consolidation of the human rights framework. From this perspective, a range of issues are included, for they affect the rights of all citizens to communicate – from community media legislation to regulations affecting content for specific groups such as children and indigenous populations (United Nations et al., 2001; United Nations et al., 2007; UNESCO, 2008). Their work progressively cements a conception of freedom of expression in line with key international documents and legislation that is different from the visions tirelessly championed by market actors and government officials worried about citizens' expression.

Transnational agencies and activism, then, are critical for the diffusion of human rights as the new norm for grounding media legislation (Berliner, 2014). Against the dominant perspectives embraced by market and political powers, local CSOs and activists are able to show that their demands are in agreement with global norms. Interviewees observe that strategic support from global organizations makes it more difficult for local activists to be dismissed as a "bunch of crazies" with strange ideas (Calleja, 2015; Gómez, 2014). By signaling that their demands are grounded in the discourse of global networks and agencies and standard international legislation, local media movements are able to reaffirm the credibility of their arguments and objectives.

Moral persuasion

Finally, international networks and organizations reinforce the strategic goals of local activists by engaging in moral persuasion. They have used their "bully pulpit" power to call on actors, particularly governments, who disregard or fail to guarantee basic rights. By doing so, they resort to symbolic sanction and praise to bring up issues and generate pressure for change. Just like human rights and other movements (Meernik et al., 2012; Murdie, 2013), they have used "naming and shaming" mechanisms to denounce violations as well as official disinterest in specific transgressions and other matters. Such actions are premised on the universal acceptance of specific norms such as equal rights to free expression. Denunciations generally remark upon inconsistencies between the behavior of specific actors, namely governments, and international and national laws and norms accepted by the global community.

Not all global organizations have had similar interest in using their platforms for moral persuasion. At times, inter-government organizations, international non-government organizations, and foundations have forcefully denounced governments for perpetrating or condoning crimes as well as failing to ensure basic rights to public expression. Certainly, such decisions are essentially political. Not all global organizations and leaders are equally interested in taking open critical positions vis-à-vis governments and domestic actors such as media owners, political parties, and activists. Strategies and positions are contingent on specific mandates as well as international and domestic circumstances. Some organizations, particularly agencies of national governments, are subjected to political imperatives that curb their ability to take open political positions. Also, offices of IGOs are enmeshed in diplomatic politics and need to be sensitive to institutional power dynamics when bringing up issues with government, as the latter are members of their organizations, such as in the case of the OAS and UN agencies such as UNESCO and the United Nations Development Program.

Still, it is important to underscore that global organizations approach moral persuasion gingerly and make careful decisions about when and how to criticize domestic authorities and other actors. Aside from being mindful of politics inside their organizations, officials are reluctant to get dragged into local politics or to be the targets of accusation of "foreign intrusion" and imperialism." Regardless of whether they have national offices or chapters, they generally work in partnership with local activists, and nurture and foreground their work. Afraid of being perceived as playing a leading role or interfering with domestic politics, they prefer to provide tactical support to local activists.

Although moral persuasion is an important aspect of the work of global organizations, not all governments are equally sensitive to denunciations. Some governments have positively reacted after criticisms. For example, Mexico's President Vicente Fox supported the transfer of the judicial investigation of violence against reporters from state to federal courts after criticisms from the CPJ prompted by a rash of attacks. Fox met with a delegation of the CPJ and other press associations to discuss the issue and the need to "federalize" the investigation of crimes (Lauría, 2015).

In contrast, other governments remained unruffled by "naming and shaming" tactics. For instance, critical documents and pronouncements about the situation of the press and public expression in Ecuador under the Correa administration and in Venezuela under the Chavez and Maduro governments produced by transnational organizations had little, if any, impact on official decisions. The UN and OAS Special Rapporteurs harshly criticized Venezuela's 2004 Ley de Responsabilidad Social en Radio y Televisión and Ecuador's 2013 Ley Orgánica de Comunicación. They pointed out that the laws threaten public expression in many ways: they ban the publication of information defined as "reserved" by the government, create censorship mechanisms, and promote media self-censorship through the inclusion of ambiguous provisions (Segura, 2014). Nevertheless, the governments of Venezuela and Ecuador not only kept the laws, but they also used them to persecute critics. A few other cases, however, suggest that even governments that have generally ignored the positions of international organizations have been receptive to criticisms in specific circumstances. In 2015, observers credited the UN Rapporteur for persuading the Correa administration to withdraw its decision to dissolve Fundamedios, the CSOs that had been a vocal critic of government media and information policies.

It is difficult to provide a simple explanation for why governments are not similarly permeable to moral persuasion by international organizations and are willing to meet with officials from regional and global organizations. Interviewees believe that some governments are more sensitive to keeping a good reputation about issues such as transparency as well as civil and political rights in international circles (Bertoni, 2015). They mind international opinion particularly after high-profile events that put the spotlight on their human rights records, such as the murders of reporters and other citizens. Sensitivity to criticism does not mean that they are solidly supportive of reforms or that they are willing to support new legislation embedded in human rights principles. Yet, under certain political junctures, some administrations have been inclined to meet with global actors and discuss courses of action under global and domestic pressure.

Why transnational activism matters

In summary, transnational networks contribute to the organizational and strategic goals of local media movements by plugging them into global communities of practice, funding programs, raising their visibility and legitimacy, bolstering discursive frames, and engaging in moral persuasion with governments, media owners, and other actors.

The experiences analyzed demonstrate the contributions of transnational organizations to domestic activism. Collaboration with global and regional organizations has helped to strengthen the organizational resources and the strategic goals of local activists. The diverse makeup of global organizations as well as international legislation and experiences helped local movements to develop strategies and technical arguments in favor of reforms. Global and regional experiences served as a treasure trove of accumulated practices that provided evidence and legitimizing references for domestic proposals and actions. Local media movements generally do not work separately from global and regional agencies and networks, and generally recognize that transnational activism is strategically important (Alianza Regional, 2013).

Although transnational activism matters in many important ways, it doesn't unilaterally lead to changes in media legislation. Activists are embedded in global networks yet they continue to be focused on domestic media policies and finding appropriate junctures for pushing reforms. We find no case of "externally" induced change driven by "global civil society" or single-handedly promoted by international organizations. This finding may not be surprising to many, but a reminder is needed in the light of exaggerated expectations about the prospects of significant and long-lasting change pushed by TANs. Nor do international organizations generally assume that they solely drive changes, as interviewees recognize (Botero, 2015; Cantón, 2015; Podesta, 2015). In fact, they are fully cognizant of the fact that they need to cultivate linkages with local movements to bolster the work of local demands and organizations.

The contributions of global organizations are grounded in their visibility and reputation among selected policy-makers as well as the ability to influence political institutions including the presidency, the courts, and Congress. Some institutions have the clout to catalyze processes and convene events among diverse interests. They are perceived as actors that can bring together political and civic actors around common interests. Other institutions have unique power to influence legislation and judicial decisions. Because their principles are considered "soft laws," the UN and OAS Freedom of Expression Rapporteurs may also contribute to defining future frameworks and legislation (Pasqualucci, 2014). Even if they are not inter-state agencies, the CRIS campaign and the Alianza have become a source of inspiration and legitimacy for local organizations. The Alianza elaborated a "model" law granting public access to official information that was used as the blueprint for the drafting of legislation in many countries (Alianza Regional, 2013). The CRIS campaign laid down the basic principles of the Right to Communication that were incorporated in the broadcasting bills and other proposals drafted by local coalitions.

Other international agencies contribute fluid access to key politicians and government officials. At times, they have connected organized citizens and the political sphere through public conferences and private meetings. Certainly, not all international actors are equally interested in or drawn to conducting advocacy because it falls outside their mission or it may become politically problematic. Other organizations, however, have been deliberately engaged in partisan politics and selectively decided when and how to intervene based on internal considerations and local circumstances.

In all cases, global organizations have basically adopted supportive roles. Although their contributions are undeniable, their actions are closely linked with domestic organizations and politics. If they spread new norms around freedom of expression, they do it in conjunction with local organizations. They constantly feed off the work done locally, particularly if they are interested in having significant influence in specific debates and policies. Local organizations are central to the "information politics" (Keck & Sikkink, 1998) that nurtures global reports, events, and priorities.

Also, just like in the cases of other global social movements (Holzhacker, 2012; Marx, Halcli & Barnett, 2012), transnational media activism typically adjusts strategies to local conditions. Specific political junctures offer opportunities for making progress or, instead, shut down possibilities for change. Local mobilization, organizations, and opportunities are essential to driving change. Variations in policy developments are mainly attributed to particular local conditions even when TANs perform valuable roles.

The evidence confirms that although the consolidation of transnational media activism has ushered in new forms of participation and norm diffusion, it doesn't transcend national politics. Although parochialism is out and cosmopolitanism is in, national politics and actors are still critical. States still have unique powers and responsibilities that are not matched by global networks and associations. States retain the power to pass and enforce legislation that defines basic components of media systems and have the obligation to guarantee the right to communicate. States remain the focus of actions, the much-needed interlocutor and the arena in which to compete for political support. The expansion of citizens' participation beyond the conventional borders of the state, as we have demonstrated, does not imply that states suddenly become irrelevant or that "national politics" dramatically lose their significance as spaces of contestation. In line with what other scholars argue (Risse, 2010), we conclude that the impact of global actors strongly depend on domestic institutional conditions and organizations. For TANs, adapting to local situations and the work of domestic organizations is indispensable to increase the chances of success. The politics of TANs in media activism is inevitably enmeshed with domestic politics and states (Shekha, 2011).

In light of the evidence, we believe that a cautious and nuanced perspective is warranted to understand the contributions of transnational activism to media reforms in Latin America. Local politics is essential to understanding current media and freedom of speech policies. This conclusion hardly breaks new theoretical ground. It needs to be reiterated, however, in light of the "global turn" in media studies. Globalization has bolstered a proto-libertarian enthusiasm that fulminates against the state and minimizes old-fashioned domestic politics. It assumes that globalization invariably overshadows local and national politics (for better or worse), and it views the state as a recalcitrant, conservative institution invariably opposed to democratic change or market freedom (see Morris & Waisbord, 2001; Flew & Waisbord, 2015).

The cases examined here suggest that TANs are not necessarily anti-state or interested in shaping alternative policy-making outside states and the international system of states. There is no doubt that states do not monopolize politics or information flows in today's networked global society, but they remain central to several processes around media legislation reforms. Although states may not be completely autonomous and sovereign in the current global order, they retain substantial capacity to determine policies that regulate media systems within a certain political–geographical space.

This is why we should not assimilate transnational activism with post-state, post-national politics. Transnational activism is geographically broad, but it doesn't render the politics of specific policy spaces irrelevant (Vicari, 2014). It represents relatively new forms of activism beyond national borders, but it continues to focus on states. Domestic media policies remain critical to strengthening the hand of powerful actors or, instead, introducing reforms for improving conditions for democratic speech.

Not surprisingly, the actions of TANs have been primarily aimed at the state and traditional aspects of policy-making – stakeholders, coalitions, influence, and results. Because state institutions, namely the presidency, Congress, and the Judiciary, continue to play critical roles in policy-making, they have been central to the strategies of global actors. This is why TANs have tried to influence various phases of policy-making – public awareness, legislative priorities and debates, congressional bills, public audiences, judicial actions, policy implementation, and monitoring. Changes in national governments as well as specific junctures have affected the priorities of TANs.

Are Latin American cases examples of the persistence of state politics in media and freedom of speech policies? It is hard to tell whether the region as a whole or the countries examined here are unusual cases suggesting the impact and limitations of TANs in the context of state politics.

Notwithstanding the growing presence of regional bodies such as the IACHR, states keep significant autonomy and decision-making power on matters of freedom of expression. Even transnational bodies such as the IACHR and the UN Freedom of Expression Rapporteurs recognize and emphasize the crucial role of states to guarantee free expression and information access. There have not been processes that have dramatically undercut or curbed the power of states. Conclusions applicable to media policy in the European Union or on issues related to global Internet governance don't necessarily apply to the specific issues discussed here in Latin America. Global and regional bodies have certainly gained influence on some areas of global policy-making such as audiovisual trade, copyright, or Internet neutrality, yet such developments do not necessarily imply that they have similar power over issues such as media ownership, funding, press laws, and others. Globalization doesn't seem to impinge significantly on states' ability to influence a range of media and information policies. More than any other actor, states still exercise unmatched influence in setting up legal and social conditions affecting public communication and media systems. Global governance neither displaces states and domestic politics nor does it bring immediate, tangible changes to the organization and functioning of media systems.

States are able to affect the prospects of community media ownership, access to public information, and public advertising management in ways that cannot substantially affect issues pertaining to Internet neutrality and international copyright laws. Whereas some administrations may favor more transparency, pluralism, and participation in media systems, others don't. Therefore, whoever occupies the presidency, alliances, support, vision, and interests as well as the configuration of domestic politics have important consequences. These are not small matters or simply the byproduct of external forces. Understanding when and why global and national forces matter is important to assess policy-making and citizens' participation and influence.

What are needed are approaches that are sensitive to the interaction between global and local power dynamics, institutions, and actors (see Price, Verhulst & Morgan, 2013). These questions redirect our attention to questions about the dynamics of state politics and the nature of collective action in a globalized world. These issues remain important for examining the power of transnational actors and globally connected citizens in media policies. Nuanced perspectives that are sensitive to local and national politics are needed to reassess assertions, fill analytical gaps, and revisit the "global turn" in media studies. Rediscovering the importance of local politics in global media studies is overdue. The stuff that makes the politics of policy-making, issue identification, participation, proposed solutions, and mobilized resources remains solidly grounded in domestic dynamics and calculations.

7 | POLICY IMPLEMENTATION

Media policy-making is not over after bills are signed into laws. A new phase in the policy process with its own particularities and complexities begins with the implementation of new legislation.

The passing of several policy reforms in recent years set in motion dynamics without precedents in Latin America. It mainstreamed principles that had remained on the fringes of policy debates and incorporated civic participation into state policies and agencies. Governments accepted institutionalizing citizen participation as an integral component of new legislation in response to demands from media movements, which had long envisioned citizen participation as a permanent feature of the policy-making process. Neither governments nor media activists, however, were seasoned in this matter. Nor did they have blueprints for successful ways of incorporating CSOs in the roll-out of new policies. For these reasons, the inclusion of participatory mechanisms in policy implementation was *terra incognita* in media governance.

Undoubtedly, recent policy innovations have repositioned CSOs in media governance. In countries where reforms were passed, CSO are no longer excluded from policy-making. Principles and proposals championed by media activists underpin the current legal frameworks of media systems and public communication in many countries, including public access to government information, "third sector" media, the regulation of ownership of broadcasting licenses, public obligations of media organizations, and the participation of civil society. CSOs representatives now sit in regulatory and consultative government agencies – positions that give them, in principle, fluid access to government officials and opportunities to provide regular input into policy implementation. Constitutional participatory mechanisms as well as specific provisos in new media legislation grant citizens opportunities and responsibilities to be actively involved. These innovations in media policy are grounded in the notion that citizen participation is essential to democratic governance. Just like in other participatory experiences, it is deemed critical to bring up diverse perspectives and contribute to effective policies and the legitimacy of new legislation, enhance government accountability and responsiveness, and deliver better services (Cameron, Herschberg & Sharpe, 2012; Olvera, 2010; Seele & Peruzzotti, 2009; Wampler, 2012).

Participatory innovations in media policy implementation raise new questions about media governance: How are participatory politics embedded in institutional mechanisms? Do they contribute to improving governance? What obstacles has citizen participation confronted? These are the questions at the center of this chapter. We address these questions by examining the implementation of freedom of information legislation, the decriminalization of public speech, and broadcasting reforms in Argentina, Ecuador, Mexico, and Uruguay.

We are interested in assessing the participation of civic society in policy implementation more than discussing the consequences of new laws on media systems and public communication. The latter is, unquestionably, an important subject, but it exceeds the analytical scope of the book. Also, determining the impact of new legislation confronts the challenge that we are only at the beginning of complex and fluid processes triggered by new policies. In most countries, laws granting freedom of information access and decriminalizing speech have been passed in the past decade, and major broadcasting reforms have been approved only in the past few years. Without the benefit of temporal distance, it is premature to draw sweeping conclusions about the overall impact of new legislation on media pluralism.

Our argument is that the participation of CSOs in policy implementation is a major turning point in the history of media governance in Latin America. The institutionalization of participatory mechanisms is a true innovation in media policy-making in the region. However, several problems persist. One common feature of the implementation of public access to government information, freedom of speech, and broadcasting legislation is the gap between legislation and implementation. Yet, even if progressive aspects of reforms have not been implemented as effectively and fast as CSOs expected, the new laws establish better opportunities for media democracy as they recognize important rights that can be demanded.

CSOs have played critical roles during the bumpy and acrimonious implementation of new legislation. They have produced technical information and participated in public audiences; they have called attention to numerous problems, including the lethargy of participatory mechanisms, and criticized public officials for selective implementation of new laws. Citizen participation, however, has been situated in a permanent tension with the political dynamics and partisan calculations that have shaped the rolling out of new laws. It has had to wrestle with several obstacles – from weak political will to prioritize progressive aspects of the legislation to the fact that some regulatory agencies are closely influenced by the Executive power. Such dynamics have generated controversy and deepened divisions in civil society about the position of CSOs vis-à-vis governments and new laws.

Access to information

The passing of new laws allowing public access to government information raised the hopes of CSOs in the region. Media activists expected the legislation to usher in a new phase in the struggle for government transparency and accountability. The laws offered valuable mechanisms to make governments more transparent in countries with chronic problems of government opacity and accountability coupled with weak or non-existent mechanisms for citizens to get information and scrutinize official actions.

Such confidence, however, has transmuted into disillusionment. In recent assessments of the implementation of the laws, the tone is definitely gloomier and the expectations more moderate. While recognizing that the existence of a legal framework is unquestionably a positive step, studies offer a grim picture of the implementation of public information laws. Certainly, many requests were successfully answered and resulted in the publication of relevant information in many countries, but the overall situation is far from ideal. It has been characterized in terms of "partial" advances, "deadlock conditions," and an "uphill battle" by activists throughout the region (CAinfo, 2014; Navarrete, 2015). The 2014 UNESCO report (2014: 10) correctly observes that "it seems that governments tend to adopt public access laws and weaken them later."

CSOs have conducted many activities to monitor policy implementation. Indeed, as in the case of Uruguay, media activists founded CAInfo deliberately to ensure the presence of an organization to monitor and help to implement the 2008 law. CSOs have raised awareness about these problems through publication and public presentations. They have held workshops to educate government officials about the implementation of the laws. They have also resorted to strategic litigation when government agencies rejected petitions or provided unsatisfactory responses.

Amidst continuous problems for implementing freedom of access legislation, CSOs have filed scores of petitions to redress grievances (Alianza Regional, 2013) and indicate problems in the implementation of the legislation. Besides specific goals for obtaining information, strategic litigation or "cause lawyering" (Sarat & Scheingold, 2006) was used to show problems in the implementation of the law. Negative or partial responses by government officials prompted CSOs to engage in litigation in municipal, federal, and international courts. Activists utilized it to denounce official responses that denied requests on the grounds that publicizing certain information would compromise the protection of personal data and national security. They have accused officials of violating laws by restricting the right to public access through Executive decrees, invoking justifications that are not contemplated in the legislation, demanding high costs and other requirements for filing requests, and using vague language to justify decisions.

In some cases, CSOs also contacted key officials and news organizations to inform them about the situation in order to "shame" public agencies and government for denying requests. To bring further visibility to the situation and stimulate better practices, organizations such as Colombia's chapter of Transparency International and other CSOs produced an index of transparency of government agencies.

It is hard to attribute these problems to the text of the legislation. National laws are consonant with progressive international standards emphasizing rights-based principles. Problems are chiefly grounded in the persistence of political-institutional contexts and dynamics that are contrary to the implementation of public access to information laws (Cejudo, López Ayllón & Ríos Cázares, 2011; Fox & Haight, 2011).

A major obstacle has been the lack of autonomy of the government units responsible for addressing requests and ensuring that information is collected and made publicly available. Units are often hampered by personal and partisan interests. In many cases, they have been improperly influenced by government officials. As long as autonomy is compromised, other considerations are prioritized over public access to information. The performance of units is also undermined by insufficient budgets, officers without adequate training, weak monitoring, technical confusion about procedures, and exemptions.

However, even when national agencies have mandated units in the Executive power and Congress to comply with requests, officials have used legal mechanisms to delay and deny responses. Government officials, including presidents, have ordered the non-disclosure of information about the use of reserved funds and travel by labeling them confidential and matters of national secrecy. Officials are not aware of the existence of the law or its implications. Changing a "culture of secrecy" has not been easy, as the former director of Uruguay's CAInfo points out (da Rosa Pírez, 2015).

At the root of these problems is the fact that official support to public access has remained weak. Studies have concluded that little has been done at different levels of government to transform a pervasive culture of secrecy and actively promote the right to public access among citizens across the region (Darbishire, 2006; Tello, Cerna & Pavón, 2009). The passing of new legislation has not been sufficient to mainstream laws in public life insofar as governments are disinterested in publicizing laws and procedures and in the context of the low quality of institutional democracy. Lack of awareness and disinterest contribute to the perpetuation of secrecy and the notion that government information belongs to public officials. Although CSOs have continued to monitor the situation and sounded alarms given official responses that flagrantly contradict new legislation, denunciations have not prompted major changes. Commitment to the public right to information is ambivalent and too weak to overhaul deep-seated problems and a tradition of political secrecy. Officialdom has largely been reluctant to turn rhetorical pledges into convincing actions in support of transparency and accountability. As long as governments remain indifferent, and continue to benefit from weak oversight mechanisms, it is improbable that major changes will happen.

Legislation has had limited impact in modifying the conditions necessary to strengthen citizen access to government information. CSOs have monitored the process and publicized problems but they have had limited impact on actual implementation. Activism has not been sufficient to transform not only the culture of secrecy but also hierarchical power structures. The same factors that legislation was intended to change, namely, vertical and opaque dynamics and structures in government, facilitate official resistance to comply with the law.

Such difficulties come as no surprise considering entrenched problems pertaining to the quality of democratic governance in the region. It would actually have been remarkable if laws had effectively transformed conditions considering the enormous challenges of government transparency and institutional responsiveness. Political scientist John Ackerman's (2008: 12) conclusion about the situation in Mexico rings true elsewhere: "Access to public information is a dull instrument to break the vicious circle of impunity, opacity, poor performance, and conflict of interests in government units." As important as they are, information access laws are just one instrument to overhaul deep-seated problems.

Cultivating a public culture of rights in both government and civil society is certainly not an easy matter. It demands continuous attention and interventions to educate citizens, administrative staff, and government officials about rights and responsibilities, effectively addressing pervasive government secrecy demands more than sporadic information campaigns and training sessions. Experiences in other regions show similar patterns of constant struggles between citizens and government officials over the collection and release of information to the public. As long as officials are able to find loopholes to keep information away from the public and suffer no penalties for not complying with the law, and citizens fail to put significant pressure on authorities, it is hard to envision how such dynamics can be broken.

The passing of legislation has capped favorable political junctures, but it has yet to materialize in substantial, wide-ranging transformations in the performance of the accountability and transparency of state agencies.

Freedom of speech laws

The situation of freedom of speech laws is vastly different across the region and cannot be summarized in brief assessments.

In Argentina, for example, significant progress has been made. Congress abolished the contempt law and eliminated the criminalization of libel and slander. Only exceptionally have government officials brought lawsuits against journalists. However, CSOs have continued to push for the elimination or reduction of civil penalties for libel and slander (Loreti & Lozano, 2014; Bertoni & Del Campo, 2012). Potential lawsuits against reporters accused of offending the "honor" of public officials threaten not only the financial situation of news organizations and reporters, but also have chilling effects. Although the CELS elaborated a proposal to reform the Civil Code on this issue and discussed it with members of Congress, the bill has not received significant attention. Observers believe that neither the government nor political parties in Congress have shown the political will to remove existing civil penalties because they do not want to lose all "legal shields" in case they are confronted with criticisms (Pochak, 2015).

In other countries, such as Ecuador and Venezuela, the conditions for free speech have significantly worsened in the past decade, as previously discussed. The law limits the publication of content, creates formal mechanisms of censorship, and establishes incentives for self-censorship, including ambiguous articles about content considered to cause "media lynching" and requirements for information (Segura, 2014). The government has hired private companies to regularly monitor media outlets and deliver reports to the SUPERCOM, the government agency tasked with monitoring the implementation of the law which is very close to the Executive. On the second anniversary of the 2013 law, Director Carlos Ochoa boasted that the SUPERCOM had opened 506 legal processes against media companies and achieved 313 legal decisions, and 185 financial sanctions (Mioli, 2015). Actions included SUPERCOM's decision to impose fines on the tabloid newspaper *Extra* for not retracting content and the daily *El Universo* for criticizing the government in a cartoon, and sanctioning a television station for airing content deemed discriminatory by the government. These actions took place amidst President Correa's continuous diatribes against the opposition media and Ochoa's assertions that the goal of the government is "to educate to avoid sanctions".

These actions confirmed the fears of freedom of expression organizations who criticized drafts of the bill discussed in Congress. Government patrolling and censorship of public speech confirmed their belief that the administration was determined to use specific articles and imprecise language in the law to stifle media dissent.

In Mexico, defamation, libel, and slander were decriminalized at the federal level, but laws are applicable only when a federal official, who feels that honor and dignity are wrongly affected, takes legal action against an individual. Most legal processes, however, take place in local courts where the situation has not significantly changed. Whereas the penalties for defamation, libel, and slander were eliminated in some districts such as Mexico City, they still exist in the majority of states and impose grave legal and financial penalties. States where defamation, slander and libel were decriminalized still impose important economic sanctions (Méndez, 2011).

More than legal persecution, violence against journalists has become the main threat to public speech, especially in states where drug-traffickers have an extensive and deep presence. As discussed in Chapter 4, CSOs successfully demanded that the federal government implement mechanisms to protect journalists and special protections, which were passed by Congress in 2012 (Meneses, 2015). However, the federalization of the investigation and protection of crimes against reporters has suffered from various problems. Mexico's Article 19 representative Ivan Baez (Knight Center, 2015) observes that:

> the mechanisms are imperfect. The staff lacks the capacity to perform the job. Financial and human resources are insufficient to meet the demand. Technological capacity is insufficient, too. Therefore, the mechanism is too slow. Many times, protection arrives when journalists no longer feel threatened or after they left their cities or the country. In fact, when we realized the mechanism was not working, we stopped submitting cases.

According to the OAS Freedom of Expression Rapporteur report, the lack of communication between federal and other agencies also undercuts the effectiveness of the law and the mechanisms. Given official deficiencies, Article 19 and other CSOs decided to step up their own efforts to protect reporters (Solís Leree, 2015).

The implementation of broadcasting reforms

Notwithstanding advances in the new broadcasting laws, numerous problems beset policy implementation. The cases of Argentina, Ecuador, Mexico, and Uruguay suggest that governments have acted slowly, particularly in relation to civic demands to strengthen participatory mechanisms and promote the "third sector." Whereas they have acted with relative brio regarding aspects of the laws linked to the political communication objectives of the Executive, governments have not shown unbridled enthusiasm or urgency to move swiftly on these issues. Only in some cases when prodded by CSOs have they shown more interest in translating the law into effective reforms.

The inclusion of participatory mechanisms in the implementation of media legislation is absolutely novel in the history of media governance in the region. Certainly, making such a principle effective has demanded new forms of interaction between CSOs and government officials, namely, cooperation, consultation, and mutual learning. This is a paradigm shift in the way that government officials conventionally understand their job as well as their relationship with CSOs and ordinary citizens. The results are mixed given that, despite some advances, numerous obstacles have conspired against broadening and strengthening citizen participation.

Argentina Two participatory institutions created by the 2009 law, the Federal Council of Audiovisual Communication (COFECA) and National Council of Audiovisual Communication and Childhood (CONACAI), have functioned relatively well. Even if some of their expectations have not been met, several CSOs representing community groups, cooperatives, educational institutions, and indigenous media have actively participated in both institutions and collaborated informally with AFSCA – the agency responsible for the implementation of the law.

There have been unjustified delays in matters related to the "third sector," specifically regarding the processing of applications and granting new licenses, producing the technical plan (which is needed to have a detailed assessment of frequencies and licensees), and addressing the chaotic situation of radio broadcasting in large urban areas that resulted from decades-long legal limbo. The AFSCA has called for applications for FM radio licenses in specific areas in the country, assigned low-power licenses, authorized low-power television stations, and digital television licenses for non-profit organizations. By December 2014, it had granted licenses or permits to 114 non-profit organizations and thirty-eight indigenous organizations, mostly in sparsely populated areas and small towns (Marino et al, 2015).

Arguably, the reluctance of the Fernández de Kirchner government to regulate the situation in metropolitan areas is grounded in the fact that any decision would have generated intense controversy because it involves current private and community stations operating in illegal conditions. CSOs representing community and alternative media urged the authorities to implement the technical plan and launch the licensing process in urban areas (Gómez & Sande, 2014).

During the first two years after the law was passed, community media associations demanded the assignation of the funding stipulated. The law establishes that 10 percent of AFSCA's annual revenues must be invested in specific projects submitted by community and indigenous media. In 2012, AFSCA began the assignation of this funding through the Fondo de Fomento Concursable para Medios de Comunicación Audiovisual (FOMECA). Due to demands from CSOs, the funding was allocated to specific issues that they believed were most urgent (Pugliese, 2014; Gerbaldo, 2013). In 2015, AFSCA conducted ten public bids and awarded loans for technical equipment, technological infrastructure, radio and television production, and community media management.

Some alternative media organizations also demanded that the AFSCA grant them temporary permits in order to function and use funding offered by the FOMECA. As a result of their negotiations with AFSCA, some of them obtained that permits without fulfillment of all the conditions required by law (Urioste, 2015). Instead, other television and radio stations have been stuck in the contradictions of the regulatory agency: they have been unable to apply for public funds because the state did not grant them legal recognition. This is not a minor problem considering the chronic economic problems of community media. In a country where few companies based in Buenos Aires and other large cities control the lion's share of media advertising expenditures, state economic support is vital to ensuring the diversification of media ownership and offerings.

After the passing of the 2009 law, activists formed the Espacio Abierto de Televisoras Populares, Alternativas y Comunitarias to participate in the implementation process. They blended protest strategies with advocacy with legislators to ensure that specific aspects of the laws affecting community media were promptly implemented. They criticized regulations for requesting high application fees and other requirements from grassroots organizations. Eventually, the

AFSCA recognized problems, delayed the call for applications, incorporated demands, and granted temporary permits for low-power stations. Instead, other organizations clustered in Red Nacional de Medios Alternativos have prioritized confrontations with the AFSCA to demand rights (Segura, 2015b).

In contrast to active citizen participation in matters related to the third sector, long delays have hampered participatory governance of public broadcasting in Argentina. The congressional commission responsible for promoting and monitoring the broadcasting law has functioned irregularly, and the parliamentary minorities did not designate their representatives to the public broadcasting board until 2012 (three years after the law was passed). Delays were criticized by two associations of communication research (the Federación Argentina de Carreras de Comunicación Social and the Red de Carreras de Comunicación y Periodismo), congressional members of the center-left Frente Amplio Progresista, and a national senator from the opposition. Members of the Honorary Advisory Council of Public Media created by law were proposed by their institutions but they were only appointed by President Fernández de Kirchner in January 2015. Because the Council did not function for several years after the law was passed, it has not held public audiences for citizens to participate in assessing proposals and demands and evaluating the functioning of public broadcasting. Neither the Fernández de Kirchner administration nor the public broadcasting board showed significant interest in expanding public participation in order to bring in diverse perspectives and institutionalize accountability mechanisms as mandated by the law.

How do we explain differences in the performance of various participatory mechanisms stipulated by the 2009 law? The reason is relatively straightforward: Whereas CSOs that originally demanded participatory mechanisms regarding the application of articles affecting community and indigenous media have remained active, there has not been a similar sustainable movement to push for the activation of citizen participation in the national public broadcasting system. Especially in the face of weak official political commitment to citizen participation in policy implementation, civil society mobilization remains critical to translating the participatory provisos included in the law into effective mechanisms. It is difficult to envision significant changes when citizen mobilization to remind the government about the content of the 2009 law is weak or non-existent.

Uruguay The 2007 Community Media Law stipulates the participation of civic society in the implementation process. With that goal in mind, the law establishes two mechanisms, the Consejo Honorario Asesor de Radiodifusión Comunitaria (CHARC) and the Comisión Honoraria Asesora Independiente (CHAI). The CHARC was created by law and was intended to ensure transparency in the assignation of licenses. It includes representatives from three Ministries (Culture, Education, and Industry), Congress, community media, public and private universities, and NGOs focused on human rights. One of its main tasks has been the production of the National Census of Community Radio, a vital document to assess the situation of the sector, respond to requests for legalization, and determine whether the applicant effectively meets the criteria stipulated by the law. Together with government agencies, the CHARC is also responsible for conducting activities to inform the public about the law and application requirements. Also, the law grants citizens the right to participate in public audiences to provide comments and opinions on proposals for licenses submitted by media organizations.

Community media organizations such as AMARC and Ecos have criticized the Frente Amplio governments for its ambivalent position – initial support for the law but followed by general inertia after the legislation was passed. While CSOs applaud the government for not trying to co-opt community media or heavy-handedly managing the process, they have criticized the lack of interest in promoting the sector. Also, there have not been significant and systematic efforts by the government to engage the public. Limited participation in public audiences conducted in recent years has been symptomatic of weak promotion efforts. It is hard to envision regular civic engagement, as stipulated by the law, without promotion.

For activists, the viability of the sector is possible only through state intervention in the form of economic subsidies, official advertising, tax exemptions, equipment, professional training, and other measures. However, actual decisions fall short of official rhetorical commitment to the sector. It is impossible for most community stations to exist without some form of public support. State inaction condemns stations to survive in extremely difficult and unequal market conditions, particularly for stations in small communities and towns. Also, it is unconceivable that stations would produce quality content to serve their communities properly and attract publics without professional capacity and support. The law alone has not solved problems or contributed to strengthening conditions for the consolidation of the "third sector."

CSOs have criticized the Frente Amplio administrations for not assigning sufficient resources to promote community media since the law was passed. They have contended that the government failed to provide the necessary institutional infrastructure, and to train government and media staff in various tasks (e.g. processing and reviewing license applications, management and financing of media), monitor and control the complex situation, and promote opportunities among media organizations to gain legal status.

CSOs have also pointed out that the CHARC lacks sufficient administrative and financial support to conduct its tasks. It could not complete the census in a timely fashion, which is a critical step for producing a comprehensive picture of the sector and enforcing decisions (e.g. shutting down stations that violate the law). Nor can the CHARC properly make recommendations during the examination and allocation of community media licenses. Administrative support has been disproportionate to the volume of work, namely over 400 petitions to address the situation of media stations. Consequently, the process has been plagued by enormous delays. Furthermore, it has lacked human and monetary resources to maintain a website with updated information to expedite the process and attend requests from applicants. Because the performance of the CHARC largely depended on work by voluntary members rather than paid representatives from Congress and the Executive, it is hard to imagine how its functioning is possible in a sustainable and effective manner, particularly given the complexity of the sector.

AMARC (2012, 2013) has also repeatedly criticized the call for applications for community television licenses which ignore the situation of community organizations in terms of operational and financial resources. It has also criticized the government for allowing private companies to bid for community television licenses, which directly contradicts the text of the law, delays in license assignment for community radio, and the absence of monitoring of the situation. One document (AMARC, 2013) affirms that "the actions and declarations of President José Mujica ignore the result of the democratization of communication, and bring back practices shaped by political junctures. The State does not own the public airwaves; instead, it has to administer the airwaves as 'property of humankind'."

Activists have also denounced the weakness of government accountability mechanisms to document, monitor, and bring up problems in policy implementation. In fact, it is hard to imagine that many problems would have become public had it not been for CSOs. Yet CSOs cannot carry out actions that are exclusively within the sphere of state agencies, such as attending to complaints, following up on technical reports and denunciations, and shutting down illegal activities.

Mexico In Mexico, the 2014 Reforma Constitucional de Telecomunicaciones, Radio y Televisión created an Advisory Council appointed by the Instituto Federal de Telecomunicaciones (IFETEL). Unlike the broadcasting laws passed in Argentina and Uruguay, the Reforma neither mandates citizen participation nor establishes quotas. Media activists considered that the IFETEL appointed "honest and knowledgeable" members (Trejo Delarbre, 2015; Meneses, 2015), even though officials control the appointment of Council members. Although CSOs believe that the conditions are not ripe for major changes in the law, they recognize that the Council was able to make valuable suggestions regarding technical and other matters in line with progressive principles (Calleja, 2015).

Media activists are also hopeful about the possibility of using participatory channels to correct policy limitations and the situation of community media. Even though the first licenses to community media were granted in 2004, only sixteen radio stations functioned legally as of 2015. This situation is partially caused by ambivalent policies. The Reforma recognizes community media, which represent a significant achievement for CSOs. The Ley Secundaria of the Reforma, however, establishes limitations in terms of reach and funding, and imposes high fines on stations operating without a license. While they were critical of these limitations, CSOs remain optimistic because IFETEL Council members are sensitive to the situation of community media, and they have produced technical and administrative guidelines to improve the conditions (Calleja, 2015).

Ecuador The challenges for civic participation in the implementation of the 2013 law are different than in Argentina and Uruguay. Put it simply, it is almost impossible to institutionalize citizen participation when the law has few and weak mechanisms, especially if the government has not prioritized them during the implementation.

The institutional architecture of the law is anchored in two agencies controlled by the Executive. The Consejo Ecuatoriano de Regulación y Desarrollo de la Información y Comunicación (CORDICOM) oversees various issues – from allocating licenses to establishing rules for content. All five members are closely tied to the Executive. In fact, the original members had worked with the Correa administration before they were appointed (Conaghan, 2015). The Superintendencia de la Información (SUPERCOM) is responsible for ensuring compliance with the law. It has controversial attributions such as monitoring, control, and imposing penalties on the media. It is headed by a person selected by the President. Neither the CORDICOM nor the SUPERCOM includes participation from CSOs or members of the National Assembly. Even though the CORDICOM has a representative of the Council of Citizen Participation and Social Control, there is no civic participation (Sierra Caballero, 2015).

Although both the Constitution and the law highlight the significance of the "third sector" in media industries, little progress has been made. A negligible number of radio licenses were granted, including new permits for Ecuador's fourteen original nations that are members of a network linked to the Ministry of Social Development. Media activists have criticized the network for its financial and organizational ties to the state (Sierra Caballero, 2015).

Onerous requirements for applying for community media licenses remain a huge obstacle. Applicants are expected to have a legal existence and present four reports: technical, communication, management, and business plans for the fifteen-year duration of the license – requirements that are similar to those for commercial media (López Vigil, 2015). According to official estimations, setting up a community radio station costs approximately $100,000. The vast majority of grassroots organizations hoping to run non-profit outlets lack the ability to raise such an amount, produce the required information, and meet several criteria. Nor has the government, media activists argue, spent considerable time promoting plans or helping organizations to prepare proposals (Tornay, 2015). Given these problems, it is not surprising that the government received a low number of applications despite the fact that Ecuador has a rich tradition of community media and officials repeatedly voiced their support for the sector (*El Comercio*, 2015). Community media organizations and other CSOs have met with legislators and public officials to demand the implementation of constitutional rights. However, they encountered little political will to grant licenses to community media (López Vigil, 2015). Whereas the Correa administration has shown remarkable zeal for policing speech and disciplining dissenters, it has relegated key demands by community media activists who, despite reservations, supported the 2013 broadcasting law.

The law is not enough

The implementation of new policies has not been a smooth process in which governments have promptly rolled out laws, created institutions and mechanisms, assigned necessary financial and human resources, and prioritized equally all aspects of new legislation. In some cases, there have been remarkable gaps between the text of the laws and the priorities and dynamics of the implementation process.

The cases of legislation dealing with public access to government information, speech laws and broadcasting reforms demonstrate a similar problem: governments have been selectively interested in the application of new policies. They have not paid similar attention to all parts of new legislation. They have not prioritized effective functioning of government agencies, strengthening participatory mechanisms and promoting the "third sector." Governments have generally moved ahead with equal doses of bureaucratic lethargy, inefficiency, and partisanship more than a solid commitment to public goals and citizen participation. Policy implementation has been rife with bureaucratic inefficiency and lack of sufficient expertise in government agencies to shepherd the process.

With few exceptions, participatory mechanisms have not received the necessary support from the state to become truly active and autonomous bodies. State agencies tasked with key functions, such as in the cases of Argentina and Ecuador, have been hobbled by influence from the Executive. The Executive casts a large shadow over public broadcasting in terms of funding, management, staff appointment, and ultimately content decisions. The application of articles dealing with community media has been noticeably slow. Most community and alternative media continue operating in illegal conditions. The vast majority of licenses remain in private hands.

These problems are not purely coincidental – a series of accidental lapses in the agenda of governments. Nor are they the unfortunate result of underperforming government agencies. Rather, they are indicative of weak political will among governments to turn citizen participation and the right to communication into top priorities during the implementation process. They reflect selective interest among governments in applying progressive legislation and deliberate political calculations to relegate certain aspects of the law. Citizen participation, community media, public media, and other terms praised by government officials became controversial subjects once the implementation phase started. They are no longer politically unambiguous or shared rallying causes. Rather, they are hotly contested in the struggle over power to determine priorities and allocate resources. They demand making choices and potentially paying political costs.

Fissures in civil society

The reactions of CSOs vis-à-vis governments during the phase of policy implementation are illustrative of fissures in civil society. The processes of policy implementation have further crystallized divisions in media activism anchored in different positions and assessments of new legislation and governments.

In Ecuador, for example, CSOs have been divided over the implementation of the 2013 law. Some, such as ALAI and CIESPAL, continued supporting the government; on the other hand, ALER, CORAPE, OCLACC, Radialistas Apasionados y Apasionadas y El Churo Comunicación have been deeply dissatisfied with the overall process, especially the lack of attention to community media (López Vigil, 2015). Media activist and writer José Ignacio López Vigil captures the sentiment as follows: "We were useful idiots in the service of a totalitarian project." Furthermore, he adds, a "[Damocles] sword hangs over CSOs critical of the government" because a 2013 presidential decree bans CSOs from participating in public policies. This is not just simply a potential threat; the Correa government has used that decree to shut down two CSOs since the decree was enacted.

The positions of media activists during the process of policy implementation can be clustered in three groups: partisan militants, critical participants, and categorical critics. Whereas "partisan militants" have been complacent with authorities, "critical participants" and "categorical critics" have called attention to troubling spots and erratic decisions. The difference between the last two is that whereas the former have continued to participate in policy implementation through institutional and other channels, the latter have not done so.

"Partisan militants" have been government cheerleaders who praised both the legislation and the implementation process. Closely identified with the party in power, they eagerly marched in step with official decisions and rarely voiced criticisms in public.

"Critical participants" have questioned aspects of policy implementation while they continued to support the process "from the inside" by participating in institutional mechanisms established by the legislation. They have voiced criticisms in public documents, street protests, and meetings with officials. While they have kept open lines of communication with the state, they have remained largely separate from governments and partisan interests. Such a position is grounded in the belief that maintaining autonomy from the state is indispensable to be able to provide critical insights into policy-making.

In this category, we find CSOs in Uruguay that originally shepherded the processes that culminated in new legislation. Although they have criticized various aspects, they have remained engaged in policy implementation. Also, many Argentine CSOs that formed the Coalición por una Radiodifusión Democrática fall into this group. Despite differences with the Fernández de Kirchner administration, they continued to support the law and participated in public audiences and other platforms. They demanded that the government accelerate the implementation of a technical plan to reorganize the media system, promote the "third sector," and force all media companies to comply with the law. In contrast, leftist organizations such as the Red Nacional de Medios Alternativos have been more publicly critical of the government. They have accused officials of duplicitous behavior: deploying a combative discourse against "media monopolies" but refusing to implement decisive actions to dismantle ownership concentration.

Aside from mechanisms and roles stipulated by the laws, "critical participants" have resorted to other strategies to voice positions and make demands. CSOs have held public events, pursued news coverage, and produced and disseminated reports to express views about various aspects of policy implementation. Civic organizations have also used administrative and judicial mechanisms to demand and act upon new rights. In Argentina, for example, CSOs participated in a public audience called by the Supreme Court to testify in favor of the constitutionality of the 2009 law (after the Clarín Group had legally challenged two of its articles, the Supreme Court reaffirmed the constitutionality of the law in 2013).

In contrast, "categorical critics" have questioned the laws and remained skeptical about the true motivations of governments in sponsoring legislative reforms. CSOs have been entangled in prolonged, acrimonious battles with governments. This has been particularly noticeable in countries where conditions for public expression have significantly worsened in recent years.

In Ecuador, the Fundación Andina para la Observación y Estudio de Medios (Fundamedios) has been the flagship civic organization opposed to the 2013 broadcasting law. It has regularly produced criticisms of the law and monitored and reported scores of abuses. The Correa administration put Fundamedios under the control of the Secretary of Communication in January 2014. It demanded that the organization stop "expressing political positions against social development." In 2015, it urged the closure of Fundamedios based on a 2013 presidential decree which establishes that the government can order the dissolution of an organization that "engag[es] in partisan political activities ... interferes in public policies, threatens the internal or external security of the State or affects public peace."

In Nicaragua, Centro de Investigación de la Comunicación (CINCO) and media activists have complained about threats and investigations ordered by the Ortega government as well as pressure the administration put on international donors to stop funding local organizations working on freedom of speech (Álvarez, 2015). In Venezuela, several CSOs such as IPyS, Provea and Espacio Público working on freedom of expression have regularly clashed with the Chavista governments and have been repeatedly the target of rhetorical and legal attacks (Balbi, 2015).

In other countries, such as Argentina, relations between "categorical critics" and the Fernández de Kirchner administration never reached similar levels of confrontation. Yet they have criticized specific aspects of the text and the implementation of the 2009 broadcasting law (e.g. the appointment of most members of the regulatory agency by the Executive, the lack of articles about the regulation of public advertising) and charged the government with the lack of a national law granting public access to government information, the persistence of discretionary practices in the management and allocation of public advertising, and other issues.

In summary, citizen mobilization has performed vital functions during policy implementation, particularly when the process was hamstrung by the lack of government will or when the legislation and its application have significant problems for freedom of expression. Whereas "critical participants" were able to shake off official lethargy in some cases, "categorical critics" were largely unsuccessful in their efforts to change official decisions as they remained ignored and/or fiercely criticized (and persecuted) by officials

Media activists have made important contributions to policy implementation by participating in various capacities. Some roles are embedded in new legislation, such as producing data to document the situation of specific media industries, meeting regularly with public officials, reviewing and discussing license applications in public audiences, and monitoring the implementation of specific articles. Also, CSOs have partnered with legislators to put the spotlight on problems in the laws and their application. They have criticized aspects of new laws that are contrary to the right to communication, denounced official delays, and demanded that governments prioritize the application of specific articles. Notwithstanding government equivocal commitment to bolstering citizen participation and accountability and prioritizing progressive aspects of the legislation, citizen participation in policy implementation reflects important innovations in media governance.

The significance of citizen participation in policy implementation

What conclusions should be drawn about citizen participation in the implementation of new media policies? Neither giddy triumphalism nor utter pessimism is warranted. The implementation of different policies across countries presents considerable variations in yielding straightforward positive or negative conclusions.

Undoubtedly, recent experiences are watershed moments in the history of media governance in Latin America. They are novel opportunities for inclusive and pluralist policy-making that reflect important shifts in the position of civil society and rights-based vision of public communication.

Certainly, the political dynamics and incentives that culminated in the passing of new legislation did not translate into policy implementation. The movement and junctures that pushed effective policy advocacy do not necessarily survive into policy implementation. The combination of factors – mobilized publics, sympathetic elites, and suitable political junctures – that resulted in the passing of laws is not sufficient to guarantee effective implementation.

The enactment of key demands by civic society has faced particular challenges. Original elite support for progressive aspects such as the promotion of the third sector, restrictions on media concentration, and freedom of information legislation subsided once bills became law. It became mostly rhetorical or, at best, ambivalent support for progressive legislation. Public officials decided to delay or sacrifice the application of specific articles. Paying lip service to progressive measures, they preferred to profit from secretive practices and legal loopholes. They failed to show significant commitment to supporting participatory mechanisms established by new legislation or be responsive to citizens' demands. Government priorities often trumped demands by CSOs.

These are not minor obstacles in the path to effective progressive policies. As important as civil society is in the emergent configuration of media governance, the state retains key roles in policy implementation. Crucial decisions about the application of the law are in the hands of political officials, namely the Executive and specific agencies that, by constitutional design or common practice, are too close to presidential strategies and partisan politics. Indeed, CSOs have deposited great hopes on state intervention to address problems through the application of new legislation.

Progressive reforms are unthinkable without effective and targeted state intervention. The state needs to guarantee the autonomy of public media in terms of management, funding, and content. It is also responsible for mandating that private corporations comply with new legislation and enforcing penalties. Likewise, the state is expected to promote the "third sector" of media systems through various mechanisms: offering operational funding and production grants, placing advertising, giving tax exemptions and favorable license terms, conducting training, and providing technical equipment. Just as states have supported the private sector over decades through financial deals, they should enact favorable measures to support community and alternative media. The difference lies in the fact that while states boosted the economic health of private media through sweetheart arrangements (e.g. condoning debts, granting long-term licenses for ridiculously low fees, throwing financial lifesavers, protecting incumbents from competition, refusing to fine delinquent companies), they need to support the "third sector" through transparent and accountability mechanisms.

How can states successfully perform these tasks in light of long-standing governance deficits? As long as presidential discretionality, opacity, and clientelism dominate state politics, it is difficult to envision the effective implementation of innovative legislation. Old politics are contrary to progressive laws. Top-down decision-making undercuts citizen participation. It eviscerates the public interest of progressive laws in favor of corruption, nepotism, and cronyism. It neutralizes the potential of critical reasoning in favor of facts and expertise that reinforce partisan and clientelistic interests. Governments may limit the spheres of participation and accountability, or apply the sheen of "citizen participation" to legislation while refusing to transform decision-making processes. These are real possibilities considering the uneven development of other contemporary participatory experiences in Latin America: despite promising developments and good intention, many initiatives aimed at bolstering citizen participation confronted the obstacles of old politics (Hetland, 2014; McNulty, 2013), and in some cases, they became absorbed into networks of "participatory clientelism" (Goldfrank, 2011).

Continuous civic mobilization is indispensable to pressure government officials to ensure that progressive laws are implemented and to jettison aspects that are contrary to democratic public communication. Civic participation remains crucial particularly when governments promote policies that are contrary to the guaranteeing speech rights, flatly ignore specific aspects of the legislation, and give ambiguous support to progressive legislation. In cases where the legislation features progressive principles, but they are not fully applied and/or are subjected to official propaganda designs, "the prestige of the law" (Graña, 2013) is in danger. The overall legitimacy of legislation suffers when governments fail to apply laws grounded in human rights principles. Citizen activism has proven to be necessary to ensure the functioning of participatory mechanisms and that legislation effectively supports the communication rights of all citizens.

CONCLUSION: THE CONTRIBUTIONS OF MEDIA MOVEMENTS

We conclude the book with a review of the contributions of media movements to three areas of media governance: citizen participation in policy-making, the institutional capacity of collective actors to shape media legislation, and the mobilization of public discourse to define the fundamental principles of public communication and media systems.

From elite-captured to participatory policy-making?

Have media movements contributed to shifting a historical pattern of elite-captured policies to participatory policy-making? Our answer is cautiously affirmative. The previous chapters show that, although there has not been a surefooted and complete transition, policy-making has changed in important ways. From being an affair largely limited to political and economic elites, it has gradually become more open to citizen participation and receptive to long-standing rights-based demands championed by media activists. Certainly, situations and developments are not similar across all countries. No generalization can do justice to the vast diversity of cases showing progress, inertia, and setbacks in the region. Blanket statements about elite-controlled or citizen-centered policy-making inevitably fail to recognize different and dynamic situations in the region.

Considering that elite-captured policy-making refers to situations when powerful political and economic interests monopolize public debates and legislative decisions, it would be misguided to use those terms to characterize the current landscape. Elite interests do not completely dominate public debates about problems and solutions. Nor do they have a complete grip on legislative deliberations and decision-making. To suggest that entrenched interests remain as dominant as ever is to ignore positive developments and dynamic scenarios. Obviously, the magnitude of the changes should not be exaggerated in light of differences in the current status of legislative proposals and actual reforms, the content of new laws, the priorities of governments, and the vigor of local media movements.

Changes are particularly visible during the first and second phases of policy-making. Citizen presence has been noticeable during public debates and the articulation of proposals to change legislation as well as during legislative deliberations and decision-making. In contrast, evidence is mixed during the phase of policy implementation. Notwithstanding auspicious developments, policy-making is still fraught with numerous problems that undercut the contributions of organized citizens to democratic media governance.

Policy debates Organized citizens have made significant gains during public debates about media policy. Even if the situation is not a level playing field, CSOs have made noticeable inroads by proposing diagnosis and solutions to the problems of contemporary public communication and media systems. Structural inequalities in public debates persist, namely, the presence of media corporations decidedly opposed to any proposals to curb their power, and public officials uninterested in transforming traditional *quid pro quo* dealings with the private sector. Corporate and government voices continue to push out dissident positions trying to redefine the basic principles of public communication. Media reforms grounded in rights-based notions are hardly a common subject of news coverage for media news giants. Not surprisingly, CSOs demanding ownership regulations and other reforms grounded in progressive ideas rarely receive close and fair attention from leading media companies.

Despite these challenges, media movements have managed to shape public debates about policy reforms. They have presented positions and conducted debates in their own offline and online communication spaces. They have also pursued and taken advantage of opportunities in the legacy media and other public forums. They have used various strategies to mobilize public opinion and make demands to legislators.

Policy formulation Organized activists have also made significant inroads during the legislative debates and the drafting of new bills. Through advocacy, they brought attention to problems and proposals to lawmakers. Although efforts did not always result in desired bills or progressive policies, activists have slowly gained access to legislative staff. Congressional committees have considered technical reports and recommendations produced by CSOs. Public officials have consulted on technical matters with CSO representatives. Citizens have been invited to give public input to bills and provide expert testimonies in congressional debates and court sessions dealing with various media and information legislation. CSOs have also participated in ad hoc mechanisms mandated by presidents on specific opportunities, such as Argentina's public consultation about the broadcasting law, Brazil's First National Conference on Communication, Mexico's civil society roundtable on broadcasting, and Paraguay's roundtable on community broadcasting.

Such opportunities for civic participation not only did not exist in the past; they were unthinkable in many countries where, until recently, governments persecuted alternative and community media organizations and legislators completely ignored CSOs with expertise on legal and technical matters.

Policy implementation Media movements have also made important contributions to policy implementation. They have used various mechanisms to ensure the correct and comprehensive application of new legislation. They have called attention to merits and shortcomings of new laws. They have monitored the work of various agencies and used legal instruments to advance reforms and indicate obstacles. They have upbraided officials for failing to comply with the laws and urged corrections. They have defended dissent as a vital component of public speech against government decisions to chill criticism and promote self-censorship among reporters through legal and political means.

In other words, just as it hard to imagine that innovative media reforms would have originally emerged without committed citizens and organizations, it is also difficult to envision how policy implementation would have happened if CSOs had not insisted on enacting specific articles of new legislation (Ávila Pietrasanta, Gutiérrez & Leree, 2002). Even when the implementation of progressive policies remains uneven, CSOs have remained important actors by demanding that officials comply with legislation and nudging authorities to act.

In summary, we find evidence of citizen participation in the three phases of the media policy-making process. This is a remarkable development in the history of media governance in Latin America. No similar period of intense mobilization and visibility has been found in the past anywhere in the region. Whereas citizens were virtually absent in the major decisions that historically defined media systems, instead, today's situation is considerably different. Citizen participation has thrived and left important marks in new legislation and policy-making processes.

In fact, it is inconceivable that contemporary media policy-making would be limited to traditional collusive practices and backroom deals between political and economic elites. Such practices, undoubtedly, persist. It would be naïve to expect that they have been dramatically reduced, let alone eliminated, in such short periods of time and against resilient obstacles. Such practices, however, are less likely to go unnoticed or unpunished, or to be considered part of the natural order of policy-making and remain unknown to the public. Indeed, activists have continued to denounce persistent collusion between government officials and corporate actors and attempts to silence citizens' voices. They have criticized egregious attempts by political and media elites to monopolize policy-making at the expense of public interests and denounced recalcitrant legislatures uninterested in debating and drafting progressive bills. Media activists have mobilized to denounce contradictions in recent media and information laws in Argentina and Mexico as well as official reluctance to apply progressive legislation in Ecuador and Uruguay. Such examples of resistance suggest shifting dynamics in media policy-making.

A stronger presence of CSOs and citizens signals the gradual incorporation of deliberative politics in media policy-making. This is a healthy development for media democracy. It represents the consolidation of democratic politics foregrounding citizens as rights-bearing actors. It materializes the double ambition of media activists to transform not only the content of media policies but the policy-making process, too. It expands the range of voices in the multilayered process of lawmaking. It crystallizes a conception of media policies as a matter of public competency rather than the exclusive jurisdiction of partisan and industrial interests. It strengthens formal and informal mechanisms of public accountability in decisions affecting public expression.

To be clear, we do not conclude that media governance *in toto* is systematically responsive to citizens' input and participation.

Significant problems persist and troubling developments demand analytical precision and caution. Participatory politics have yet to become standard features of media policy-making. Institutional innovations have only been gradually incorporated. Mobilized citizens still have to elbow their way into the process by reminding legislators about new rights and pointing out official negligence to support participatory processes. Media policy-making has become more pluralist even if lawmakers have not uniformly pledged support for deliberative politics or dramatically turned to citizen-driven politics. Changes have largely happened because activists were determined to find opportunities to get involved, shake off official disinterest, and denounce attempts to lock citizens out of the process.

A series of successful and failed experiences have contributed to CSOs building a sense of ownership and empowerment – the conviction that media policy-making might be more inclusive if media activists become engaged.

Strengthening institutional competencies

It is also important to acknowledge another important contribution of media movements to media governance: Strengthening institutional competencies related to media policy-making. This is an unintended yet significant contribution of media movements. As Mario Giugni (1998) suggests, it is important to recognize positive effects of social movements even if they are not prominent in activists' agenda or are deliberately pursued. They are "spillover outcomes" (Meyer & Whittier, 1994) or "indirect" and "unintended" consequences (Giugni, 1998) that demonstrate the broad impact of collective action (Bosi & Uba, 2009).

In our case, institutional competencies are intrinsic to the "political capabilities" (Williams, 2004) that citizens need to be active members in a democracy. These refer to developing and maintaining organizational scaffolding and strategic knowledge that can be utilized in support of various policy-making processes and participatory governance. These are collective democratic goods that are critical for democratic governance and social change.

As a result of participation in policy-making processes, they have gained valuable knowledge and expertise. CSOs across all countries have the capacity to advocate for legal reforms, practice-based understanding of administrative and policy-making processes, institutional memory built upon previous experiences, and technical expertise in specific areas. Such capacities are fundamental for democratic media governance and integrating civil society in the policy-making process in different roles. This is essential for foregrounding and weaving citizens' voices into processes of deliberation and decision around media policies.

Like other recent participatory experiences in Latin America (Altschuler & Corrales, 2013; Cornwall & Shankland, 2013), media movements have contributed to enhancing the institutional texture and performance of civil society and the state. These contributions go beyond media policy-making; they provide critical resources for democratic citizenship and governance, such as civic institutional capacity and state participatory mechanisms. Socio-cultural outcomes include fostering a legacy of activism, participatory skills, and citizens' knowledge of specific issues (Giugni, 2008). Other outcomes are clustered in terms of impact on participatory politics, such as engendering subsequent forms of participation, and shared leadership and structures (Meyer & Whittier, 1994).

Media movements have also contributed to institutional strengthening in both civil society and the state by enhancing institutional capacity and cultivating collaboration and learning. Institutional capacity not only refers to the presence of institutions in the public sphere that may channel citizen participation, it also includes the honing of strategic competencies related to mobilization and advocacy among CSOs. What matters is that the participation of citizens and CSOs in particular policy-making processes have shaped a legacy of technical and advocacy capacity that can be mobilized in support of other initiatives.

As a result of participatory experiences, CSOs have gained valuable expertise related to technical matters, policy-making process, and strategic thinking about positioning and advocating for media reforms. They have accumulated individual and organizational competencies including technical matters (e.g. national and international legislation), legislative knowledge, advocacy skills, coalition-building expertise, and partnership development. Collectively, these organizations provide a reservoir of institutional capacity to be tapped by similar media movements in the region.

Further, other citizen initiatives have borrowed from media movements to form organizations and strategic actions. In Argentina, the Coalición stimulated the formation of other organizations pursuing reforms in other media and cultural issues and policies (Prato & Segura, 2014; Prato, Traversaro & Segura, 2015). At the regional level, the Coalición's structure became a point of reference for organizations with similar goals in other countries. CSOs pushing for broadcasting reforms in Ecuador (Colectivo Ciudadano de Comunicación), Mexico (Coalición por el Derecho a la Comunicación) and Uruguay (Coalición por una Comunicación Democrática) have drawn inspiration from the Argentine case to form coalitions during the processes that culminated, respectively, in the 2013 communication law, the 2014 telecommunication, radio, and television law, and the 2014 broadcasting law. Activists in these countries also proposed that Congress solicit input from citizens to draft and debate proposals.

Policy-making processes have mixed consequences for strengthening institutional capacity – that is, the presence of institutions with the necessary skills to engage citizens in public life by developing and implementing strategic actions to advance their causes.

Just as citizens' participation in the elaboration and implementation of policies is a catalyst for activation of CSOs, they may weaken and dissolve civil society institutions. Both consequences are visible in the aftermath of the policy-making processes analyzed here. Just as some organizations gained visibility and reputation as the consequence of participating in policy-making processes, others dissolved after the passing of legislation. Although the organizations that were members remained active, the coalitions did not consolidate as long-lasting institutional platforms. These should not be considered "institutional failures," however. The coalitions were not intended to last beyond the achievement of specific policy objectives (de Rosa Pírez, 2015; Villanueva, 2015).

Media movements also contributed to strengthening the institutional capacity and participatory mechanisms of the state. Since the early 2000s, many countries have implemented mechanisms to engage citizens in democratic politics through referendums, forums, collaborative governance, audiences, and participatory budgeting. Media movements have utilized several mechanisms included in new media laws as well as platforms created by constitutional reforms.

These experiences gave unprecedented opportunities to CSOs to develop capacities about the functioning of participatory mechanisms, draft proposals with input from other organizations and political elites, present proposals to government officials, and shepherd initiatives through congressional procedures. By doing so, they gained valuable skills to utilize a host of participatory mechanisms to remain engaged in policy advocacy.

These experiences cultivated institutional cultures of collaboration and learning among CSOs and between CSOs and state agencies. Collective action fosters knowledge and trust with other civil society institutions that were (and in some cases, remain) allies in specific policy reform movements. Past collaboration and mutual learning become important resources for further democratization (Ramos, 2013).

Participation in the development of new policies and the implementation of legislation offered opportunities for collaboration and learning. A case in point is the experience of Argentina's Coalición during the process that led to the 2009 law and its implementation. CSOs and citizens interacted with state officials both formally and informally. Because the law stipulated the participation of civil society in the implementation phase in three new participatory institutions, it provided opportunities for consultation and cooperation between CSOs and state officials. The same processes apply to the application of new media legislation in Mexico and Uruguay. Representatives of CSOs gained valuable knowledge about the functioning of state agencies and public policies. Expected to interact regularly with ordinary citizens, public officials had to develop new skills and build trust with new partners. These experiences were particularly significant to overcome mutual distrust between the parties (Segura, 2015b).

Certainly, these relations were not free from tensions and conflicts, yet they offered unique openings for collective work across organizations. In fact, the relations between governments and media movements are illustrative of the shifting and complex dealings between governments identified with the Left and progressive social movements in the region. Rather than absolute and consistent agreements premised on supposed ideological communion, the relationships have featured alliances, tensions, and conflicts (Prevost, Campos & Vanden, 2012).

The mainstreaming of the rights-based discourse of public communication

A third contribution of media movements is the affirmation of a rights-based discourse about public communication and media systems. Through participating in media policy-making, they have cultivated and disseminated a rights-based discursive framework to define problems and propose solutions about public communication and policy reforms. Frames offer specific ways of understanding problems by attributing causes and responsibilities, identifying solutions, calling citizens to action, and making moral and legal appeals. Bringing in new frames and shifting conventional discourses to understand, debate and address social issues are key contributions of social movements (Gamson, 1998).

The discursive framework of Latin American media movements is anchored in the notion of the right to communication as a fundamental human right. Citizens are defined as bearers of communication rights. This has been the cornerstone of activists' discourse – their vocabulary to interpret the reality of public communication and media systems and the rallying cry to call for policy reforms. They have championed the right to communication as the normative basis of public communication – the fundamental principle guiding the structure and the performance of media and information systems in democracy. This framework is steeped in the narratives and the work of human rights movements and landmark declarations by global movements during the past decades and echoes key principles of the NWICO debates and the MacBride Report.

It is hard to imagine that the rights-based framework would have achieved its current position in public discourse and legislation without citizen mobilization. Whereas this discourse was largely limited to activists, academics, and policy experts in the past, it has been mainstreamed in recent years. Today, a rights-based conception of public communication underpins major legal frameworks that set the basis for ordering media systems and public information. It is the "law of the land" in many countries in the region. It has appeared and been extensively discussed in public meetings, media coverage, and congressional sessions. It permeates the public discourse of governments as found in official pronouncements, public speeches, and the news coverage of official media. It has also been appropriated by other social movements focused on a range of social issues. These examples reflect shifts in public discourse about communication and media systems that can be legitimately credited to the actions of social movements.

While CSOs in the region have long championed rights-based discourse about public communication, activists credit Argentina's Coalición for broadcasting reform for laying down clear proposals for reform. The public debates during the process prior to congressional debates as well as parliamentary sessions bolstered the visibility of the discourse of communication as a human right and articulated basic aspects of legislation steeped in a rights-based perspective. The Coalición's proposal was based on the paradigm of communication and culture as human rights and condition for democracy and the development of the people.

This language is also found in citizens' proposals and legislation elsewhere in the region. Recommendations and justifications submitted by Argentine activists about issues such as the tripartite division of licenses (public, commercial, and community), the de-concentration of media companies, the promotion of the "third sector" through a variety of strategic state interventions, and the need to ensure the autonomy of public broadcasting were borrowed by CSOs in Ecuador, Mexico, and Uruguay during discussions that culminated in the drafting of new proposal and legislative bills.

The consolidation of a rights-based discourse offers an alternative to market and statist views that have historically dominated public discourse about media legislation and policies. Media movements have catapulted to the center of media policy-making the notion that media systems and public communication should maximize opportunities for public expression and ensure the right to communication of all citizens. This discourse furnishes CSOs and media movements with a vocabulary and rationale to assess problems, articulate demands, and justify proposals. As it has gained public salience and resonance in the political and legal matrix, it can be tapped by various media movements to make claims and defend positions. Undoubtedly, this represents a significant landmark in the history of media governance in the region, and constitutes a major triumph for media movements.

Questions for media policy research

What are the lessons from the cases analyzed here for media policy scholarship? The experiences of media movements in Latin America raise questions that need further attention. It is necessary to go beyond bright-eyed and doctrinal views about citizen participation in media governance in order to tackle more complex questions to refine theoretical arguments and concepts.

One issue pertains to questions about the desirable role of civil society in matters dealing with legislation about public communication and media systems. Civil society is not ideologically seamless about possible roles of media activism in media governance. The evidence from Latin America demonstrates that CSOs held different views about government, legislation, and proposals and took dissimilar positions throughout various phases of policy-making across countries. Further attention is needed for the following questions (Rodríguez, Ferron & Shamas, 2014): What position should CSOs take vis-à-vis power? Should they be uncompromising critics who monitor policy decisions and shed light on problems that contradict rights-based principles? Should they take critical yet pragmatic positions by constantly seeking out elite allies to promote change? Should they hitch political plans to the party in power based on the conviction that it might represent the best hope for reforms?

Given the heterogeneity of political visions and positions in civil society about a host of policy issues, it is necessary to address these questions with a fine-grained analytical brush to produce nuanced understandings about different conceptions of citizen participation. To simply reaffirm that citizenship matters in media policy-making or to celebrate participation is unlikely to render novel insights. Only the examination and comparison of empirical cases reflecting the multiple roles and positions of citizen engagement in media governance might produce nuanced analyses and theoretical breakthroughs.

Second, citizens' participation in media policy-making needs to be analyzed within specific institutional contexts. Just to champion the value of citizens' voice in abstract is insufficient for the simple reason that participation in media policy-making is institutionally bounded. Opportunities and limitations are nestled in the particular structures and dynamics of institutions. Our study shows that citizens voiced different perspectives in many institutional arenas affecting policy-making – public audiences, news coverage, street theater, legislative debates, courts, international organizations, advocacy meetings. Principles and demands may not be different, but the style and the purpose of communication acts vary according to the norms of different institutions. The openness of specific institutional spaces such as the news media, courts, and congressional committees, shapes, constrains, and facilitates different types of citizen expression. Therefore, it is important to grapple with questions about where and how citizens express demands and articulate proposals for policy reform.

Third, because the institutional contexts for participation in policy-making processes are embedded in the state, it is necessary to compare opportunities for public expression among states. Our study shows that states are central arenas for the discussion of policies and the mobilization of citizens in pursuit of policy reforms. Further work is needed to compare how the design and performance of state institutions affects the prospects of citizen participation in media policies. At a time of intriguing and promising innovations in state-sanctioned forms of citizen participation in Latin America and other regions, it is important to compare the strengths and limitations of different forms of citizen participation in media policy-making.

No doubt, the institutionalization and the deepening of rights-based policy reforms continue to confront many obstacles in Latin America. Media governance in the region remains burdened by a long history of anti-democratic policy-making (Levine & Molina, 2011). Many governments generally continue to champion policies to favor media corporations and public officials. Other governments wrap themselves in the flag of rights-based communication, but they have tried to silence critics and colluded with private corporations, thereby exacerbating chronic problems for equal conditions for public expression and dissent. Executive discretionality remains a big challenge notwithstanding the recent push for transparency and accountability. Media policy-making is not a flattened process in which all voices in society have similar chances to be expressed and heard. It is bounded by the conventions of representative democracy and shaped by profound power asymmetries.

In closing, media movements have made three significant contributions. They have invigorated public and legislative debates about media reforms, brought in a new perspective to ground media legislation, and made key contributions to policy implementation. They have strengthened the institutional competencies in both civil society and the state by developing forms of collaboration and expertise. They have contributed to recasting the foundational principle of democratic media governance by foregrounding the notion of communication as a human right. By doing so, media movements have enriched public dialogue and legislative instruments to transform public communication. These achievements are a touchstone for media governance and a pivotal moment for media activism in the region.

The changes discussed in this book do not warrant unbounded optimism about the prospects of media pluralism. Much remains to be done to dismantle anti-democratic patterns of policy-making. The ascendancy of citizen participation in media governance reflects dynamic policy scenarios that are still fraught with many problems. Media democracy is beleaguered by various problems. Patrimonialism persists as demonstrated by the continuation of *quid pro quo* practices by governments and private companies where they exchange favors to obtain political and economic benefits. Private companies have continued to use legal tactics and backdoor maneuvers to pressure governments to ignore and eliminate reforms directly affecting their interests, such as ownership de-concentration and the strengthening of the third sector. Corporate hostility to reforms is not surprising. Many companies have neither accepted changes quietly nor abandoned the shibboleth that the absence of regulations is the best policy for media industries. Certainly, it has not helped that governments have continued to dither over progressive reforms and/or opposed demands for media pluralism. Some governments have approached reforms tentatively as they were afraid of private backlash or disinterested in making democratic communication a priority. Others were duplicitous as they favored a soaring rhetoric in support of progressive communication while leaving basic problems untouched, practicing media patrimonialism, and/or implementing measures to strengthen arbitrary official interference in public speech.

The achievements of media movements remain precarious and vulnerable to political shifts and recalcitrant structures. Backsliding is always possible; success is never guaranteed. The steadfast commitment of media movements remains as necessary as ever. They are needed to continue to agitate for passing and implementing progressive reforms, challenge corporate and official efforts to undo achievements, and remind governments about rights-based international and national legislation.

At the time of completing this book in late 2015, we believe that a cautious outlook is imperative given the fragility of policy reforms, notorious obstacles to public expression, and the historical averseness and outright opposition of political elites and market interests to progressive media legislation. Yet we remain modestly hopeful given remarkable changes and the energies of media activism in the region. By bringing in critical and deliberative politics, citizen activism has been a counterpoint to power hierarchies and spearheaded important innovations in contemporary media governance.

REFERENCES

ABC Color. (2014, 22 September). Paraguay, el número 100. *ABC Color.*

Abraham-Dowsing, K., Godfrey, A. & Khor, A. (2014). Reframing the Evidence Debates: A View from the Media for Development Sector. *BBC Media Action.* http://downloads. bbc.co.uk/rmhttp/mediaaction/pdf/ research/working_paper_reframing_ the_evidence_debates.pdf.

Abramovich, V. & Courtis, C. (2000). El acceso a la información como derecho. *Anuario de Derecho a la Comunicación, 1*(21), 231.

Ackerman, J. (2008). Introducción: Mas allá del acceso a la información. In J. Ackerman (Ed.), *Más allá del acceso a la información: transparencia, rendición de cuentas y estado de derecho* (pp. 11–32). Mexico: Siglo XXI.

Acosta, F. M. (2014). *El acceso a la información pública en Argentina y México. Un análisis desde la perspectiva de la accountability social.* Buenos Aires: Universidad de Buenos Aires.

Agencia de Noticias. (2012, November 5). *Uruguay: Gobierno ordenó el cierre de 74 radios comunitarias.* http://www. agenciadenoticias.org/uruguay- gobierno-ordeno-el-cierre-de-74- radios-comunitarias/.

Alianza Regional. (2013). *Fuerza Colectiva: Aprendizajes de la Alianza Regional para la incidencia.* Montevideo: Alianza Regional por la Libertad de Expresión y el Derecho a la Información

Almeida, P. & Ulate, A. C. (2015). Social Movements Across Latin America. In P. Almeida & A. C. Ulate (Eds.), *Handbook of Social Movements across Latin America* (pp. 3–10). Berlin: Springer.

Altschuler, D. & Corrales, J. (2013). *The Promise of Participation: Experiments in Participatory Governance in Honduras and Guatemala.* New York: Palgrave Macmillan.

Álvarez Ugarte, R. (2013). Una mirada desde los movimientos sociales al pasado, presente y futuro de la Ley de Servicios de Comunicación Audiovisual. *Revista Argentina de Teoría Jurídica, 14.*

Álvarez, L. (2015, 27 June). Gobierno cerró el cerco a ONG, La Prensa. *La Prensa.*

Alvarez, S. E. (2014). Ambivalent Engagements, Paradoxical Effects: Latin American Feminist and Women's Movements And/ in/against Development. In C. Verschuur, I. Guérin & H. Guétat- Bernard (Eds.), *Under Development: Gender* (pp. 211–235). London: Palgrave Macmillan.

Alvarez, S., Dagnino, E. & Escobar, A. (1998). *Cultures of Politics, Politics of Cultures: Re-visioning Latin American Social Movements.* Boulder: Westview Press.

AMARC Uruguay. (2012, 11 October). AMARC reclama atención a las radios comunitarias.

AMARC Uruguay. (2013, 30 July). Carta abierta Amarc Uruguay al CHARC y URSEC.

Amenta, E. (2006). *When Movements Matter: The Townsend Plan and the Rise of Social Security.* Princeton, NJ: Princeton University Press.

Amenta, E. (2014). How to Analyze the Influence of Movements. *Contemporary Sociology, 43*(1), 16–29.

Amenta, E., Caren, N., Chiarello, E. & Su, Y. (2010). The Political Consequences of Social Movements. *Annual Review of Sociology, 36*, 287–307.

Anheier, H. K., Kaldor, M. & Glasius, M. (2006). *Global Civil Society 2006/2007*. London: Sage

Animal Político. (2014, 27 April). La cadena humana contra la ley telecom, en fotografías y videos. *Animal Político.*

Arango-Forero, G., Arango, M. F., Llaña, L. & Serrano, M. C. (2010). Colombian Media in the XXI Century: The Re-conquest by Foreign Investment. *Palabra Clave, 13*(1), 59–76.

Arroyo, L., Becerra, M., García Castillejo, A. & Santamaría, O. (2012). *Cajas mágicas. El renacimiento de la televisión pública en América Latina.* Washington: World Bank.

Article 19. (2007, 3 August). Uruguay: Senate must approve Community Broadcasting Bill. https://www.article19.org/data/files/pdfs/press/uruguay-broadcasting-pr.pdf.

Asociación de Comunicadores Calandria. (2013). *Construyendo desarrollo y ciudadanía desde la comunicación.* Lima: Asociación de Comunicadores Calandria.

Asociación por los Derechos Civiles. (2004). *Una radiodifusión pública para la democracia.* Buenos Aires: ADC.

Asociación por los Derechos Civiles & Open Society Institute. (2005). *Una censura sutil. Abuso de publicidad oficial y otras restricciones a la libertad de expresión en Argentina.* Buenos Aires: ADC.

Asociación por los Derechos Civiles & Open Society Institute. (2008). *The Price of Silence: The Growing Threat of Soft Censorship in Latin America.* New York: ADC & Open Society Justice Initiative.

Ávila Pietrasanta, I., Calleja Gutiérrez, A. & Solís Leree, B. (2002). *No más medios a medias: Participación ciudadana en la revisión integral de la legislación de los medios electrónicos.* México: FES; Senado de la República.

Badillo, A., Mastrini, G. & Marenghi, P. (2015). Teoría crítica, izquierda y políticas públicas de comunicación: el caso de América Latina y los gobiernos progresistas. *Comunicación y Sociedad, 24*, 95–126.

Baiocchi, G., Braathen, E., & Teixeira, A. C. (2013). Transformation Institutionalized? Making Sense of Participatory Democracy in the Lula Era. In K. Stokke & O. Törnquist (Eds.), *Democratization in the Global South: The Importance of Transformative Politics.* Basingstoke, Hampshire: Palgrave Macmillan.

Baranchuk, M. & Rodríguez, Usé, J. (2011). *Ley 26.522: Hacia un Nuevo paradigma en comunicación audiovisual.* Lomas de Zamora: AFSCA-UNLZ.

Barclay, S., Jones, L. C. & Marshall, A. M. (2011). Two Spinning Wheels: Studying Law and Social Movements. In A. Sarat (Ed.), *Special Issue Social Movements/Legal Possibilities, 54*, 1–16.

Barrett, G. & Gaventa, J. (2012). Mapping the Outcomes of Citizen Engagement. *World Development, 40*(12), 2399–2410.

Becerra, M. (2008, 23 April). Los medios salen del placard. *Página/12.*

Becerra, M. (2009, 10 October). Las cuentas pendientes de los medios. *La Nación.*

Becerra, M. (2015). *De la concentración a la convergencia: Políticas de medios en Argentina y América Latina.* Buenos Aires: Paidós.

Becerra, M. & Lacunza, S. (2012). *Wiki Media Leaks. La relación entre medios y gobiernos en América Latina bajo el prisma de los cables de WikiLeaks.* Buenos Aires: Ediciones B.

Becerra, M. & Mastrini, G. (2009). *Los dueños de la palabra. Acceso, estructura y concentración de los medios en la América Latina del siglo XXI.* Buenos Aires: Prometeo.

Becerra, M. & Mastrini, G. (2015). Nuevas reglas de juego en telecomunicaciones en la Argentina. *Observacom.* http://observacom.org/nuevas-reglas-de-juego-en-telecomunicaciones-en-la-argentina/.

Becerra, M. & Waisbord, S. (2015). *Principios y "buenas prácticas" para los medios públicos en América Latina.* Montevideo: UNESCO.

Beltrán, L. R. (1993). Comunicación para el desarrollo en Latinoamérica, una evaluación sucinta al cabo de cuarenta años. *IV Mesa Redonda sobre Comunicación y Desarrollo.* Lima: IPAL.

Beltrán, L. R. (2007). La comunicación para el desarrollo en Latinoamérica: un recuento de medio siglo. In Loreti, D., Mastrini, G. & Baranchuk, M. (Eds.), *Participación y democracia en la Sociedad de la Información* (pp. 149–187). Buenos Aires: Prometeo Libros.

Bennett, W. L. (2004). Social Movements beyond Borders: Organization, Communication, and Political Capacity in Two Eras of Transnational Activism. In D. della Porta & S. Tarrow (Eds.), *Transnational Protest and Global Activism* (pp. 203–226). Lanham, MD: Rowman & Littlefield.

Bennett, W. L. & Segerberg, A. (2013). *The Logic of Connective Action: Digital Media and the Personalization of Contentious Politics.* New York: Cambridge University Press.

Berliner, D. (2014). The Political Origins of Transparency. *The Journal of Politics, 76*(2), 479–491.

Berliner, D. & Erlich, A. (2015). Competing for Transparency: Political Competition and Institutional Reform in Mexican States. *American Political Science Review, 109*(1), 110–128.

Bertoni, E. (2012). Freedom of Information: Three Harmless Words? The Role of the Media and Access to Information Laws. *Derecho Comparado de la Información, 19,* 29–94.

Bertoni, E. & Del Campo, A. (2012). *Calumnias e injurias: a dos años de la reforma del Código Penal Argentino.* Buenos Aires: CELE.

Biblioteca del Congreso Nacional de Chile (BCN). (2014). *Televisión digital – ley fácil.* http://www.bcn.cl/leyfacil/recurso/television-digital.

Boersner, D. (2005). Gobiernos de izquierda en América Latina: tendencias y experiencias. *Nueva Sociedad, 197,* 100–113.

Bosi, L. & Uba, K. (2009). Introduction: The Outcomes of Social Movements. *Mobilization, 14*(4), 409–415.

Boulding, C. & Wampler, B. (2010). Voice, Votes, and Resources: Evaluating the Effect of Participatory Democracy on Well-Being. *World Development, 38*(1), 125–135.

Brock, K. & McGee, R. (2012). *Knowing Poverty: Critical Reflections on Participatory Research and Policy.* Routledge.

Brunner, J. J. & Catalán, C. (1995). *Televisión: libertad, mercado y moral.* Santiago: Editorial Los Andes.

Buchanan, C. (2015). Revisiting the UNESCO debate on a New World Information and Communication Order: Has the NWICO been achieved by other means? *Telematics and Informatics, 32*(2), 391–399.

Bulla, G. (2011). Participación: concepto clave en la Ley de Servicios de Comunicación Audiovisual. In M. Baranchuk & J. Rodríguez Usé (Eds.), *Ley 26522. Hacia un nuevo paradigma en comunicación audiovisual* (pp. 93–104). Buenos Aires: AFSCA-UNLZ.

Buquet, G. & Lanza, E. (2011). *La televisión privada comercial en Uruguay*. Montevideo: FES.

Burch, S. (2014). The Democratization of Communication: Latin American Perspectives and Initiatives. In C. Padovani & A. Calabrese (Eds.), *Communication Rights and Social Justice: Historical Accounts of Transnational Mobilizations* (pp. 115–134). New York: Palgrave Macmillan.

Burch, S., León, O. & Tamayo, E. (2004). *'Se cayó el sistema'. Enredos de la Sociedad de la Información*. Quito: ALAI

Burstein, P. (1999). Social Movements and Public Policy. In M. Giungi, D. McAdam & C. Tilly (Eds.), *How Social Movements Matter* (pp. 3–21). Minneapolis, MN: University of Minnesota Press.

Burstein, P. & Sausner, S. (2005). The Incidence and Impact of Policy-Oriented Collective Action: Competing Views. *Sociological Forum, 20*(3), 403–419.

Burstein, P., Einwohner, R. & Holla, J. (1995). The success of political movements: A bargaining perspective. In J. C. Jenkins & B. Klandermans (Eds.), *The Politics of Social Protest: Comparative Perspectives on States and Social Movements* (pp. 275–295). Minneapolis: University of Minesota Press.

Bush, S. (2015). *The Taming of Democracy Assistance: Why Democracy Promotion Does Not Confront Dictators*. New York: Cambridge University Press.

Cabezas, A. (2014). Transnational Feminist Networks Building Regions in Latin America. *Latin American Policy, 5*(2), 207–220.

CAinfo. (2014). *Tras seis años de ley de acceso a la información pública persisten desafíos en materia de transparencia activa*. Montevideo: Cainfo. http://www.cainfo.org.uy/2014/09/tras-seis-anos-de-ley-de-acceso-a-la-informacion-publica-persisten-desafios-en-materia-de-transparencia-activa/.

Calabrese, A. (2004). The Promise of Civil Society: A Global Movement for Communication Rights. *Continuum. Journal of Media and Cultural Studies, 18*(3), 317–329.

Calleja, A. (2015). *El movimiento de la radiodifusión comunitaria y su institucionalización*. Typescript.

Cameron, M. A. & Herschberg, E. (2010). *Latin America's Left Turns: Politics, Policies, and Trajectories of Change*. Boulder, CO: Lynne Rienner.

Cameron, M. A., Hershberg, E. & Sharpe, K. E. (Eds.). (2012). *New Institutions for Participatory Democracy in Latin America: Voice and Consequence*. New York: Palgrave Macmillan.

Campbell, C., Cornish, F., Gibbs, A. & Scott, K. (2010). Heeding the Push from Below: How do Social Movements Persuade the Rich to Listen to the Poor? *Journal of Health Psychology, 15*(7), 962–971.

Capoccia, G. & Kelemen, R. D. (2007). The Study of Critical Junctures: Theory, Narrative, and Counterfactuals in Historical Institutionalism. *World Politics, 59*(3), 341–369.

Capriles, O. (1976). *El Estado y los medios de comunicación en Venezuela*. Caracas: Instituto de Investigaciones de la Comunicación-ININCO.

Casey, J. (2004). Third Sector Participation in the Policy Process: A

Framework for Comparative Analysis. *Policy & Politics*, 32(2), 241–257.

Castañeda Menacho, M. (2008). *Campaña de incidencia público-política sobre la ley de radio y televisión: Afirma tus derechos por una comunicación de calidad*. Lima: Calandria.

Cejudo, G., Ayllón, S. L. & Cázares, A. R. (2011). An Assessment of Transparency in Mexico: Lessons from the 2010 Metrics of Transparency. *Transparencia y privacidad*, 1 (1), 1–36.

Cerbino, M. & Ramos Ávila, I. (2009). Medios de comunicación y despolitización de la política en Ecuador. In A. Cañizález (Ed.), *Tiempos de Cambio: Política y Comunicación en América Latina* (pp. 47–62). Caracas: Universidad Católica Andrés Bello – ALAIC.

Chartock, S. (2011). How Movement Strength Matters: Social Movement Strength and the Implementation of Ethnodevelopment Policy in Ecuador and Peru. *Studies in Comparative International Development*, 46(3), 298–320.

Checa-Godoy, A. (2012). La Banca y La Propiedad de Los Medios: El Caso de Ecuador. *Revista Latina de Comunicación Social*, 67(2), 6–22.

Coelho, V. S. (2014). A Brief Reflection on the Brazilian Participatory Experience. *Journal of Public Deliberation*, 10(1), 1–4.

Conaghan, C. (2015). Surveil and Sanction: The Return of the State and Societal Regulation in Ecuador. *European Review of Latin American and Caribbean Studies*, 98, 7–27.

Conway, J. (2006). *Praxis and Politics: Knowledge Production in Social Movements*. New York: Routledge.

Couldry, N. (2010). *Why Voice Matters: Culture and Politics After Neoliberalism*. Los Angeles: SAGE.

Cornwall, A. & Shankland, A. (2013). Cultures of Politics, Spaces of Power: Contextualizing Brazilian Experiences of Participation. *Journal of Political Power*, 6(2), 309–333.

Cornwall, A., Robins, S. & Von Lieres, B. (2011). States of Citizenship: Contexts and Cultures of Public Engagement and Citizen Action. *IDS Working Papers* (363), 1–32.

Cornwall, M., King, B., Dahlin, E. & Schiffman, K. (2007, September). Signals or Mixed Signals: Why Opportunities for Mobilization are not Opportunities for Policy Reform. *Mobilization*, 12(3), 239–254.

Cruz, A. (2009). Building Political Will for Enhanced Citizen Access to Information: Lessons from Latin America. In C. Malena (Ed.), *From Political Won't to Political Will: Building Support for Participatory Governance* (pp. 227–244). Sterling, VA: Kumarian Press.

Dahlgren, P. (2013). *The Political Web: Media, Participation and Alternative Democracy*. New York: Palgrave Macmillan.

Darbishire, H. (2006). El Derecho a la Información en América Latina. *Anuario de Derechos Humanos*, 259–274.

Darling, J. (2014). Community Radio and Free Expression in Late Twentieth-Century El Salvador. *American Journalism*, 31(1), 49–70.

Dauvergne, P. & LeBaron, G. (2014). *Protest Inc.: The Corporatization of Activism*. Cambridge: Polity.

de la Torre, C. & Lemos, A. O. (2015). Populist Polarization and the Slow Death of Democracy in Ecuador. *Democratization*, 23(2), 1–21.

de Lima, V. (2011). Brasil: Politicas de comunicações no governo Lula (2003–2010). In A. Koschutzke & E. Gerber (Eds.), *Progressismo e politica de comunicações: Maos a obra* (pp. 49–66). Buenos Aires: Ebert Foundation.

del Bianco, N. R., Esch, C. E. & Moreira, S. V. (2012). Radiodifusão pública: Um desafio conceitual na América Latina. *Revista Estudos em Comunicação*, *10*(4), 155–181.

Diani, M. & Bison, I. (2004). Organizations, Coalitions, and Movements. *Theory and Society*, *33*, 281–309.

Donders, K., Pauwels, C. & Loisen, J. (2014). *The Palgrave Handbook of European Media Policy*. New York: Palgrave Macmillan.

Dorcé, A., Vega, A., Trejo Delarbre, R. & Ortega Ramírez, P. (2014). Telecommunications and Broadcasting Reform in Mexico in 2013: Key Elements of the Process. *Critical Studies in Media Communication*, *5*(31), 356–364.

Doyle, M. M. (2015, 27 July). Los pueblos indígenas en la Ley SCA: antecedentes, transformaciones y desafíos. *VIII Seminario Regional (Cono Sur) ALAIC*. Córdoba.

Dryzek, J. (2006). *Deliberative Global Politics: Discourse and Democracy in a Divided World*. Cambridge: Polity.

Edwards, M. (2009). *Civil Society*. 2nd edition. Cambridge: Polity.

Edwards, M. & Gaventa, J. (2014). *Global Citizen Action*. London: Routledge.

El Nacional. (2015, 6 August). Centro Carter abandona Venezuela. *El Nacional* (Venezuela). http://www.el-nacional.com/politica/Centro-Carter-abandona-Venezuela_0_677932428.html.

El País. (2015, 19 April). Andebu enfrenta a la ley de Medios. *El País* (Uruguay).

El Universo. (2015, 11 February). Carlos Ochoa: Regulación a redes sociales necesita antes un gran debate en el país. *El Universo* (Ecuador).

El Universo. (2015, 21 March). Cordicom buscará creación de más medios comunitarios. *El Universo* (Ecuador).

Ellner, S. (2013). Latin America's Radical Left: Challenges and Complexities of Political Power in the Twenty-first Century. *Latin American Perspectives*, *40*(3), 5–25.

Espacio Público (2015). Situación general de la libertad de expresión e información en Venezuela. *Comunicación*, *170*, 20–29.

Etchemendy, S. (2008). ¿Izquierda de actores o de política social? El dilema del progresismo en América Latina. *Umbrales*, *5*, 103–112.

Exeni, R. J. L. (2002). Reinventando La Utopía: Políticas De Comunicación En/Para El Siglo XXI. *VI Congreso Latinoamericano de Investigadores de la Comunicación*. ALAIC-ABOIC-UPSA.

Fernández, C. & Paxman, A. (2000). *El Tigre: Emilio Azcárraga y su imperio Televisa*. Grijalbo Mondadori Sa.

Fernández Christlieb, F., Ortega Ramírez, P. & Solís Leree, B. (2013, September). La aportación de la academia a la reforma constitucional de 2013: un recuento histórico. *Revista Mexicana de Comunicación*, *26*(135), 33–39.

Fisher, D. (1982). *The Right to Communicate: A Status Report*. Paris: United Nations Educational, Scientific and Cultural Organization, Department of Mass Communication.

Fishkin, J. (2009). *When the People Speak Deliberative Democracy and Public Consultation*. New York: Oxford University Press.

Flew, T. (2013). Academics and Activists in the Policy Process: Engagement with Australian Media Inquiries 2011–2013. In *The Role of Advocacy in Media and Telecom Policy* (pp. 1–39). Washington, DC: New America Foundation.

Flew, T. & Waisbord, S. (2015). The Ongoing Significance of National Media Systems in the Context of

Media Globalization. *Media, Culture & Society*, 37(4), 620–636.

Fligstein, N. & McAdam, D. (2011). Toward a General Theory of Strategic Action Fields. *Sociological Theory*, 29(1), 1–26.

Fogarty, E. (2011). Nothing Succeeds Like Access? NGO Strategies Towards Multilateral Institutions. *Journal of Civil Society*, 7(2), 207–227.

Fox, E. (Ed.) (1988). *Media and Politics in Latin America: The Struggle for Democracy*. Thousand Oaks: SAGE.

Fox, E. (Ed.) (1990). *Días de Baile: el Fracaso de la Reforma de la Televisión de América Latina*. Mexico City: FELAFACS-WACC.

Fox, E. & Waisbord, S. (Eds.) (2002). *Latin Politics, Global Media*. Austin, TX: University of Texas Press.

Fox, J. & Haight, L. (2011). Mexico's Transparency Reforms: Theory and Practice. In S. Maret (Ed.), *Government Secrecy (Research in Social Problems and Public Policy)* 19 (pp. 353–379). Bingley, UK: Emerald Group.

Fraser, N. (2014). *Transnationalizing the Public Sphere* (K. Nash, Ed.). Malden, MA: Polity.

Frau-Meigs, D., Nicey, J., Tupper, P., Palmer, M. & Pohle, J. (2012). *From NWICO to WSIS: 30 Years of Communication Geopolitics: Actors and Flows, Structures and Divides*. Bristol: Intellect.

Freedman, D. (2008). *The Politics of Media Policy*. Cambridge: Polity Press.

Fuenzalida, V. (1998). Situación de la Televisión Pública en América Latina. *Diálogos de la Comunicación, 53*, 1–20.

Gamson, W. (1975). *The Strategy of Social Protest*. Belmont, CA: Wadsworth.

Gamson, W. (1998). Social Movements and Cultural Change. In M. G. Giugni, D. McAdam & C. Tilly (Eds.), *From Contention to Democracy* (pp. 57–77). Lanham, MD: Rowman & Littlefield.

Gamson, W. & Modigliani, A. (1989). Media Discourse and Public Opinion On Nuclear Power: A Constructionist Approach. *American Journal of Sociology*, 95(1), 1–37.

Ganz, M. (2010). *Why David Sometimes Wins: Leadership, Organization, and Strategy in the California Farm Worker Movement*. New York: Oxford University Press.

Gaventa, J. & Barrett, G. (2012). Mapping the Outcomes of Citizen Engagement. *World Development*, 40(12), 2399–2410.

Geissel, B. & Newton, K. (2011). *Evaluating Democratic Innovations: Curing the Democratic Malaise?* New York: Routledge.

Gilson, J. (2011). Transnational Advocacy: New Spaces, New Voices. *Alternatives: Global, Local, Political*, 36(4), 288–306.

Ginosar, A. (2013). Media Governance: A Conceptual Framework or Merely a Buzz Word. *Communication Theory*, 23(4), 356–374.

Gitlin, T. (2003). *Letters to a Young Activist*. New York, NY: Basic Books.

Giugni, M. (1998). Was it Worth the Effort? The Outcomes and Consequences of Social Movements. *Annual Review of Sociology*, 24, 371–398.

Giugni, M. (1999). How social movements matter: Past research, present problems, future developments. In M. Giugni, D. McAdam & C. Tilly (Eds.), *How Social Movements Matter* (pp. xiii–xxxii). Minneapolis: University of Minnesota Press.

Giugni, M. (2004). Personal and Biographical Consequences. In D. Snow, S. Soule & K. Hanspeter (Eds.), *The Blackwell Companion to Social*

Movements (pp. 489–507). Malden, MA: Blackwell.

Giugni, M. (2008). Political, Biographical, and Cultural Consequences of Social Movements. *Sociology Compass*, 2(5), 1582–1600.

Giugni, M. & Yamasaki, S. (2009). The Policy Impact of Social Movements: A Replication Through Qualitative Comparative Analysis. *Mobilization*, 14(4), 467–484.

Giugni, M., McAdam, D. & Tilly, C. (1999). *How Social Movements Matter*. Minneapolis: University of Minnesota

Goldfrank, B. (2011). *Deepening Local Democracy in Latin America: Participation, Decentralization, and the Left*. University Park, PA: Penn State University Press.

Gómez, F. & Sande, M. (2014, 19 November). Consolidar lo logrado. *Página/12*.

Gómez, G. (2007). *Uruguay – Senado aprueba proyecto de ley sobre medios comunitarios*. AlterInfos América Latina. http://www.alterinfos.org/spip.php?article1852.

Gómez García, R. & Treré, E. (2014). The #YoSoy132 movement and the struggle for media democratization in Mexico. *Convergence: The International Journal of Research into New Media Technologies*, 20, 496.

Gómez García, R. & Sosa Plata, G. (2006). Reforma de la legislación en radio, televisión y telecomunicaciones en México. *Quaderns del CAC*, 25, 99–138.

Gonçalves, S. (2014). The Effects of Participatory Budgeting on Municipal Expenditures and Infant Mortality in Brazil. *World Development*, 53, 94–110.

Goodwin, J. (2011). Conclusions: Are Protesters Opportunists? Fifty Tests. In J. Jasper & J. Goodwin (Ed.), *Contention in Context: Political

Opportunities and the Emergence of Protest* (pp. 277–302). Stanford: Stanford University Press.

Gramsci, A. (1971). *Selections from the Prison Notebooks*. (Q. Hoare & G. N. Smith, Eds.) New York: International Publishers.

Graña, F. Ed. (2013). *Medios comunitarios: El fin de una larga noche*. Montevideo: Universidad de la República.

Graziano, M. (1986). Política o ley: debate sobre el debate. *Espacios*.

Guerin, M. (2013). *Pensar la Televisión Pública*. Buenos Aires: La Crujía.

Guerrero, M. A. (2010). Broadcasting and Democracy in Mexico: From Corporatist Subordination to State Capture. *Policy and Society*, 29(1), 23–35.

Guerrero, M. A. & Márquez-Ramírez, M. (Eds.) (2014). *Media Systems and Communication Policies in Latin America*. New York: Palgrave Macmillan.

Gumucio Dagron, A. (2003). Arte de equilibristas: La sostenibilidad de los medios de comunicación comunitarios. *Punto Cero*, 10(10), 1–31.

Haas, P. M. (1992). Epistemic Communities and International Policy Coordination. *Internatonal Organization*, 46(1), 10–35.

Hailer, M. (2014). *Coronelismo eletrônico: Partidos contra a regulação da mídia são os campeoes de concessão em rádio e TV*. Revista Forum Semanal. http://revistaforum.com.br/digital/179/coronelismo-eletrônico-partidos-contra-regulação-da-midia-sao-os-campeoes-de-concessão-em-radio-e-tv/.

Hallin, D. C. & Mancini, P. (2012). *Comparing Media Systems: Three Models of Media and Politics*. New York: Cambridge University Press.

Harlow, S. & Harp, D. (2012). Collective Action on the Web: A Cross-cultural Study of Social Networking Sites and Online and Offline Activism in the United States and Latin America. *Information, Communication & Society*, 15(2), 196–216.

Haug, C. (2013). Organizing Spaces: Meeting Arenas as a Social Movement Infrastructure between Organization, Network, and Institution. *Organization Studies*, 34(5–6), 705–732.

Haughney, D. (2012). Defending Territory, Demanding Participation: Mapuche Struggles in Chile. *Latin American Perspectives*, 39(4), 201–217.

Heller, P. (2013). *Challenges and Opportunities: Civil Society in a Globalizing World*. Providence, RI: Human Development Report Office, United Nations Development Programme.

Hernández, D. (2006). La nueva ley venezolana de Responsabilidad Social en Radio y Televisión. *Cuadernos Electrónicos Derechos Humanos y Democracia*, 2, 1–18.

Hetland, G. (2014). The Crooked Line: From Populist Mobilization to Participatory Democracy in Chávez-Era Venezuela. *Qualitative Sociology*, 37(4), 373–401.

Hintz, A. (2011). From Media Niche to Policy Spotlight: Mapping Community-Media Policy Change in Latin America. *Canadian Journal of Communication*, 36(1), 147–159.

Hintz, A. & Milan, S. (2012). Struggling for Open Information Environments: Civil Society, Initiatives for Media Policy Change. *iConference '12*. Toronto.

Hirschman, A. (1970). *Exit, Voice, and Loyalty*. Cambridge, MA: Harvard University Press.

Holzhacker, R. (2011). National and Transnational Strategies of LGBT Civil Society Organizations in Different Political Environments: Modes of Interaction in Western and Eastern Europe for Equality. *Comparative European Politics*, 10(1), 23–47.

Huerta-Wong, J. E. & García, R. G. (2013). Concentración y diversidad de los medios de comunicación y las telecomunicaciones en México. *Comunicación y sociedad* (19).

Human Rights Watch (2013). Venezuela: Chávez's Authoritarian Legacy: Dramatic Concentration of Power and Open Disregard for Basic Human Rights. https://www.hrw. org/news/2013/03/05/venezuela-chavezs-authoritarian-legacy.

Jiménez, C. & Muñoz, J. (2008). Estructura de los medios de comunicación en Chile. *Razón y Palabra*, 13(60).

Jobert, B. & Kohler-Koch, B. (2008). *Changing Images of Civil Society: From Protest to Government*. London: Routledge.

Jung, W., King, B. & Soule, S. (2014). Issue Bricolage: Explaining the Configuration of the Social Movement Sector, 1960–1995. *American Journal of Sociology*, 120(1), 187–225

Kaplún, G. (2010). *La nueva ley de Radiodifusión Comunitaria en Uruguay: el largo camino de la democratización de las comunicaciones*. Montevideo: UNESCO.

Kaplún, G. (2014, August). *Diez años de (lentos) avances en la reforma de las comunicaciones en Uruguay*. Observatorio Latinoamericano 14. Buenos Aires: Instituto de Estudios de América Latina y el Caribe, Facultad de Ciencias Sociales, Universidad de Buenos Aires.

Karam Cárdenas, T. (2014/15). Presentación del Dossier sobre telecomunicaciones. *México Interdisciplinario/Interdisciplinary Mexico*, 7, 4–12.

Keck, M. & Sikkink, K. (1998). *Activists beyond Borders: Advocacy Networks in International Politics*. Ithaca, NY: Cornell University Press.

Kitzberger, P. (2012). The Media Politics of Latin America's Leftist Governments. *Journal of Politics in Latin America*, 4(3), 123–139.

Knight Center. (2015). *A pesar de amenazas, periodista asesinado en Ciudad de México no recibía protección, ¿qué pasa con el mecanismo de protección?* Austin, TX: Knight Center – The University of Texas at Austin. https://knightcenter.utexas.edu/blog/oo-16162-sanctions-against-independent-media-continue-supercom-marks-2-years-ecuador.

Kolb, F. (2007). *Protest and Opportunities: The Political Outcomes of Social Movements*. Chicago, IL: University of Chicago Press.

Kriesi, H. (1995). The Political Opportunity Structure of New Social Movements. In J. C. Jenkins & B. Klandermans (Eds.), *The Politics of Social Protest* (pp. 167–198). Minneapolis, MN: University of Minnesota Press.

Krohling Peruzzo, C. M., Tufte, T. & Vega Casanova, J. (2011). *Trazos de una otra Comunicación en América Latina: Prácticas comunitárias, teorías y demandas sociales*. Barranquilla: ALAIC.

Lanza, Edison (2015). Relatoría Libertad de Expresión: la Ley Audiovisual de Uruguay cumple con los estándares internacionales y la Convención Americana de Derechos Humanos. Observacom. http://observacom.org/relatoria-libertad-de-expresion-la-ley-audiovisual-de-uruguay-cumple-con-los-estandares-internacionales-y-la-convencion-americana-de-derechos-humanos/.

Lázzaro, L. (2010). *La batalla de la comunicación. De los tanques mediáticos a la ciudadanía de la información*. Buenos Aires: Colihue.

Leach, M. & Scoones, I. (2007). *Mobilising Citizens: Social Movements and the Politics of Knowledge*. Sussex: IDS – University of Sussex.

León, O., Burch, S. & Tamayo, E. (2005). *Movimientos sociales y comunicación*. Quito: ALAI.

Levine, D. H. & Molina, J. E. (2011). *The Quality of Democracy in Latin America*. Boulder, CO: Lynne Rienner Publishers.

Light, E. (2013). Sputtering to a start: The history and future of radio spectrum regulation in Uruguay. *Journal of Latin American Communication Research*, 3(2), 83–115.

Lizama, V. (2014). 8 Reasons Why Latin America's Media Market Is Set to Skyrocket. http://latinlink.usmediaconsulting.com/2014/06/8-reasons-why-latin-americas-media-market-is-set-to-skyrocket/

López Vigil, J. I. (1995). ¿Qué hace comunitaria a una radio comunitaria? *Chasqui*, 52, 51–54.

López Vigil, J. I. (2013, October). Lo bueno, lo malo y lo feo de la Ley de Comunicación de Ecuador. *Envio (Nicaragua)*.

Loreti, D. & Lozano, L. (2014). *El derecho a comunicar: Los conflictos en torno a la libertad de expresión en las sociedades contemporáneas*. Buenos Aires: Siglo XXI.

Loreti, D. & Zommer, L. (2005). Debates en torno a la libertad de expresión y el acceso a la información. In CELS (Ed.), *Derechos Humanos en Argentina—Informe 2005* (pp. 393–423). Buenos Aires: Siglo XXI.

Loreti, D., Lozano, L. & Pochak, A. (2014). El acceso a la información como herramienta para garantizar el derecho a la verdad. In D. Loreti & L. Lozano (Eds.), *El Derecho a comunicar: Los conflictos en torno a la libertad de expression en las sociedades contemporáneas* (pp. 237–271). Buenos Aires: Siglo XXI.

Lozano, L. & de Charras, D. (2012, 25 September). Los desafíos del pluralismo. *Página/12*.

Lugo-Ocando, J. (2009). *The Media in Latin America.* Maidenhead: Open University Press.

Lugo-Ocando, J. & Cañizález, A. (2010). When Magic Realism confronted Virtual Reality: Online News and Journalism in Latin America. In G. Meikle (Ed.), *News Online: Transformations and Continuities* (69–83). New York: Palgrave Macmillan.

Lugo-Ocando, J., Cañizález, A. & Lohmeier, C. (2010). When PSB is delivered by the hand of God: The case of Roman Catholic broadcast networks in Venezuela. *International Journal of Media & Cultural Politics,* 6(2), 149–167.

Luna Vásquez, C. I. (2014). Concentración del sistema de medios de comunicación en Panamá y sus relaciones con el poder económico y político. *Comunicación y sociedad,* 22.

Manheim, J. (2011). *Strategy in Information and Influence Campaigns.* New York: Routledge.

Marcelo, C., Mediano, A. P. & Tello, C. (2009). Acceso a la información pública: los desafíos del Consejo de la Transparencia. *Anuario de Derechos Humanos,* 5, 193–204.

Marino, S., Mastrini, G., Becerra, M., Rubini, C. & Espada, A. (2015). *Diagnóstico sobre el acceso del sector sin fines de lucro a medios audiovisuales en la Argentina 2014. Licencias, autorizaciones, permisos y fondos concursables.* Typescript.

Martin Barbero, J. (2001). Claves de Debate/ Televisión pública, televisión cultural: entre la renovación y la invención. In C. A. Bello (Ed.), *Televisión pública: del consumidor al ciudadano* (pp. 35–69). Bogotá: FES/Promefes.

Marx, C., Halcli, A. & Barnett, C. (2012). Locating the Global Governance of HIV and AIDS: Exploring the Geographies of Transnational Advocacy Networks. *Health & Place,* 18(3), 490–495.

Mastrini, G. (2014). Argentina Digital: Una ley hecha a medida del poder de turno. *Infobae.* http://www.infobae. com/2014/11/11/1607973-argentina-digital-una-ley-hecha-medida-del-poder-turno.

Mastrini, G. & Becerra, M. (2001). 50 años de concentración de medios en América Latina: del patriarcado artesanal a la valorización en escala. In F. Quirós & F. Sierra (Eds.), *Globalización, comunicación y democracia: Crítica de la economía política de la comunicación y la cultura.* Sevilla: Comunicación Social Ediciones y Publicaciones.

Mastrini, G. & Becerra, M. (2006). *Periodistas y magnates: Estructura y concentración de industrias culturales en América Latina.* Buenos Aires: Prometeo.

Mastrini, G. & Becerra, M. (2009). *Los Monopolios de la verdad: Descifrando la estructura y concentración de los medios en Centroamérica y República Dominicana.* Buenos Aires: Prometeo.

Mastrini, G. & de Charras, D. (2005). 20 años no es nada: del NOMIC a la CMSI o el mismo amor, la misma lluvia. *Anuario Ininco,* 17(1), 217–240.

Mastrini, G. & Loreti, D. (2007). Integración comercial o diálogo cultural ante el desafío de la Sociedad de la Información: Un espacio de diálogo, pensamiento y construcción. In D. Loreti, G. Mastrini & M. Baranchuk (Eds.), *Participación y democracia en la sociedad de la información: actas III Congreso Panamericano de Comunicación* (pp. 9–18). Buenos Aires: Prometeo.

Mastrini, G. & Mestman, M. (1996). *¿Desregulación o re-regulación? De la derrota de las políticas a la política de la derrota.* Cuadernos de Información y Cultura 2. Madrid: Universidad Complutense de Madrid.

Mata, M. C., Carro, P., Córdoba, M. L., Monjo, D., Navarro, J., Segura, M. S. & Simo, J. C. (2005). *Condiciones objetivas y subjetivas para el desarrollo de la ciudadanía comunicativa* (1–58). Centro de Competencia en Comunicación para América Latina.

Matos, C. (2012). *Media and Politics in Latin America: Globalization, Democracy and Identity.* London: I. B. Tauris.

Mattelart, A. (2005). "Sociedad de la información". Premisas, nociones e historia de su constitución. Claves para comprender el Nuevo Orden Internacional. In M. C. Mata, M. L. Córdoba & L. Nicolino (Eds.), *Democracia y ciudadanía en la sociedad de la* información*: Desafíos y articulaciones regionales* (21–41). Córdoba: ECI-UNC/Delegación Regional de Cooperación para el Cono Sur y Brasil de la Embajada de Francia.

Mattelart, A. (2007). Pasado y presente de la "Sociedad de la Información": entre el nuevo orden mundial de la información y la comunicación y la "Cumbre Mundial de la Sociedad de la Información." In D. Loreti, G. Mastrini, M. Baranchuck & P. Alabarces (Eds.), *Participación y democracia en la sociedad de la información: Actas III Congreso Panamericano de Comunicación* (pp. 19–42). Buenos Aires: Prometeo.

Mauersberger, C. (2012). To Be Prepared When the Time Has Come: Argentina's New Media Regulation and the Social Movement for Democratizing Broadcasting. *Media, Culture & Society, 34*(5), 588–605.

McAdam, D. & Boudet, H. (2012). *Putting Movements in Their Place: Explaining Variation in Community Response to the Sitting of Energy Projects.* New York: Cambridge University Press.

McAdam, D. & Sewell, W. (2001). Temporality in the study of social movements and revolutions. In R. Aminzade, J. Goldstone, D. McAdam, E. Perry, W. Sewell, S. Tarrow & C. Tilly (Eds.), *Silence and Voice in the Study of Contentious Politics* (pp. 89–125). New York: Cambridge University Press.

McAdam, D., McCarthy, J. & Zald, M. (1996). *Comparative Perspectives on Social Movements: Political Opportunities, Mobilizing Structures, and Cultural Framings.* New York: Cambridge University Press.

McAdam, D., Tarrow, S. & Tilly, C. (2001). *Dynamics of Contention.* New York: Cambridge University Press.

McCarthy, J. & Mayer, Z. (1977). Resource Mobilization and Social Movements: A Partial Theory. *American Journal of Sociology, 82,* 1212–1241.

McNulty, S. (2013). Participatory Democracy? Exploring Peru's Efforts to Engage Civil Society in Local Governance. *Latin American Politics and Society, 55*(3), 69–92.

Meernik, J., Aloisi, R., Sowell, M. & Nichols, A. (2012). The Impact of Human Rights Organizations on Naming and Shaming Campaigns. *Journal of Conflict Resolution, 56*(2), 233–256.

Méndez, A. (2011, 28 February). Difamación, injuria y calumnia aún son delitos en 25 estados del país. *La Jornada.*

Meyer, D. (2004). Protest and Political Opportunities. *Annual Review of Sociology, 30,* 125–145.

Meyer, D. (2005). Social Movements and Public Policy: Eggs, Chicken, and Theory. In D. Meyer, V. Jenness, H. Ingram (Eds.), *Routing the Opposition: Social Movements, Public Policy, and Democracy* (pp. 1–26). Minneapolis, MN: University of Minnesota Press.

Meyer, D. & Whittier, N. (1994). Social Movement Spillover. *Social Problems, 41*(2), 277–298.

Michels, A. (2012). Citizen Participation in Local Policy Making: Design and Democracy. *International Journal of Public Administration, 35*(4), 285–292.

Michener, G. (2011). FOI Laws Around the World. *Journal of Democracy, 22*(2), 145–159.

Milan, S. & Hintz., A. (2013). Networked Collective Action and the Institutionalized Policy Debate: Bringing Cyberactivism to the Policy Arena? *Policy & Internet, 5*(1), 7–26.

Mioli, T. (2015). Sanctions against independent media continue as Supercom marks 2 years in Ecuador. Knight Center - The University of Texas at Austin. https://knightcenter.utexas.edu/ blog/00-16162-sanctions-against-independent-media-continue-supercom-marks-2-years-ecuador.

Mitchell, G. E. & Schmitz, H. P. (2013, October). Principled instrumentalism: A theory of transnational NGO behaviour. *Review of International Studies,* 1–18.

Monckeberg, M. O. (2009). *Los magnates de la prensa: Concentración de los medios de comunicación en Chile.* Santiago: Random House Mondadori.

Morris, N. & Waisbord, S. (2001). *Media and Globalization: Why the State Matters.* Rowman & Littlefield.

Moyses, D., Valente, J. & Silva, S. P. (2009). Sistemas públicos de comunicação: panorama analítico das experiências em doze países e os desafios para o caso brasileiro. In *Sistemas Públicos de Comunicação no Mundo: A Experiência de Doze Países e o Caso Brasileiro* (pp. 291–319). San Pablo: Intervozes/Paulus.

Murdie, A. (2013). The Ties That Bind: A Network Analysis of Human Rights International Nongovernmental Organizations. *British Journal of Political Science, 44*(1), 1–27.

Nabatchi, T., Gastil, J., Weiksner, G. & Leighninger, M. (2012). *Democracy in Motion: Evaluating the Practice and Impact of Deliberative Civic Engagement.* New York: Oxford University Press.

Natanson, J. (2010). Medios y 'Nueva Izquierda': algunos apuntes impresionistas. In O. Rincón (Ed.), *¿Por qué nos odian tanto? Estado y medios de comunicación en América Latina* (pp. 15–21). Bogotá: FES.

Navarrete, J. (2015, 9 June). Ley de acceso a información "en punto muerto." *Confidencial.* http://www.confidencial. com.ni/archivos/articulo/21958/ley-de-acceso-a-informacion-quot-en-punto-muerto-quot.

Navas Alvear, M. & Villanueva, E. (2004). *Hacia una América Latina transparente. Las experiencias de Ecuador y México.* Quito: Coalición Acceso.

Nazareno, M. (2010). ¿Hace la izquierda la diferencia? La política socio-económica en el "giro a la izquierda" de América Latina. *Estudios, 23–24,* 175–191.

O'Briain, D. & Bartley, K. (2003). *The revolution will not be televised.* Documentary.

Oberschall, A. (1993). *Social Movements: Ideologies, Interests, and Identities.* New Brunswick, NJ: Transaction.

Olvera, A. (2006). El discurso de la sociedad en el espacio public internacional. Lecciones para planificadores. Mexico: PRODEV.

Olvera, A. (2010). *La democratización frustrada. Limitaciones institucionales y colonización política de las instituciones garantes de derechos y de participación ciudadana en México.* México: Centro de Investigaciones y Estudios Superiores en Antropología Social.

Organization of American States. (2002a). *Informe anual de la Relatoría para la Libertad de Expresión.* Washington, DC: Organization of American States.

Organization of American States. (2002b, 10 May). *La Comisión Intermericana de Derechos Humanos finaliza su visita a la República Bolivariana De Venezuela. Comunicado de Prensa.* Washington, DC: Organization of American States.

Organization of American States. (2013). *Chapter II: Evaluation of the state of freedom of expression in the hemisphere, Annual Report of the Office of the Special Rapporteur for Freedom of Expression 2013.* Washington, DC: Organization or American States. http://www.oas.org/en/iachr/expression/docs/reports/annual/monitoring/ChII_Annual_REport_ENG_2013.pdf.

Padilla, A. (2010). A Venezuela na idade mídia. In C. Medina (Ed.), *Liberdade de expressão. Direito à informação nas sociedades latino-americanas.* São Paulo: Fundação Memorial da América Latina.

Panizza, F. (2005). Unarmed Utopia Revisited: The Resurgence of Left-of-Centre Politics in Latin America. *Political Studies, 53,* 716–734.

Parkinson, J. & Mansbridge, J. (2013). *Deliberative Systems: Deliberative Democracy at the Large Scale.* New York: Cambridge University Press.

Parthasarathy, S. (2010). Breaking the expertise barrier: Understanding activist strategies in science and technology policy domains. *Science and Public Policy, 37*(5), 355–367.

Pasquali, A. (1991). *¿Qué es una radiodifusión de servicio público?* Venezuela: Monte Ávila Editores.

Pasquali, A. (1995). *Reinventar los servicios públicos.* Caracas: Nueva Sociedad.

Pasqualucci, J. (2014). *The Practice and Procedure of the Inter-American Court of Human Rights.* New York: Cambridge University Press.

Pateman, C. (2012). Participatory Democracy Revisited. *Perspectives on Politics, 10*(1), 7–19.

Pérez, A. M. (2007). *La radio en Iberoamérica: evolución, diagnóstico, prospectiva.* Sevilla, Spain: Comunicacion Social.

Peruzzotti, E. (2005). *La política de accountability social en América Latina.* Working Document, Universidad Torcuato Di Tella, Buenos Aires.

Peruzzotti, E. & Smulovitz, C. (2000). Societal Accountability in Latin America. *Journal of Democracy, 11*(4), 147–158.

Philip, G. & Panizza, F. (2011). *The Triumph of Politics: The Return of the Left in Venezuela, Bolivia and Ecuador.* Cambridge: Polity.

Picco, E. (2013). Sistemas mediáticos subnacionales argentinos: heterogeneidad y diferencias en contextos neopopulistas. *Íconos – Revista de Ciencias Sociales, 45,* 83–100.

Pickard, V. (2010). Reopening the Postwar Settlement for U.S. Media: The Origins and Implications of the Social Contract Between Media, the State, and the Polity. *Communication, Culture & Critique*, 3(2), 170–189.

Pickard, V. (2013). *America's Battle for Media Democracy: The Triumph of Corporate Libertarianism and the Future of Media Reform*. Cambridge: Cambridge University Press.

Piven, F. F. (2006). *Challenging Authority: How Ordinary People Change America*. Lanham, MD: Rowman and Littlefield.

Pogrebinschi, T. & Samuels, D. (2014). National Public Policy Conferences. *Comparative Politics*, 46(3), 313–332.

Prato, A. V. & Segura, M. S. (2014, 5 May). Las nuevas disputas culturales. *Página/12*.

Prato, A. V., Traversaro, N. G. & Segura, M. S. (2015, October). La sociedad civil argentina y la "batalla cultural." De la Ley de Servicios de Comunicación Audiovisual al proyecto de Ley Federal de Culturas. (2009–2014). *Estado y políticas públicas*, 5, 81–96.

Prevost, G., Campos, C. O. & Vanden, H. (2012). *Social Movements and Leftist Governments in Latin America: Confrontation or Co-option?* London: Zed.

Price, M. E. & Verhulst, S. (2015). Introduction. In M. E. Price, S. Verhulst & L. Morgan (Eds.), *Routledge Handbook of Media Law* (pp. 1–14). New York: Routledge.

Price, M. E., Verhulst, S. & Morgan, L. (Eds.) (2015) *Routledge Handbook of Media Law*. New York: Routledge.

Puppis, M. (2010). Media Governance: A New Concept for the Analysis of Media Policy and Regulation. *Communication, Culture & Critique*, 3(2), 134–149.

Putnam, R. (2001). *Bowling Alone: The Collapse and Revival of American Community*. New York: Simon & Schuster.

Raboy, M. & Landry, N. (2005). *Civil Society, Communication, and Global Governance: Issues from the World Summit on the Information Society*. New York: Peter Lang

Ramírez Alvarado, M. D. (2005). La participación ciudadana desde la óptica de la ley de responsabilidad social en radio y televisión de Venezuela. *Comunicar, 25, 283*–300.

Ramírez Alvarado, M. D. (2007). Escenarios de comunicación en una Venezuela polarizada: del Grupo Cisneros a la Ley Resorte. *Zer, 22*, 283–300.

Ramírez Cáceres, J. D. (2009). La concentración de la propiedad radial en Chile: las exigencias de nuevos paradigmas entre globalidad y localidad. *Revista de Estudios para el Desarrollo Social de la Comunicación*, (5), 309–328.

Ramírez Cáceres, J. D. (2010). Radios Comunitarias en Chile: las paradojas de su propiedad. *Revista Austral de Ciencias Sociales*, (19), 63–74.

Ramonet, I. (2009, 4 October). La prensa diaria se muere. *Le Monde Diplomatique* (Santiago de Chile).

Ramos, I. (2013, August). Trayectoria de democratización y desdemocratización de la comunicación en Ecuador. *Íconos: Revista de Ciencias Sociales*, 67–82. DOI: 10.17141/iconos.46.2013.133.

Relly, J. & de Bustamante, C. G. (2014). Silencing Mexico: A Study of Influences on Journalists in the Northern States. *International Journal of Press/Politics*, 19(1), 108–131.

Rey, G. (2003). *Veedurías y observatorios. Participación social en los medios de comunicación*. Buenos Aires: Colectivo La Tribu.

Risley, A. (2006). The Political Potential of Civil Society: Advocating for Freedom of Information in

Argentina. *The Latin Americanist*, 49(2), 99–130.

Risley, A. (2015). *Civil Society Organizations, Advocacy, and Policy Making in Latin American Democracies*. New York: Palgrave Macmillan.

Risse, T. (2010). Rethinking Advocacy Organizations? A Critical Comment. In A. Prakash & M. K. Gugerty (Eds.), *Advocacy Organizations and Collective Action* (pp. 283–294). New York: Cambridge University Press.

Rodrigues, M. G. (2011). Rethinking the Impact of Transnational Advocacy Networks. *New Global Studies*, 5(2). DOI: 10.2202/1940-0004.1124.

Rodríguez, C., Ferron, B. & Shamas, K. (2014). Four Challenges in the Field of Alternative, Radical and Citizens' Media Research. *Media, Culture & Society*, 36(2), 150–166.

Royo, S. Yetano, A. & Acerete, B. (2011). Citizen Participation in German and Spanish Local Governments: A Comparative Study. *International Journal of Public Administration*, 34(3), 139–150.

Russell, S. (2011). Determinants of Latin American Activism: Domestic and Transnational Political Opportunities and Threats. *Sociology Compass*, 5(8), 747–762.

Sáez Baeza, C. (2008). *Tercer sector de la comunicación: Teoría y praxis de la televisión alternativa. Una mirada a los casos de España, Estados Unidos, y Venezuela*. Barcelona: Universidad Autónoma de Barcelona.

Santos, S. (2013). Coronelismo eletrônico versus convergência das comunicações: poder e negociação na relação entre comunicação e democracia no Brasil. In L. Albornoz et al. (Eds.), *Comunicación, políticas e industria: Actas del VIII Congreso Internacional de la Unión Latina de Economía Política de la Información,*

la Comunicación y la Cultura (pp. 55–81). Bernal: Universidad Nacional de Quilmes.

Sarat, A. & Scheingold, S. (2006). *Cause Lawyers and Social Movements*. Stanford: Stanford University Press.

Scholte, J. A. (2014). Reinventing Global Democracy. *European Journal of International Relations*, 20(1), 3–28.

Scott, J. (1988). *Weapons of the Weak*. New Haven, CT: Yale University Press.

Seele, A. & Peruzzotti, E. (Eds.) (2009). *Participatory Innovation and Representative Democracy in Latin America*. Baltimore, MD: John Hopkins University Press.

Segura, M. S. (2008a). Comunicación y Ciudadanía en los estudios latinoamericanos de comunicación. *Publicación del CIFFyH*, 6(5), 705–723.

Segura, M. S. (2008b, December). México: Legisladores y ciudadanía frenan la Ley Televisa. Los argumentos le ganaron al poder mediático. *Umbrales. Crónicas de la Utopía*, 9, 142–144.

Segura, M. S. (2010, September). Democratizando las comunicaciones globales: nuevos sujetos, nuevas prácticas. *Rastros*, 13, 55–68.

Segura, M. S. (2011a). De lo alternativo a lo público. Las tomas de posición de las organizaciones sociales en vistas a democratizar las comunicaciones (Argentina, 2001–2009). *Derecho a Comunicar*, 1(2), 205–226.

Segura, M. S. (2011b). Democracia y derechos humanos en la reforma comunicacional: Los argumentos y sus condiciones de producción. *Sociodicea*, 42–51.

Segura, M. S. (2011c). La sociedad civil y la democratización de las comunicaciones en la Argentina: La experiencia de la Coalición por una Radiodifusión Democrática. *Argumentos. Revista de Crítica Social*, 13, 1–26.

Segura, M. S. (2011d). *Las disputas por democratizar las comunicaciones. Las tomas de posición de las organizaciones sociales (Córdoba, 2001–2009)*. Doctoral Thesis, Universidad de Buenos Aires, Buenos Aires.

Segura, M. S. (2012, 30–31 August). La sociedad civil ecuatoriana en la disputa por una nueva ley de comunicación. Comparación con el proceso argentino. *I Coloquio de Comunicación para la Transformación Social*, 1–13.

Segura, M. S. (2013a). "Democratization of the media in Latin America: Views from the inside and the outside. *7th Nordic Conference on Latin American Research*. Oslo: University of Oslo.

Segura, M. S. (2013b). Contigo o sin ti: medios no lucrativos y Estado desde la Ley 26.522. *Austral Comunicación*, 2(2), 145–185.

Segura, M. S. (2014). Democratización de la comunicación y nuevas leyes de radiodifusión en América Latina. Algunos ejes de comparación con estándares internacionales y propuestas de la sociedad civil. *XII Congreso Latinoamericano de Investigadores de la Comunicación*. Lima: ALAIC.

Segura, M. S. (2015a). Civil society participation and public media. The Argentinian case. *PANAM*. Montreal.

Segura, M. S. (2015b). La relación con el Estado como diferencia. Los medios sin fines de lucro y la reconfiguración del sistema a partir de la Ley 26.522. In R. Costa & T. Mozejko (Eds.), *Hacer la diferencia. Abordaje sociocrítico de prácticas discursivas* (pp. 1–38). Villa María: EDUVIM.

Segura, M. S., Nicolino, L. & Córdoba, L. (2005). Los periodistas en la construcción de agenda pública. *III Congreso Panamericano de Comunicación*. UBA.

Shawki, N. (2011). Organizational Structure And Strength and Transnational Campaign Outcomes: A Comparison of Two Transnational Advocacy Networks. *Global Networks*, 11(1), 97–117.

Shekha, K. R. (2011). Determinants of Latin American Activism: Domestic and Transnational Political Opportunities and Threats. *Sociology Compass*, 5(8), 747–762.

Sivak, M. (2013). *Clarín, el gran diario argentino. Una historia*. Buenos Aires: Planeta.

Skocpol, T. (2004). *Diminished Democracy: From Membership to Management in American Civic Life*. Norman, OK: University of Oklahoma Press.

Snow, D. A., Soule, S. A. & Kriesi, H. (2004). Mapping the Terrain. In D. A. Snow, S. A. Soule & H. Kriesi (Eds.), *The Blackwell Companion to Social Movements* (pp. 3–16). Malden, MA: Blackwell.

Solís Leree, B. (Ed.) (2004). *La relación sociedad/medios en el marco de la reforma del Estado en México*. México: Universidad Autónoma Metropolitana.

Sorj, B. (Ed.) (2010). *Usos, abusos y desafíos de la sociedad civil en América Latina*. Buenos Aires: Siglo XXI.

Sousa, C. B. (2014). *Comunicação e igualdade racial: Atuação de movimentos negros na 1ª Conferência Nacional de Comunicação*. Dissertation (Master's in Communication).

Speer, J. (2012). Participatory Governance Reform: A Good Strategy for Increasing Government Responsiveness and Improving Public Services? *World Development*, 40(12), 2379–2398.

Staggenborg, S. (2010). Research on Social Movement Coalitions. In N. van Dyke & H. J. McCammon

(Eds.), *Strategic Alliances: Coalition Building and Social Movements* (pp. 316–330). Minneapolis: University of Minnesota Press.

Stahler-Sholk, R., Vanden, H. E. & Becker, M. (2014). *Rethinking Latin American Social Movements: Radical Action from Below.* Lanham, MD: Rowman & Littlefield.

SUBTEL. (2013, 15 October). *Ley de Televisión Digital abierta y gratuita se convierte en realidad.* Santiago: Subsecretaría de Telecomunicaciones del Gobierno de Chile. http://www.subtel.gob.cl/ley-de-television-digital-abierta-y-gratuita-se-convierte-en-realidad/.

Sunkel, G. & Geoffroy, E. (2001). *La Concentración Económica de los Medios de Comunicación en Chile.* Santiago: LOM Ediciones.

Tarrow, S. (1994). *Power in Movement: Social Movements, Collective Action and Mass Politics in the Modern State.* New York: Cambridge University Press.

Tarrow, S. (1996). States and opportunities: The political structuring of social movements. In D. McAdam, J. D. McCarthy & M. N. Zald (Eds.), *Comparative Perspectives on Social Movements: Political Opportunities, Mobilizing Structures, and Cultural Framings* (pp. 41–61). New York: Cambridge University Press.

Tarrow, S. (2005). *The New Transnational Activism.* New York: Cambridge University Press.

Tarrow, S. (2012). *Strangers at the Gates: States and Movement in Contentious Politics.* New York: Cambridge University Press.

Tate, W. (2013). Proxy citizenship and transnational advocacy: Colombian activists from Putumayo to Washington, DC. *American Ethnologist, 40*(1), 55–70.

Tello, C. E., Cerna, M. G. & Pavón, A. M. (2009). Acceso a la información pública: los desafíos del Consejo de la Transparencia. *Anuario de Derechos Humanos,* 5. DOI: 10.5354/0718-2279.2009.11528.

Tilly, C. (1986). European Violence and Collective Action since 1700. *Social Research, 53*(1), 159–184.

Tilly, C. (1999). From Interactions to Outcomes in Social Movements. In M. Giugni, D. McAdam, C. Tilly, M. Giugni, D. McAdam & C. Tilly (Eds.), *How Movements Matter: Theoretical and Comparative Studies on the Consequences of Social Movements* (253–270). Minneapolis, MN: University of Minnesota Press.

Tilly, C. (2004). *Social Movements, 1768–2004.* New York: Routledge.

Tornay, M. C. (2015, 18 August). Las emisoras comunitarias del Ecuador, a la espera de un nuevo escenario comunicacional. *Revista Pueblos.* http://www.revistapueblos.org/?p=19646

Torres, J. L., Muente, A., Hanlin, P., Stevens, M., Clinton, A., McCarthy, S. & Souza, L. K. (2013). Perspectives on Protest in Latin America. In K. Malley-Morrison, A. Mercurio & G. Twose (Eds.), *International Handbook of Peace and Reconciliation* (pp. 237–246). New York: Springer.

Trejo Delarbre, R. (2006). *Una ley para Televisa: Crónica de una regresión política.* México DF: FES.

Trejo Delarbre, R. (2010). Muchos medios en pocas manos: concentración televisiva y democracia en América Latina. *Intercom – Revista Brasileira de Ciências da Comunicação, 33*(1), 17–51.

Treré, E. (2015). Reclaiming, Proclaiming, and Maintaining Collective Identity in the #YoSoy132 Movement in Mexico: An Examination of Digital Frontstage and Backstage Activism

Through Social Media and Instant Messaging Platforms. *Information, Communication & Society, 18*(8), 901–915.

Turnhout, E. & Van der Zouwen, M. (2010). "Governance without Governance": How Nature Policy Was Democratized in the Netherlands. *Critical Policy Studies, 4*(4), 344–361.

United Nations, Organization of American States and Organizaton for Security and Cooperation in Europe. (2001). *Desafíos a la libertad de expresión en el nuevo siglo.* Amsterdam. OSCE.

United Nations, Organization of American States, Organization for Security and Cooperation in Europe and African Commission on Human and Peoples' Rights. (2007). *Declaración conjunta sobre diversidad en la radiodifusión.* Amsterdam. OSCE.

UNESCO. (2008). *Media Development Indicators: A Framework for Assessing Media Development.* Paris: UNESCO.

UNESCO. (2014). *World Trends in Freedom of Expression and Media Development.* Paris: UNESCO.

Uranga, W. (2010). La transición a la democracia apenas está empezando. *Página/12.* http://www.pagina12.com.ar/diario/dialogos/21-146677-2010-05-31.html.

Urioste, J. (2015). A 6 años de la ley audiovisual: Un estudio de las radios comunitarias de Córdoba. In M. S. Segura (Ed.), *Los medios sin fines de lucro desde la Ley Audiovisual* (pp. 122–134). Córdoba: Universidad Nacional de Córdoba.

Van Dyke, N. & McCammon, H. J. (2010). Introduction: Social Movement Coalition Formation. In N. Van Dyke & H. J. McCammon (Eds.), *Strategic Alliances: Coalition Building and Social Movements* (pp. xi–xviii). Minneapolis, MN: University of Minnesota Press.

Van Laer, J. & Van Aelst, P. (2010). Internet and Social Movement Action Repertoires: Opportunities and Limitations. *Information, Communication & Society, 13*(8), 1146–1171.

Vicari, S. (2014). Networks of Contention: The Shape of Online Transnationalism in Early Twenty-First Century Social Movement Coalitions. *Social Movement Studies, 13*(1), 92–109.

Villanueva, G. R. (2014). *Estado de la libertad de expresión en Nicaragua.* Managua: CINCO.

Vinelli, N. (2014). *La televisión desde abajo. Historia, alternatividad y periodismo de contrainformación.* Buenos Aires: El Topo Blindado; El Río Suena.

Waisbord, S. (2000). *Watchdog Journalism in South America: News, Accountability, and Democracy.* New York: Columbia University Press.

Waisbord, S. (2007). Democratic Journalism and "Statelessness." *Political Communication, 24*(2): 115–129.

Waisbord, S. (2010). Press and the public sphere in contemporary Latin America. In P. Norris (Ed.), *Public Sentinel: News Media and Governance Reform* (pp. 305–328). Washington, DC: The World Bank.

Waisbord, S. (2011). Between Support and Confrontation: Civic Society, Media Reform, and Populism in Latin America. *Communication, Culture & Critique, 4*(1), 97–117.

Waisbord, S. (2013). *Vox Populista.* Buenos Aires: Gedisa.

Wampler, B. (2012). Entering the State: Civil Society Activism and Participatory Governance in Brazil. *Political Studies, 60*(2), 341–362.

Welp, Y. & Wheatley, J. (2012). The uses of digital media for contentious politics in Latin America. In E. Anduiza, M. J. Jensen & L. Jorba

(Eds.), *Digital Media and Political Engagement Worldwide: A Comparative Study* (pp. 177–199). New York, UK: Cambridge University Press.

Williams, R. (1962). *The Existing Alternatives in Communications.* London: Fabian Society.

Williams, G. (2004). Towards a repoliticization of participatory development: Political capabilities and spaces of empowerment. In S. Hickey & G. Mohan (Eds.), *Participation: From Tyranny to Transformation? Exploring New Approaches to Participation in Development* (pp. 92–108). London: Zed.

Wolfson, T. (2013). Democracy or Autonomy? Indymedia and the Contradictions of Global Social Movement Networks. *Global Networks, 13*(3), 410–424.

Wong, W. H. (2012). *Internal Affairs: How the Structure of NGOs Transforms Human Rights.* Ithaca: Cornell University Press.

Woodford, M. R. & Preston, S. (2013). Strengthening Citizen Participation in Public Policy-Making: A Canadian Perspective. *Parliamentary Affairs, 66*(2), 345–363.

Zibechi, R. (2010). *Dispersing Power: Social Movements as Anti-state Forces.* Oakland, CA: AK Press.

INTERVIEWS

Interviews were conducted by the authors. When the same individual was interviewed several times, the date of the last conversation is indicated.

Acevedo, Jorge (2015). Professor and researcher, Universidad Católica del Perú. 20 August.

Alarcón Llontop, Luis Rolando (2015). Professor and researcher, Centro de Estudios Sociales y Mediáticos de la Universidad Señor de Sipán, Perú. 4 August.

Álvarez Ugarte, Ramiro (2015). Advisor, Asociación por los Derechos Civiles (ADC), Argentina. 22 June. Personal Communication.

Balbi, Marianela (2015). Executive Director, Instituto de Prensa y Sociedad (Venezuela), 30 April.

Banfi, Karina (2015). Former Executive Director, Alianza para la Libertad de Expresión, 11 May.

Behrens, Peter-Alberto (2015). Former representative for Latin America, Konrad Adenauer Foundation, 4 May.

Belforte, Liliana (2014). Representative, Regional Council AMARC; Member, Consejo Federal de Comunicación Audiovisual, Argentina, 3 June.

Bertoni, Eduardo (2015), Former Special Rapporteur for Freedom of Expression, Organization of American States, 12 May.

Botero, Catalina (2015). Former Special Rapporteur for Freedom of Expression, Organization of American States, 1 May.

Brown, Vonda (2015). Senior Program Officer, Open Society Foundations, 1 April.

Calleja, Aleida (2015). Former President, Asociación Mexicana por el Derecho a la Información; former representative, AMARC-México, Board member of Observacom, México, 12 August.

Canela, Guilherme (2015). Communication and Information Advisor, UNESCO Uruguay, 18 March.

Cantón, Santiago (2015). Former Special Rapporteur for Freedom of Expression, Organization of American States, 2 April.

Cortés Castillo, Carlos (2015). Former Executive Director, Fundación para la Libertad de Prensa, Colombia, 30 April.

Da Rosa Pírez, Tania (2015). Former Director, Centro de Archivos y Acceso a la Información Pública (CAInfo), Uruguay, 29 September.

Fernández, José (2013). Member of Red Nacional de Medios Alternativos (RNMA), Argentina, 13 September.

Gerbaldo, Judith (2013). Training Coordinator, Foro Argentino de Radios Comunitarias (FARCO), Argentina, 13 September.

Gómez, Gustavo (2014). Former representative, AMARC Uruguay; former Regional Director AMARC-ALC; former Director Nacional de Telecomunicaciones; Director, Observacom, Uruguay, 21 October.

Güida, María Clara (2015). Professor and researcher, Universidad de Buenos Aires, Argentina, 21 September. Personal Communication.

Lanza, Edison (2015). Special Rapporteur for Freedom of Expression, Organization of American States, 19 May.

Lauría, Carlos (2015). Senior Americas Program Coordinator, Committee to Protect Journalists, United States, 30 March.

López Vigil, José Ignacio (2015). Director, Radialistas Apasionados y Apasionadas, Ecuador, 15 September.

Lozano, Luis (2015). Former Director of Communication, Centro de Estudios Legales y Sociales (CELS), Argentina, 24 April. Personal Communication.

March, Carlos (2015). Director of Strategic Communication, AVINA, Argentina, 26 March.

Meneses, María Elena (2015). Professor and researcher, Monterrey Institute of Technology and Higher Education; member Asociación Mexicana de Investigadores en Comunicación, Mexico, 3 August.

Michi, Gabriel (2015). Vice-president, Foro de Periodismo Argentino (FOPEA), Argentina, 28 September.

Navas Alvear, Marco (2015). Former member, Coalición Acceso, Ecuador, 8 October.

Olivera Paulino, Fernando (2014). Former member, organizing committee of CONFECOM, Brazil, 12 May.

Pochak, Andrea (2015). Former Adjunct Executive Director, Centro de Estudios Legales y Sociales, Argentina, 4 September.

Podesta, Don (2015). Manager, National Endowment for Democracy, United States, 5 May.

Prats, Martin (2015). President, CAInfo, Uruguay, 26 August.

Pugliese, Mariela (2014). President, FARCO, Argentina, 22 May.

Rincón, Omar (2015). Friedrich Ebert Foundation, Colombia, 12 May.

Saba, Roberto (2015). Founder and former Executive Director, Asociación por los Derechos Civiles, Argentina, 10 September.

Sánchez, Moisés (2015). Executive Director, Alianza Regional para la Libertad de Expresión, 18 May.

Sierra Caballero, Francisco (2015). General Director, Centro de Investigación y Estudios Superiores en Comunicación para América Latina (CIESPAL), Ecuador, 26 August.

Solís Leree, Beatriz (2015). Former President, AMEDI, México, 19 August.

Trejo Delarbre, Raúl (2015). Former President, AMEDI, México, 7 August.

Vaca Villareal, Pedro (2015). Former Executive Director, Fundación para la Libertad de Prensa, Colombia, 1 June.

Valente, Jonas (2015). Member of Intervozes, member of Conselho Deliberativo of Fórum Nacional Pela Democratização da Comunicação (FNDC), Brazil, 31 July.

Villanueva, Ernesto (2015). Former member of Grupo Oaxaca, Mexico, 25 September.

Vinelli, Natalia (2013). Member, Espacio Abierto de Televisoras Alternativas, Populares y Comunitarias (EATAPC), Argentina, 9 July.

INDEX